COLONISTS AND CANADIENS
1760-1867

Toronto   Macmillan of Canada   1971

Edited by
J. M. S. CARELESS

COLONISTS
CANADIENS
1760-1867

ISBN 7705-0339-X

Library of Congress Catalogue Card No. 70-155261

Cover illustration by Alan Daniel

Reprinted 1972

Printed in Canada for
The Macmillan Company of Canada Limited
70 Bond Street, Toronto, Ontario

Contents

ON LOAN
MACMILLAN FCO

Introduction   vii

1. The 1760s by Cameron Nish   1
2. The 1770s by George Rawlyk   20
3. The 1780s by Leslie Upton   41
4. The 1790s by S. F. Wise   62
5. The 1800s by Jean-Pierre Wallot   95
6. The 1810s by Alan Wilson   122
7. The 1820s by Michael Cross   149
8. The 1830s by G. M. Craig   173
9. The 1840s by Jacques Monet, S.J.   200
10. The 1850s by J. M. S. Careless   226
11. The 1860s by P. B. Waite   249

Index   273

Introduction

Between 1760 and 1867 a group of provincial societies developed in the territories held by Great Britain in the northern half of North America, societies which formed the basis of the transcontinental Canadian state that emerged thereafter. Even for the French-Canadian community, sprung from the days of New France, the century after 1760 saw the distinctive growth of a provincial society. It was the most distinctive of all, in fact, because it had necessarily to exist in a cultural dualism and within English-dominated political and economic patterns. As for the anglophone colonists dwelling alongside their *Canadien* fellow-subjects—or to the east of them on the Atlantic coasts, or west in the interior lakelands—whether they were drawn from the older British American empire or from the British centre of empire itself, they equally shared in building distinctive provincial societies, each with an individual character of its own. Perhaps the Canadian Endless Quest for identity has obscured the very real existence of these individual identities that still mark the country. And perhaps the anxious search would be eased if one examined Canadian historic growth less as a linear (or even bi-linear) development and more as a continued encounter of particularisms, each with its own well-rooted outlook, though with sufficient overlapping interests and experience to enable them to come together, if only to sustain themselves.

That, at any rate, is the approach of this volume. While repeatedly treating the common experiences and shared associations of the peoples of the British North American provinces, it deals with their wide-ranging diversity and at times parochial isolation. It eschews any central theme of seeing Canadian history in this period by hindsight, as the working out of manifest destiny for Ontario—or Quebec. If the central areas of the country enter at some length, it is simply because of their significance in people and power; but other regions come to the fore as well because of their inherent contributions to the multiple course of growth. The focus essentially is on the people of the provinces, colonists and *Canadiens*, and on the developments—political, economic, social or cultural—that largely shaped their lives. They are dealt with decade by decade by individual authors. Each of these cross-sections in time thus itself provides a frame of unity.

Naturally decades are not neat and tightly packaged units, and naturally individual authors will find their own perspective for each of them. Yet the time-span of a decade is sufficient to bring out a distinct pattern of development without neglecting the elements of continuity that are also there, while the authors' perspectives not only illuminate the variety of the story, but reinforce its enduring aspects besides.

Accordingly, the whole study is constructed as follows. Cameron Nish, Director of the Centre de Recherche en Histoire Economique du Canada Français at Sir George Williams University, describes the decade that began with the British military conquest of Canada in 1760, while George Rawlyk, of the History Department of Queen's University, examines the 1770s, that witnessed the American Revolution, and Leslie Upton, of the Department of History, University of British Columbia, the 1780s, era of Loyalist migration. S. F. Wise of Carleton University, and Director of the Canadian Armed Forces Directorate of History, treats the 1790s, when the newer colonies of British North America were fast taking shape. The 1800s are analysed by Jean-Pierre Wallot of the Department of History, University of Toronto, against their compelling background of world conflict between Britain and France. Alan Wilson of the Department of History, Trent University, then deals with the 1810s, that brought the War of 1812 further to affect the provinces.

The 1820s and 1830s, times of British immigration and mounting political and social strain, fall to Michael Cross and Gerald Craig respectively, both members of the University of Toronto's Department of History. Jacques Monet, S.J., of the History Department of the University of Ottawa, then covers the 1840s, the day of the coming of responsible government and the union of the two Canadas. The 1850s era of boom, sectional clash in Canada and opening new horizons, are my own particular concern. Finally, Peter Waite of the Department of History, Dalhousie University, closes with the 1860s, which were, of course, the concluding phase for old British North America as well as the founding years of a new Canadian federal union.

It remains to thank the above authors (including J. M. S. Careless of the Toronto Department of History) for their co-operation, their willing patience with the editorial tasks of co-ordinating the work as a whole; though in thanking them also for the value of their contributions, I will here properly stand excluded. In any case, it may be hoped that this volume will serve, as was intended, as an effective counterpart and complement to the previously published work, *The Canadians 1867–1967*, edited by Craig Brown of the Toronto Department and myself, which carries the story onward decade by decade to the Canadian society of the present era.

J. M. S. Careless

1: The 1760s

CAMERON NISH

To style the 1760s as both the first decade of British rule in Canada and the sixteenth from the beginnings of French settlement expresses the fact that it saw vital continuity as well as drastic change. The change, of course, came in the transfer of France's North American empire to British control through military conquest in 1759-60 and the Treaty of Paris in 1763. The continuity above all lay in the survival of the French-speaking community of the St. Lawrence valley. Whatever the expectations of the British conquerors, the *Canadiens* would endure as a firmly rooted people with a language, culture and social organization of their own, even when English-speaking colonists came to settle about them or in their midst.

In a general sense, English Canada did thus begin with the 1760s. Yet it is true that here, too, there were elements of continuity reaching back much earlier. In the Atlantic areas east of the St.

Lawrence region the English had established settlements in New-foundland from the early seventeenth century, and since 1713 the peninsula of Nova Scotia had been a British province wrested from French-held Acadia. To the west and north of the St. Lawrence and its tributary Great Lakes, there had long been British fur trade posts on the shores of Hudson and James Bay, as well as a British claim to all the western territory that drained into these waters, embodied in the Hudson's Bay Company charter of 1670. Hence much of the Canada of the future was already under British sway by 1760—even though, until the fall of New France, the French had by no means given up thought of altering that fact.

Nevertheless, these northern reaches of British territory were essentially empty realms of the fur trade or of scattered fishing settlements on coastal fringes. They did not contain any substantial colony of both farming population and thriving town life, such as the French had developed along the St. Lawrence from Quebec to Montreal, unless perhaps around the British naval base of Halifax founded in 1749. The English American empire of settlement in 1760 still lay southward, in the rich, well-populated Thirteen Colonies extending down the Atlantic seaboard from New England to Georgia, or in the British-held sugar islands of the Caribbean. There was, in fact, no thought that the huge northern territories would one day themselves be formed into a single outstretched union under the name of Canada.

In the 1760s, the very term Canada applied only to the former French realm of the St. Lawrence. No one then could have con-ceived of a distinctive northern country composed both of French Canadians and British colonists and separate from the older British American empire of the Thirteen Colonies. None the less, one of the most significant features of the 1760s was the fact that French- and English-speaking elements in the north were now to live within one common political framework—which ultimately, by the 1860s, would lead to a federal union of both colonists and *Canadiens*.

That was the course ahead for Canadian history. But in the first and sixteenth decade of the northern peoples, the major theme for the 1760s was the dislocation caused by conquest and the adjust-ment to it: the introduction of British rule over the *Canadiens,* the small but influential influx of English-speaking merchants into their St. Lawrence domain, and still the survival and growth of the French Canadians themselves. There were only about 65,000 of them in 1760; yet theirs was the one sizeable community of settlement in all the sparsely populated northern lands, where they would long remain in the majority. Consequently, although there were significant developments in the Atlantic areas in the sixties, and in the western world of Indians and fur traders, one must examine this decade in the part of British America that would eventually become Canada, by focusing primarily on the people of the St. Lawrence valley.

First, they faced the harshest stages of the imperial conflict, known from its European counterpart as the Seven Years' War, and the final collapse of French power in North America. In 1759 the city of Quebec, the very heart of French empire, had fallen after the British victory of September 13 on the Plains of Abraham. The Marquis de Vaudreuil, the first Canadian-born governor of New France, had retired to Montreal with the remaining French regulars and *Canadien* militia commanded by the Chevalier de Lévis. In the spring of 1760, Lévis indeed took the offensive, and besieged the British, now under General James Murray as governor of Quebec, in their turn in that badly battered city. In fact, the French sharply worsted Murray at the battle of Ste Foye on April 28 outside the walls of Quebec; but lacked the strength to follow up their success. And when the ice cleared from the St. Lawrence waterway, British seapower and British reinforcements reached up the river to Quebec once more. The French again had to retreat to Montreal.

There the position grew hopeless, as British armies converged on the city from Quebec, Lake Champlain, and Lake Ontario. Cut off and virtually surrounded, Vaudreuil signed the Capitulation of Montreal on September 8, 1760, surrendering the last major French force in continental America, and signalling the effective occupation of French Canada by British power. The ultimate fate of the colony, however, was still not known. Fortunes of war, political alignments in Europe, the needs of allies and the necessity of compromise on the part of the belligerents were all factors that might alter the final disposition of New France.

The terms of the Capitulation were the usual ones granted to a white, Christian, European power conquered by force of arms. The French in New France were granted neither more nor less than was normal in eighteenth-century warfare. The dominant note was double-cleffed: the conquered became the subjects of Great Britain's king, and substantial changes of policy awaited the king's pleasure. In any case, despite the delay and uncertainty regarding the final peace settlement, a displacement and reconstruction took place in the years 1760-63, and that continued through the first decade after the conquest. French military control of the colony and its western hinterland ended. Inasmuch as the French posts around the Great Lakes, in the Ohio country and beyond, were also trading posts, important changes took place as well in the fur trade and in its corollary, relations with the western Indians. Within three years, the latter would bring about a new Indian-European conflict, Pontiac's Rebellion.

The French and *Canadien* political, administrative, commercial and social elite left the colony, most within a short period after 1760, but some in an eighteenth-month period of grace permitted by the final peace treaty in 1763. The families that had dominated the colony for several generations by their control of the administration, Superior Council, seigneurial system, fur trade and commerce retired to France. Some would continue their careers in the service of the French; others besieged the Minister of Marine for pensions, usually granted, and lived the lives of gentlemen. The social vacuum in New France would be filled by British officials and merchants, and by some *Canadien* associates—Old and New Subjects of "His Britannick Majesty."

The colony thus far still potentially belonged to France, but was under British military administration. The initial response of the British was to use existing machinery where possible, and to retain to a large extent the French governmental jurisdiction of Quebec, Three Rivers and Montreal. Shortly after the Capitulation of Montreal, Murray was thus continued in the post of governor of Quebec; Colonel Ralph Burton was named governor of Three Rivers and Colonel Thomas Gage was appointed to the same post in the government of Montreal. By 1763, Burton had assumed the

gubernatorial post in Montreal, and a Swiss, French-speaking soldier
of fortune was governor of Three Rivers, Frederick Haldimand,
who would have an important later career in governing Canada.

A most significant feature of this military interregnum was the
reports on the three governments prepared by the British governors
of the three areas, and in particular that of Murray, dated June 5,
1762, since his views composed an influential picture of the French-
Canadian community Britain had come to rule. The immediate
objective of a military leader in a newly conquered area is security,
and the pacification of an alien people to that end. Murray's concern for his temporary New Subjects was pragmatic, at times benevolent, but principally derived from a militaristic and imperialistic
ideology not unexpected for an eighteenth-century soldier-governor,
whether French or British. Some of its roots indeed were buried in
the humus of anti-French and anti-papist biases quite natural to
British wartime sentiments, and some of them in what a later critic
might term "jingoism."

In Murray's report, the British military establishment was his
first concern. Some of the incumbents of military posts in 1762,
such as Paulus Aemilius Irving, Hector Theophilus Cramahé,
Thomas Mills, Samuel Holland and Adam Mabane, wou'd remain
the governor's close associates after the introduction of the civil
regime that followed the peace of 1763. Murray next described the
government of New France quite accurately. He decried the arbitrary powers that had been accorded the intendant; they had been
consistently abused. He also claimed that the officers of justice were
almost all metropolitan French, (which was false), and that they
were so dominated by their personal interests that their judicial
decisions were little respected, but provided no evidence for this
assertion. He further deprecated the old Superior Council, declaring that the governor, intendant and bishop seldom attended its
meetings. His last two comments on the government of the colony
prior to the conquest noted the Norman origins and litigious nature
of the populace. He did, however, recommend the lowering of the
age of majority (25 under the French regime) as this would afford
the youth of the colony greater freedom.

Murray's remarks on the ecclesiastical organization of the colony

contained all the elements of future British policy for French
Canada. According to the governor, the people were ignorant and
attached to their clergy. The upper hierarchy of the Church in New
France had been of metropolitan origin; *Canadiens* should be
encouraged to take up the ecclesiastical state. He suggested that the
British government subsidize the re-building of churches: it would
attach the citizens to their new masters. But the Jesuits, one of
whose members would be described in the newly founded *Quebec
Gazette* of September 13th, 1764, as ". . . a soft, insinuating,
whining and subtle member of that Society," were neither loved
nor esteemed by the people. However, their property might be used
to support a bishop and the Chapter of Quebec, the diocesan executive of the city. Murray expressed great respect for the female religious communities. Nonetheless, he believed that they should be
properly influenced by the British government as to numbers and
dowry required.

Agriculture and commerce came under review. Murray foresaw a
rapid increase in the commercial value of the colony now that it
was to be wisely administered. Useful employment could be provided for women and children during the long winter months: they
could prepare hemp and flax for export. As to the all-important fur
trade, while it was true that merchants from New York and
Pennsylvania now shared in it, it would probably still be centred
at Quebec. The general thrust of his report was to lay great stress
on the economic integration of the newly conquered area into the
Empire.

The military governor's last section was concerned with a characterization of the populace and the society. The *ancien régime* was
composed of four groups or orders: the upper class, or gentry; the
clergy; the merchants or commercial class; and the peasantry,
called habitants. The upper class was made up of military and civil
administrators. Most were poor. They were vain, despised the commercial class and were "great tyrants" to their vassals. As for the
clergy, Murray's main suggestion was that it be "canadianised."
This would result in a docile and satisfied group. He also noted that,
in the short time since the conquest, the people were less subject to
the influence of their clergy. The merchants could be subdivided:

wholesale commerce had been in the hands of the metropolitans from France; retail trade was controlled by the *Canadiens*. All merchants held a mass of bills of exchange which they were desperately trying to collect.

By far the longest of Murray's observations concerned the habitants, the agricultural mass of the population. He viewed them as a strong and healthy race, virtuous and temperate; but generally speaking, excessively ignorant and much under the domination of their former rulers. Murray blamed the old administrators for the people's misconceptions regarding the English, namely that the latter were brutes who would govern the French with rods of iron. The general populace had to be reassured of the good intentions of the English. This done, they would become good and faithful subjects of the king.

Murray's assessment has been both endorsed and challenged by later historians. Regardless of its accuracy, however, it became the accepted characterization of the *ancien régime* of New France. It was on the basis of the reports of Murray, Gage and Burton, and imperial needs that permanent British policy for the colony would be formulated, when the Treaty of Paris of February 10, 1763, ended the war at last, and ceded New France to Great Britain.

II

The treaty, and the Proclamation which Britain subsequently issued on October 7, 1763, were imperial in scope. The St. Lawrence colony was only one part of a global settlement. In North America, France definitely ceded all Acadia, Newfoundland and Canada, holding only the island of St. Pierre and Miquelon off Newfoundland as a base for her Atlantic fisheries, along with fishing rights around the western shores of the great island. Various West Indies islands were acquired by Britain, some returned to France. Indeed in the Caribbean, France retained what then seemed to be her most valuable areas: much more valuable as tropical sugar islands than Canada's wilderness of snow.

The concern of the British Proclamation of 1763 that followed the treaty was to integrate all of the New Subjects in the Americas into an expanded empire. A newly created Province of Quebec was announced, under James Murray as "Captain-General & Governor in Chief." Its boundaries were drawn to cut off Labrador in the east, the great hinterland beyond the Ottawa on the west, making Quebec thus comprehend the French St. Lawrence area of settlement alone. On the east Labrador, Anticosti and the Magdalen islands were annexed to Newfoundland (the fishing industry was to be controlled by British and British Americans) and the Province of Nova Scotia was given all the area that the French had known as Acadia, including the present New Brunswick and Prince Edward Island; on the west, New France's old fur trade hinterland became both an Indian preserve under direct imperial control and an economic entity in which Quebec and British American merchants would only be granted the right to trade by licence.

To protect and pacify this western Indian country the Proclamation forbad settlement beyond the line of the Appalachian mountains. This effectively closed off the Ohio valley to pioneers spreading from the Thirteen Colonies, which caused mounting irritation there in years ahead with this "Proclamation Line." The hope and intention of the British authorities, however, was to turn the flow of expanding English-speaking settlement northward, to consolidate the gains made from the French.

That did occur to some extent, as far as Nova Scotia was concerned. There, the expulsion of the French Acadians in 1755, at the outset of the climactic Anglo-French imperial struggle, had left fertile farmlands vacant in the Annapolis valley and around the Minas Basin. From 1760 New England settlers increasingly moved in. They took up much of Nova Scotia's southern shores as well, created "fishing townships" on the Atlantic coast, and established themselves in the St. John valley. By 1763 Nova Scotia looked like a northern version of Massachusetts; and it had already been granted its own representative assembly in 1758, the earliest in Canada-to-be. Much of this northward New England migration, however, had been influenced by war and postwar disorders in the continental interior that did not make any westward movement too inviting. By the time of the Proclamation of 1763 Nova Scotia's population had risen above 8,000, but the influx soon began to slow. By 1767 it had some 13,500 inhabitants; yet these also included English and German settlers in or near Halifax, and remnants of the Acadians, particularly in Cape Breton Island or areas of the future provinces of New Brunswick and Prince Edward Island.

Hence the Proclamation of 1763 had only limited success in bringing British American colonists up to Nova Scotia. It proved to have still less as far as the new province of Quebec was concerned. Few New Englanders, New Yorkers or others wanted to move to the homeland of their former foes, to settle beside a foreign people, Roman Catholic instead of Protestant in religion, French in language, and with a different social structure and land system, the seigneurial system, based on tenant-holdings rather than the individual farm-ownership they knew. Hence, despite promises in the Proclamation, to be noted later, English-speaking settlers did not flock to Quebec.

The few who did come were merchants rather than farm-colonists, the first of them often contractors and suppliers for the occupying British forces. They settled in Quebec and particularly Montreal. Thanks to their British and American business connections (now that those of France had been cut off) they largely took the lead in controlling the economic life of the colony, and especially its basic fur trade with the interior. Limited in numbers but strong in economic power, this rising Anglo-American commercial class might contend vigorously with British bureaucrats, military men and governors, who came to see them as trouble-making demagogues, grasping self-seekers intolerantly claiming superiority as Old Subjects over the New. They were "licentious fanaticks" to Murray, who much preferred the "docile," orderly French. Yet both the merchants and the British officials remained alien to the mass of the *Canadiens* of the countryside, who certainly did not become absorbed into a newly English province of Quebec, but continued in the old, largely unbroken ways of their farming and parish life.

Nevertheless, the intent and basic orientation of the Proclamation of 1763 was assimilatory. Quebec was a part of the Empire, one more of the British provinces in the northern part of America. In restricting its boundaries to create a temporary French-Canadian enclave, an infusion of English-speaking, Protestant Old Subjects was expected to dilute the French element. This, coupled with the example of the advantages of being British subjects, would serve to break old loyalties. In the decade of the sixties, loyalty was conceived not in terms of the nation, but the king. Hence French and English would both identify with their king, now George III.

The Proclamation made a crucial general provision respecting government and law. British institutions were promised in the new colonies, to attract Old Subjects as settlers, which would involve establishing representative government as well as the pattern of law and land ownership they knew. The established format was to be that prevalent in the British-American colonies, under the civil and criminal law of Great Britain. All of the New Subjects, whether those of Grenada, Dominica or Florida, as well as those of Quebec, became British subjects on the same basis. Roman Catholics were indeed confirmed in their right to worship, but were denied any and all political positions. This provision was not new. It was the established law of Great Britain. A similar provision and policy had had the same effect on the few Protestants present in New France before 1760, and the Protestants in France since the days of Cardinal Richelieu. It did raise the question, however, as to whether French Canadians would be able to sit in a representative assembly, even though Murray did not keep them out of all government posts. The Proclamation took effect on August 10, 1764, and the regime of civil government began. Murray was instructed to establish a council, which he did, and at an appropriate time, to call an assembly. The appropriate moment never occurred, given mounting conflict between the governor and the merchants, his fear of them controlling the assembly, which they demanded as of right, and his hesitancy even to establish a full pattern of English law since, like an assembly, it was foreign to French experience and would chiefly benefit the small English group.

The major role played by military needs and military men till the implementation of the Proclamation was to be expected. One of the unforeseen results of the provisions of that document, however, was to endow the governor with a focus of power that his *ancien régime* counterpart had never possessed, unchecked by an intendant or a relatively independent Superior Council. In this first decade, the governor and the governor's party dominated the life of Quebec, be it Governor Murray or his successor, Sir Guy Carleton. Francis Maseres, who would be Attorney-General of Quebec later in the decade, best described what he called "Murray's Party": "Those who were zealous for him are the persons whom he had raised and given office to . . ."

There was some overt nepotism, too, and official posts kept to members of the in-group. Such an accumulation of political, economic and judicial functions in relatively few hands indeed had been a characteristic of the French regime. Prevalent in the British-American colonies as well, it also became a feature of the British regime in Quebec. Murray's party, whose members were physically located in Quebec city, was thus a dominant interest group among the other interest groups. The opposition to him, political and economic, was more pronounced in mercantile Montreal than the political capital. Time, ulterior events and hindsight has led to characterizing the parties of the first decade as a French party, opposed by an English or merchants party. Murray's opposition, however, was essentially anti-Murray and anti-Murray's policies, rather than anti-French.

The implementation of the Proclamation in 1764 did not create the crises of Murray's last years in the colony, but it did bring them into focus. In part, the problems of the colony involved the use of power and privilege by the governor's party; in part, the interests of retail trade as against those of wholesale commerce. The economy of the fur trade did not always meld easily with that of the fishing industry. Serious differences of political principle arose between the military-official outlook exemplified by Murray and his cohorts, and the constitutionalist viewpoint prevalent among his opponents. In the colony this problem was compounded by diverse British opinions regarding the role of the crown as against the role of Parliament in colonial affairs. Questions of legal systems, land tenure, language and religious rights were all thrown into one bubbling, boiling cauldron. While some in the colony, both English and French, wanted an assembly, some, in particular Murray and his party, did not. Was the common law of Great Britain to be rigidly applied, moreover, not applied at all, or modified and applied in combination with the *Coutume de Paris*? Every alternative had its adherents. French Catholics should participate in the courts and serve in the army; or again, they should do so only upon renouncing their religion. Murray was unwilling and unable to solve all these problems, to satisfy diverse and contradictory interests. The resolution of some issues, such as the pattern of law, did not depend solely upon him, but rather upon the metropolitan authorities. His principal contribution to the legal system was to delay the full implementation of the provisions regarding law embodied in the Proclamation. Roman Catholic institutions and French civil law still operated within a court structure based on British common law.

The governor's most significant achievement after 1763 was the integration of the Roman Catholic Church, and its adherents, into the imperial framework. The Church, along with all of the other social structures of the colony, had suffered some dislocation after the conquest. Its bishop, Pontbriand, had died in June 1760; no new priests could thus be consecrated. The British government did not permit the immigration of new recruits from France, since the cloth and collar covered a Frenchman as well as a Catholic. Some, but not many, clerics returned to France. The British distrusted the two principal male religious orders, the Sulpicians and the Jesuits, and the latters' extensive estates were subsequently confiscated. However, Church and churchmen, unlike other elite groups of the *ancien régime*, changed less in personnel and policy in the first decade than did the government.

As early as 1759, the Church inaugurated a policy of cooperation with the British. Pontbriand had told the parish priests of the conquered area that Protestant services could take place in their churches, after the Catholic service. By 1762, Jean Olivier Briand, a French-born canon of the Quebec cathedral chapter, was already working closely with Murray, advising him on clerical appointments. Briand became Murray's man, and Murray Briand's. In 1766, after being elected by the chapter and consecrated by the Papacy, the governor named him Superintendent of the Church in Quebec —bishop in all but name. The ecclesiastical hierarchy had a leader again.

A quiet pragmatist, a "courtier priest," Briand occupied himself with the material as well as spiritual organization of his diocese. Murray personally advanced some money and convinced the British government to do so as well. The French crown and clergy also granted the Canadian Church an annual *pension* of 3,000 *livres* in 1765. But the important point was that the British state had reached a lasting accommodation with the French Catholic Church, giving the former increased credence with the firmly Catholic *Canadien* population.

Church and state relations had been satisfactorily settled. But those of the governor and his party with the merchant element— and their friends in London—only grew worse, as merchants continued to demand the English laws and assembly promised in the Proclamation, and Murray still baulked, fearing that the "fanaticks" might thus be put in control. The French and British regimes in Canada responded in a similar fashion to such conflicts of personality or policy in the colony: recall the governor. Murray left Quebec on June 28, 1766. His legacy in Quebec included assets and liabilities. A bishop and the integration of the Church into the Empire was a decided accomplishment. The governor's refusal to completely exclude the New Subjects from government, despite the prohibition on Catholics holding office under British law, was a realistic policy; the sheer force of numbers combined with the lack of Old Subject immigrants made it imperative. Yet he left his successor, Guy Carleton, three major unresolved problems: the legal system, the form of government, and the rooted dissatisfaction of the merchants. None of these would be settled during the remainder of this first decade.

Like Murray, Carleton was a soldier-aristocrat (Anglo-Irish instead of Scots) who had served at the siege of Quebec. He came to Canada ostensibly as a sympathizer with the merchants; but his origins and military outlook soon moved him closer to his predecessor's views. He began by reshaping the governor's council into his own party. Then he turned to the legal system: officially British but unofficially an unsatisfactory mixture of French and English laws and usages. He asked François-Joseph Cugnet, the son of a late chief councillor of the Superior Council of New France, to pre-

pare a report on the laws of the *ancien régime*. His new attorney-
general, Francis Maseres, also submitted a report on the laws of
Quebec, but Carleton rejected its findings. He would reach a definitive solution of the legal issue only in the next decade. Carleton
also took up the question of the structure of government, as Murray
had before him, and quickly came to similar conclusions regarding
the ineffectiveness of the Proclamation. In one important aspect,
however, he differed from Murray. The ex-gove nor had postulated
many of his policies on the future anglicization of Quebec. Carleton
believed that the colony would remain French forever, or at least
for the foreseeable future. But again, his definitive policy on government, derived from that opinion, would not mature until the 1770s.

III

In the first decade, the economic life of the St. Lawrence valley
community continued familiar patterns but also saw the inaugura-
tion of new associations. There was still the staple fur trade, seigneurial farming and fishing in the lower St. Lawrence and Gulf.
But there was also the fact that the colony was now tied to a new
economic metropolis in London, to British imperial traffic, and to
an Anglo-American merchant element.

One purpose of the British conquest had been to acquire dominance over the economic empire of the St. Lawrence. The essential
importance of St. Lawrence commerce influenced policy in both the
French and English regimes. British-American free trade enthusiasts, once located physically and commercially in the valley of the
St. Lawrence, rapidly became converted to a belief in the monopo-
listic trading pattern of the *ancien régime*. And whatever changes
did take place, the basic economic structure of the English colony
continued to resemble that of the old French colony, as was indicated by the state of trade in the 1760s. During the French regime,
imports had exceeded exports. The same was true of the first decade
of the British regime. The imbalance in trade was partly the result
of postwar reconstruction: the economy was being capitalized. The
new merchants, Old Subjects but at first lacking both stocks and

capital, had to expend larger sums as they took root in Quebec's economy.

The relatively low exports of the sixties, both in furs and other products, was notably due to the restricted hinterland imposed by the Proclamation and to the competition of British American merchants operating from the Thirteen Colonies. These effects of economic integration into the British Empire became evident shortly after the conquest. Fur exports from New York at a minimum doubled between 1760 and 1770; at a maximum they increased by over 500 per cent. The exports from Hudson Bay, however, notwithstanding the conquest, remained constant in the first decade. Quebec's economic competition for furs really came from the south.

The basic fur trade was thus a problem in the decade. Currency was another. The already badly inflated money system of the *ancien régime* had collapsed in 1759-60, and the initial policy of the British authorities had been to discredit the enemy's currency. By 1763, due to an honest concern for the holders of French obligations, and because Old Subjects were speculating in French bills, the British government undertook negotiations for the redemption of French money. The French government finally agreed to a settlement by which the balance to be redeemed was 46 million *livres*.

The generalized results of the unsettled currency situation were twofold: the old currency was a useless asset until such time as it was, if ever, redeemed; also, other sources of capital had to be found. More directly, the final result of the collapse of the former currency system was a minimum reduction of money assets in Quebec by 30 per cent, and at times, as much as 50 per cent. Economic adjustment after the conquest was indeed a problem for both Old and New Subjects. Both the legitimate recipients of the old currency, and those who speculated in it, suffered the consequences of the years of uncertainty. French-Canadian entrepreneurs faced a more complex adjustment than did the Old Subject entrepreneurs, since the English were in contact with the British market and capital system, while the French had lost their traditional economic organization. New contacts for both markets and capital, as well as supplies, had to be established.

In Carleton's regime as in Murray's, economic problems were also

linked to the political system. Problems of government and constitutional provisions had economic effects. There existed a coincidence of interests between Old and New Subjects on some of these
issues. For instance, the competition of New York traders affected
both French and English merchants. The currency problems also
affected conqueror and conquered, though not always equally. And
the general fall in Quebec's economy was a problem for all, as were
troubles in the hinterland. Both groups championed a revision of the
boundaries, to open the Indian country more effectively again to
Canadian interests; and both felt western trade suffer from Pontiac's
rebellion of 1763-65.

In the western lands of the Ohio valley and Great Lakes region,
the Indian tribes did not necessarily return to quiet when the Seven
Years' War ended. Many had been French allies; indeed, the
British American colonists called the conflict the French and
Indian War. Many Indians resented the British taking over the
western posts once held by the French, fearful for their lands and of
the spread of English settlement. The British military authorities,
including Murray at Quebec, did not pay sufficient heed to the
Indian problem. When they did, they included in the Proclamation
of 1763 the provisions for checking settlement, and for setting aside
the Indian country, apart from Quebec or other colonies, so that
the tribes could be pacified and the fur trade supervised. But this
came too late to prevent an uprising by Pontiac, a chief of the
Ottawas, who with Senecas, Hurons, Chippewas and others sought
to drive the British out of the western forts.

Michilimackinac, key to the Upper Lakes trade, was taken in
June 1763, and so were other posts. Pontiac failed to surprise the
major base of Detroit, but laid siege to it for several months, until
the Indians learned that no help would be sent from France. The
ill-organized rising gradually fell apart, but the Indian frontiers
remained dangerously restive until peace negotiations were concluded between British and Indians in 1765, further confirmed by
a treaty at Fort Stanwix in 1768.

In consequence, it is not surprising that Quebec's fur trade suffered during the sixties. Traders, in fact, were excluded from the
Indian country until the revolt ended in 1765, and found the

licensing system then set up expensive and restrictive. The restrictions were gradually relaxed, and full freedom to trade restored in 1768. As a result, Montreal rapidly advanced its influence in the interior, thanks to its commanding position on the superb St. Lawrence water route to the upper country. Furthermore, English-speaking traders based on Montreal—often in partnership with *Canadiens* and using skilled French-Canadian *voyageurs* as their canoemen—men such as Alexander Henry, began more and more to penetrate the interior. It was still a hard life, as this contemporary description of the fur trade in the 1760s shows:

> The adventurer in the Indian trade must have his goods ready at Montreal in the month of April, consequently they must be arrived from England at Quebec on or before the month of November the preceeding year, from there during the winter they must be transported to Montreal where they are prepared for the Indian Voyage by being put in packages not exceeding one hundred pounds weight each. . . . The birch canoes with their complements of six men each being ready, the goods are put on board and so they proceed (the first week in May) on the voyage by the River Ottawaes to the port of Michilimackinac . . . As they must unload and load their canoes every night and during the course of the voyage carry them on their backs in 35 different places some of which are a league long . . . it is generally the middle of June before the earliest canoes arrive. The remainder of this month, July, August and September is all the time the traders have to dispose of their goods and to carry their furs to Montreal. If in this time they cannot finish their business and they are obliged to stay all winter, they are sure to make a loseing [sic] voyage.

The combination of French knowledge of the Indians and the *pays d'en haut* with English trade goods and commercial connections was to prove a potent one; especially when it led northwest beyond the Great Lakes, where the greatest destiny of the Canadian fur trade was to lie. In this far northwest, the French fur traders had reached to the Saskatchewan in the later days of New France. In 1768, following the lifting of the licensing restrictions, the first English trader from Canada, James Finlay, arrived to winter there. As yet the lordly Hudson's Bay Company which officially owned the Saskatchewan plains as part of Rupert's Land, the country draining into Hudson Bay, had little to fear from such Canadian interlopers. The Bay Company was pleased enough to be relieved of warlike threats to its holdings from New France. It was not concerned about fur trade competition rising overland from Canada, when it had its short sea route from the Bay to British markets, and its well-established posts on the shores to which the Indians brought the furs themselves. Still, the Company was probing down further into the James Bay area as the 1760s ended; and even reached northward towards the Arctic, when in 1769 it sent Samuel Hearne on the first of three epic journeys into the tundra of the Barren Lands.

His achievements there would come in the next decade, just as the Canadian northwest fur trade would also take shape then. In fact, that was widely true of the 1760s: many of its developments or problems would reach their outcome later. This first and sixteenth decade was not rich in decisive accomplishments—other than in the conquest of Canada itself.

Returning to that conquest, and the centrally important theme of Quebec, one should not underestimate the bare military aspects of that event. Force and circumstance brought a long-existing conflict to a final resolution: Canada would be British, first as part of a large British-American unit; later as a remnant of the First British Empire. Moreover, Murray's regime, shaping the first years of British rule, was more significant than Carleton's in the later years of the decade. Murray had sincerely believed that the colony should be, and would be, anglicized in the long run. Neither he nor his opponents disputed the rights of Roman Catholics to practise their faith. The recognition of the Church, and the consecration of an all-but bishop were believed to be temporary expedients, just, but not enduring. The instituting of an assembly and British laws were put off, because it seemed that the *Canadien* majority would then be too much at the mercy of an intolerant mercantile minority. Murray, however, interpreted tolerance as his personal prerogative. His policy led beyond tolerance to autocratic establishment. He personally set aside the constitutional promises of the Proclamation and his own Instructions, a mode of political behaviour that enraged the constitutionalist-minded English-speaking Old Subjects.

The most serious general problem faced by the French New

Subjects was still that of adjustment. While there was some continuity in the political, economic, religious and social structures of the *ancien* and new regimes, the symbols and representatives of authority had been disrupted and replaced. The ingrained pattern of social relationships, the natural social responses to authority based on unquestioned assent, had to be adjusted. The crown and monarch no longer meant France and Louis, but England and George. Colonial rulers were of another nation, faith and language, looking to London, not to Paris or Rome.

Still, the province was at peace, and increasingly prosperous, as the costs of war and conquest were overcome, as agriculture steadied, and the fur trade expanded anew. The outlook in 1770 was still uncertain for *Canadiens* and colonists. But it was not as violent and fearful as when the decade opened.

2: The 1770s

GEORGE RAWLYK

If any single historical event significantly stamped its mark upon the 1770s and also gave the decade its own peculiar character and coherence, it was the refusal of the British colonies north of New York and Massachusetts to join the American Revolution. The inhabitants of Newfoundland and most of those residing on what would later be known as Prince Edward Island were never seriously tempted to follow the American example. They were effectively protected from the revolutionary threat from the south by their powerful British orientation, the isolated nature of their primitive settlements and also by British warships. On the other hand, especially in 1775 and 1776, many Nova Scotia and Quebec residents were under considerable pressure to join the American "rebels" in their attempt to shatter the existing framework of the British North American colonial system.

Instead of triggering a major, indigenous, pro-American political and military outburst in Nova Scotia, however, the revolutionary crisis helped to precipitate one of the most important social movements in Nova Scotia history—the widespread religious revival known as the Great Awakening.

In the inland colony of Quebec, even though the "Yankee" liberators were turned back and the revolutionary ideology rejected, the Revolution helped to intensify certain existing class and racial tensions in the colony. And furthermore, partly as a result, many French Canadians felt "in a manner emancipated" by the ebb and flow of unanticipated events. The distant northern regions of the fur trade, of the Hudson's Bay Company in Rupert's Land, were affected much less directly by the events of the Revolution, although here, too, the decade witnessed developments of considerable consequence.

At the easternmost extremity of British North America, Newfoundland during the 1770s continued to be regarded by the British government "as a great English ship moored near the banks during the fishing season for the convenience of the English fishermen." According to a 1698 act of Parliament, the Newfoundland ship was to be manned only during the spring and summer months, as all permanent settlement on the inhospitable island was expressly forbidden. It was hoped that by the terms of the act the Newfoundland fishery would become the "nursery of the British Navy" and thus provide "a number of seamen for the speedy manning of our fleets in time of danger."

In theory, settlement may have been prohibited but in actual practice it had not been. By the 1770s there were probably over fifteen thousand permanent residents, seven-eighths of whom lived in a narrow ribbon of civilization running along the coast of the peninsula between Trinity and Placentia Bays on the eastern tip of the island. The men outnumbered the women by almost nine to one during the winter months, and by almost twenty to one during the fishing season because of the yearly temporary influx of almost ten thousand fishermen. There was a clear distinction drawn between the permanent Newfoundland settlers, and the fishermen who returned to Great Britain each autumn. The two groups, how-

ever, had at least three major things in common. First, their liveli-
hoods were dependent upon "the knob-headed, richly fat, and suc-
culent codfish." Second, their racial and regional composition was
virtually identical. Almost all of them came from either the West
Country of England, or from Ireland. Third, the inhabitants and the
fishermen had their basic interests divided between Newfoundland
and the British Isles. Newfoundland was not, therefore, a North
American colony. It remained instead a British economic and
strategic outpost.

Newfoundland life in the 1770s was totally absorbed in the
fishery. Agriculture and stock-raising were in a most rudimentary
state and any attachment to the soil, unlike in the other North
American colonies, hardly existed on the island. Society was characterized by deep class, racial and religious divisions and a large
number of permanent residents found themselves in a state of semi-
vassalage. These people were callously manipulated by the prominent members of Newfoundland society—the merchants, liquor-
sellers, storekeepers and boatkeepers. It was realized by many of
the elite that it was to their economic advantage to encourage the
inhabitants to mortgage their next year's wages for supplies and
liquor consumed during the long interval between the end of one
season and the beginning of the other. It is not surprising that the
"winter-slaves," as they were called, locked into a hopeless economic
situation, turned to rum and debauchery to escape from the grim
realities of their primitive existence. Mostly illiterate and completely
ignorant of and indifferent to the political issues agitating many
Americans, these men were oblivious to the revolutionary movement.
Rhetoric proposing fundamental political and constitutional reforms
would have made no impression on the minds of these people, whose
prime concern was mere existence. Economic bondage had produced a peculiar Newfoundland fatalism.

An unusual quantity of liquor was consumed by its inhabitants;
in 1775 there were no fewer than eighty grog shops in St. John's,
the capital. Because of the shortage of women and the long despair-
ing winter months of inactivity, prostitution was also widespread,
as was the quaint custom of exchanging and sharing wives. Little
could be done by the handful of Church of England missionaries

and the justices of the peace to deal with the widespread "blasphemy, profaneness, breach of the Sabbath, adultery, fornication, polygamy, incest, swearing and drunkeness."

A further ingredient in Newfoundland's social turmoil was the often bitter racial and religious tension existing between the Roman Catholic Irish and the Protestant West Countrymen. The total population was divided almost equally into the two opposing camps. To exacerbate still further this friction imported from the Old World to the New, the Roman Catholic Irish were expressly forbidden by statute to worship publicly on the island. They were thus thrust to the bottom of Newfoundland's social scale—only a notch, however, below the Protestant West Countrymen.

Once the American Revolutionary War broke out, the Irish appeared, to the authorities at least, to be the only group on the island capable of disloyal behaviour. Almost everyone else could be trusted. The government officials and the English permanent residents had always shared a strong British orientation. But in sharp contrast to this, the Irish had enthusiastically supported the French in their invasion of Newfoundland in 1762. Three years later, quite independently of the Stamp Act crisis in the New England colonies, they had also "raised a formidable riot in Conception Bay." But there was little reason for any official anxiety regarding the possible disaffection of the Irish or any other group in Newfoundland. The presence of four or five British warships in Newfoundland waters during the early war years, and of a relatively strong garrison ashore, must have overawed most islanders and therefore considerably strengthened the forces of continuity underlying the status quo. The depredations committed by freebooting American privateersmen in various settlements after 1776, as well as the unexpected prosperity ushered in by the war, merely confirmed most Newfoundlanders in their pro-British stance or, at least, in their apathy.

The response to the Revolution of the other British island colony, the tiny St. John's Island (Prince Edward Island), was similar to that of Newfoundland and for many of the same reasons. In 1765 St. John's Island had been divided into sixty-seven townships or lots of twenty thousand acres each. Two years later these lots were distributed among proprietors who in exchange for the land were obliged to settle within ten years one hundred persons per lot and also to pay a quit-rent of from two to six shillings for each hundred acres. In 1779, twelve years after the grand lottery and ten years after the island had become a separate colony, in forty-nine of the sixty-seven lots there was not even one settler. Furthermore, most of the proprietors had carefully avoided paying one shilling in quit-rents for their land.

The population of the island had grown from approximately three hundred in 1768 to about thirteen hundred a decade later. Of this thirteen hundred, it has been estimated, nine hundred had landed between 1770 and 1775 and at least three hundred were Acadian French-speaking inhabitants and their families who had escaped expulsion during the Seven Years' War. The immigrants who arrived between 1770 and 1775 were Scots, such as those hundreds of Highlanders from South Uist brought over in 1772 by the proprietor Captain John MacDonald, laird of Glenaladale and Glenfinnan. MacDonald's Highlanders, who had been driven from their homes in Scotland, looked to him as their saviour. As was later observed by the Earl of Selkirk, they esteemed "it the most sublime degree of virtue to love their Chief and pay him a blind obedience." When MacDonald in 1775 volunteered to join the British army "to help prevent the Scots Highlanders . . . being seduced by the Congress," his island tenants automatically adopted his anti-revolutionary position. The Scots tenants of other "Proprietor-Chiefs," responded in a similar manner. These recent immigrants had no desire to abandon their lands to chase after ephemeral constitutional issues.

Only the Acadians, as a group, seemed to be disaffected; and a few, especially after the French decided to support the Americans in 1778, openly advocated a Franco-American invasion. Such an attitude was certainly understandable when the traumatic impact upon the Acadians of the "Expulsion" is taken into account. Revenge, fear of the new immigrants, and a desire to return to their "Golden Age" influenced their attitude towards hostilities. But fully aware of military realities, they were unwilling to take any initiative; instead, they waited for others to liberate them. They waited in vain.

The only noteworthy military engagement on the island in the 1770s was the comic-opera invasion of Charlottetown, the capital, in November 1775, by two American privateers. After plundering a number of houses and stores, the Massachusetts freebooters captured Attorney-General Phillips Callbeck, the acting governor, and two other officials, and proudly carried them off to General George Washington at Cambridge. Washington had no use for the captives and immediately despatched them back to St. John's Island by way of Nova Scotia. The Charlottetown attack persuaded the British authorities to devote some attention to the defence of the island. Consequently, the Newfoundland fleet was augmented to ensure the protection of the neighbouring island, and a seven-gun battery was built at Charlottetown and reinforcements sent to defend it.

An immediate effect of the American Revolution was to discourage further immigration to the island. But this was not all. War also meant that many of the settlers had good prices for their produce and excellent wages for their labour. It was noted early in 1780 by the returning Governor Patterson, who had left the island five years earlier, that "They [the inhabitants] are comfortable in their situation, have large stocks of cattle, and abound with all the necessaries of life as far as they regard the table."

II

By 1770 the influx of Yankee fishermen and farmers into Nova Scotia had virtually come to an end and an outflow back to New England had begun. Immigration from Great Britain, however, continued and even expanded. As a result, more than a thousand Yorkshiremen, some destitute Highlanders and Irish Roman Catholics entered the colony before the outbreak of the Revolution and significantly strengthened the non-Yankee elements of the population. By 1776, of an estimated total population of seventeen to twenty thousand, only approximately one-half was of New England origin. Nova Scotia in 1776, therefore, was not a homogeneous New England colony. Rather, it was little more than a political expression for a number of widely scattered and isolated communities stretching from Pictou on Northumberland Strait to the Acadian villages on Cape Breton Island, to Canso and then to Halifax and Yarmouth, and along the Bay of Fundy coast to Maugerville on the St. John River and the tiny outpost of Passamaquoddy on the St. Croix.

During the revolutionary decade, there were at least two distinct Nova Scotias, Halifax and the outsettlements. The actual influence of the capital was largely restricted to the Bedford Basin region. Petty political squabbling, graft and corruption, economic and social stagnation seemed to characterize Halifax life in the pre-revolutionary years. Governor William Campbell, and Francis Legge who replaced him in 1773, were in constant trouble with the Halifax commercial elite. Both were eventually hounded out of the governorship by their persistent and unscrupulous critics. Being forced to leave the capital was, in many respects, something to be looked forward to. Halifax, which in 1775 had a population of almost two thousand, was described by one eyewitness as being

> little more than a hamlet; at best it was a miserable village, inhabited chiefly by fishermen . . . most of the houses were in a dilapidated state, letting in the bleak winds of the season through manifold chinks, hardly a room having ever known the luxury of being plastered.

Apart from Yorkshiremen and Scotch-Irish residing in the Chignecto-Minas Bay region, the Highland Scots of Pictou and the "Foreign [German-speaking] Protestants" of Lunenburg, the outsettlements were dominated by the Nova Scotia "Yankees." These inhabitants of the coastal strip of the southern half of peninsula Nova Scotia and of the valley of the St. John River had strong cultural and economic ties with their former homeland. They also were suspicious of the small clique of Halifax merchants who controlled the legislative and executive functions of government and who attempted to impose centralized control over the isolated townships. Consequently, when the revolutionary crisis engulfed North America, the Halifax authorities, not without reason, expected their "bitter bad subjects" to flock to the American side. Only in the vicinity of the two western frontier settlements of Maugerville and

Cumberland, however, was there any indigenous revolutionary activity. The "contagion of disaffection" infected merely a minority of the population of this area, and then only for a period of a few months in 1776. Even then, the "disaffection" was probably more than anything else proof, as the Maugerville rebels put it, of "our . . . Desire to submit ourselves to the government of the Massachusetts Bay."

These two indigenous revolutionary movements came into being in Maugerville and the Chignecto Isthmus quite independently of one another. The first was led by the Reverend Mr. Seth Noble, a Congregational minister recently arrived from New England, who had been able to convince his parishioners "that as tyranny ought to be Resisted in its first appearance . . . the united Provinces are just in their proceedings." On the Chignecto Isthmus Jonathan Eddy and John Allan, leading public figures and successful farmers, were the ringleaders.

Towards the end of November and in early December of 1775, Noble, Eddy and Allan were certain that the Nova Scotia government had prepared the way for revolution by passing two extraordinarily unpopular acts. The first stipulated that one-fifth of the militia was to be called out to defend the colony and the other imposed a tax for the support of the militia. Almost immediately the legislation was denounced throughout the "Yankee" regions by those who violently objected to the new tax and to the possibility of being compelled, as one petition emphasized, to "march into different parts in arms against their friends and relations." Just at the moment when it seemed likely that the profound discontent would be channelled into a violent confrontation, Governor Legge promptly suspended the two contentious acts.

Failing to grasp the significance of Legge's decision in undermining the base of their potential support, Eddy and Allan decided in early 1776 that the time was ripe for fomenting a major insurrection. They badly misjudged public opinion. When they sounded out their neighbours regarding the viability of rebellion, they were apparently genuinely shocked to discover that most "Yankees," even though they "would have welcomed an army of invasion," had no enthusiasm for participating in an independent insurrection. Ground between the millstones of contending forces and values, most of the Chignecto "Yankees," like those New Englanders in other areas of Nova Scotia, did not want to commit themselves. A well-known petition from the Yarmouth inhabitants to Governor Legge cogently expressed this point of view:

> We do all of us profess to be true Friends and Loyal Subjects to George our King. We were almost all of us born in New England, we have Fathers, Brothers and Sisters in that country, divided betwixt natural affection to our nearest relatives, and good Faith and Friendship to our King and Country, we want to know if we may be permitted at this time to live in a peaceable State. . . .

The "Yankees" would patiently wait, aloof from the conflict, until they were "liberated" and absolutely certain which side would gain effective control of Nova Scotia.

In February 1776 Eddy, with fourteen supporters, left Chignecto to persuade Washington and the Continental Congress to send an "army of Liberation" to Nova Scotia. Eddy's mission failed but he, nevertheless, refused to abandon his scheme. In early August he was in Machias where he was able to recruit a twenty-eight man liberating army for the planned invasion of Nova Scotia. After picking up a few more volunteers at Passamaquoddy and Maugerville, at which latter place the inhabitants were "almost universally . . . hearty in the cause," Eddy's eighty-man army made its way to the Chignecto Isthmus. The immediate military target was Fort Cumberland, the British fort at the Bay of Fundy side of the narrow isthmus.

The supporters of Eddy and Allan on the isthmus understandably "expressed their uneasiness at seeing so few invaders . . . and those unprovided with Artillery." They vehemently argued that, in view of British strength, there was no possible chance of success. Eddy was therefore forced to resort to outright intimidation in order to compel his former supporters to join the invading force. In late November the invading force was driven from the Chignecto by British troops. Eddy and his men retreated westwards to Maugerville and then to Machias and to oblivion. The following year in Maugerville the inhabitants, under British pressure, abandoned their American sympathies and submitted themselves once again to

George III. In the Chignecto, by 1777, most of the supporters of revolution had emigrated to Massachusetts thus destroying the local movement.

In both areas there were four phases in the collective response to revolution on the part of a large number of inhabitants. There was, prior to 1775, a prevailing apathy concerning the political and economic questions that were disturbing New Englanders. The Nova Scotia "Yankees," by emigrating in the early 1760s, had missed a critical decade in the ideological development of the New England colonies. And consequently, most of them were incapable of comprehending the arguments used during the immediate pre-revolution period. In a sense then, their political thinking had congealed before the Stamp Act crisis. The second phase occurred in late 1775 and early 1776. During these months, the government's militia policy precipitated a crisis which, together with the underlying sympathy for family and friends in New England, was used by politically aware leaders to bring the local revolutionary movement into public view. There followed a period of a number of months when the leaders attempted to broaden the base of support, in the Chignecto by bringing in an invading force and by intimidation, and in Maugerville by persuasion. Then in 1777, most of the remaining settlers quickly reverted to their British allegiance.

Most other Nova Scotians, even though they probably never passed beyond the earliest phase of the Maugerville–Chignecto reaction to the Revolution, still must have shared the basic vacillation and confusion of that reaction. In a very real sense the essence of Nova Scotia's response to the Revolution was acute confusion. The activities of American privateers merely added to the existing chaos. Almost every Nova Scotia settlement, with the exception of Halifax, was ravaged by American privateersmen. Here indeed was a strange way to make American converts of Nova Scotians!

It is too simplistic, however, to conclude that the New England privateering raids drove the wavering Nova Scotia "Yankees" into the welcoming arms of the mother country. Some of the well-to-do merchants, who bore the brunt of the expeditions, probably did move in this direction. But the majority of "Yankee" inhabitants, who had little of any value to lose to freebooters, certainly did not.

These men must have been able to distinguish clearly between the rapacious privateersmen and the people and governments of the independent states. Moreover, the ordinary Nova Scotia inhabitants had as much to fear from the press-gangs as from the privateers. For example, even after having lost a number of their ships to American privateers and having suffered depredations ashore, the people of Liverpool, "much Discouraged," wanted to return to New England. They blamed their plight, it should be noted, not on the Americans but on the indifference of the British authorities in Halifax who seemed far more interested in impressing Nova Scotians into the British navy than in defending them.

As in Newfoundland and St. John's Island, the Revolution brought to Nova Scotia a sudden burst of economic prosperity. Halifax, as always during periods of war, sucked in huge sums of money for military purposes; some of this money made its way to the outsettlements, as did revenue from the considerable illicit trade carried on with the Americans. This commercial activity, however, did little to neutralize the general feeling of uneasiness, fear and puzzlement concerning the war. Until local leaders were able to make some sense out of the confusing contemporary situation, the Nova Scotians were bound to have remained in a troubled frame of mind, as they desperately searched for a new sense of identity to replace their disintegrating dual loyalty to both Old and New England. As one contemporary observer perceptively noted in the autumn of 1776: the "inhabitants . . . were reduced to the shocking dilemma of Being Either plundered and butchered by their friends or of incurring the highest displeasure of their own Government."

III

Henry Alline was one Nova Scotian who was able to perceive a special purpose for his fellow colonists in the midst of the confused revolutionary situation. He was the charismatic leader of the intense religious revival which swept the colony during the war period. This revival was not merely a "retreat from the grim realities of the world to the safety and pleasantly exciting warmth of the revival meeting." Nor was it basically a revolt of the outsettlements against Halifax or an irrational outburst against all forms of traditionalism and authority. The Great Awakening of Nova Scotia may be viewed as an attempt by many inhabitants to appropriate a sense of identity. Religious enthusiasm in this context, a social movement of profound consequence in the Nova Scotia situation, was symptomatic of a collective identity crisis as well as a searching for an acceptable and meaningful ideology. Resolution of the crisis came not only when the individuals were absorbed into what they felt was a dynamic fellowship of true believers, but also when they accepted Alline's analysis of contemporary events and his conviction that their colony was the centre of a crucial cosmic struggle.

Alline was born in Newport, Rhode Island, in 1748, and in 1760 moved with his parents to Falmouth in the Minas Basin region of Nova Scotia. Like most young people in the settlement, he was brought up in a pious Christian atmosphere. His morbid sense of introspection and the pressure he was under to commit himself one way or another in the revolutionary struggle helped to precipitate a psychic crisis and conversion in 1775. As Alline observed in his *Journal*:

> my whole soul seemed to be melted down with love; the burden of guilt and condemnation was gone, darkness was expelled, my heart humbled and filled with gratitude, and my will turned of choice after the infinite God . . . my whole soul seemed filled with the divine being . . . my whole soul was filled with love, and ravished with a divine ecstacy beyond any doubts or fears . . . for I enjoyed a heaven on earth, and it seemed as if I were wrapped up in God.

Under a compulsion to have others share with him this traumatic religious experience, Alline resolved "to go forth, and enlist my fellow-mortals to fight under the banners of King Jesus." He considered himself to be more than an evangelist or even a prophet; he believed he was, rather, Nova Scotia's and the world's second John the Baptist. It was Jesus Christ and Alline, not George III or George Washington, who were alone worthy of blind obedience.

Eventually Alline visited almost every settlement in Nova Scotia; and only Halifax, Chester and Lunenburg were unaffected by the revival he largely articulated into existence. Almost single-handed,

Alline was able to draw the isolated communities together and to impose upon them a feeling of unity. They each were sharing a common experience; he was providing them with answers to disconcerting and puzzling contemporary questions. For Alline, the Nova Scotia revival was an event of world significance. The social, economic and political backwater that was Nova Scotia was the new centre of the Christian world. He thus was attempting to lift Nova Scotians from their parochial surroundings and to thrust them into the middle of the world stage.

In his sermons preached as he criss-crossed the colony, Alline developed the theme that the Nova Scotia "Yankees," in particular, had a special predestined role to play in bringing about the millennium. It must have required special effort for the preacher to convince Nova Scotians of their world role. But Alline, striking deep into the Puritan New England tradition that viewed self-abnegation and frugality as virtues, contended that the relative backwardness and isolation of the colony had removed the inhabitants from the prevailing corrupting influences of New England and Britain. As a result, Nova Scotia was in an ideal position to lead the world back to God. As far as he was concerned, the revival was convincing proof that the Nova Scotians were "a people on whom God had set his everlasting Love" and that their colony was "as the Apple of His Eye."

The implication of the conjunction of events, of civil war in New England and an outpouring of the Holy Spirit in Nova Scotia, was obvious to Alline and the hundreds who flocked to hear him. God was passing New England's historical role of Christian leadership to Nova Scotia. With two powerful Protestant nations furiously battling one another, the whole course of events since the Reformation seemed to be ending in a meaningless tangle. In the world view of those New Englanders fighting for the revolutionary cause, Old England was corrupt and the Americans were engaged in a righteous and noble cause. There was therefore some meaning for hostilities. But to Alline the totally "inhuman war" had no such meaning. Rather, along with all the other signs of the times, it could only indicate one thing, that the entire Christian world, apart from Nova Scotia, was abandoning the way of God.

What was regarded as the tragic backsliding of New England had presented Nova Scotia with an opportunity to put things right. Alline was determined that the new "Citty upon a Hill" would lead the world back to the pristine purity of the Christian faith. By permeating his Evangelical preaching with this mission-oriented rhetoric, he provided his audience with what he later termed "an omnicient eye" to read the "map of the disordered world." A new collective identity—an awareness of being Nova Scotian—was emerging in the late 1770s, especially in the "Yankee" areas of the colony.

IV

In 1770 the governor of Quebec, Guy Carleton, left for a visit to England; his sojourn there was to last four years. Carleton's main concern was to persuade the imperial authorities to impose upon that province a new governmental framework that would ensure, to use his own words, "perfect subordination from the first to the lowest." His proposals closely reflected the views of the French-Canadian seigneurs and priests who wished to see established in Quebec a hierarchial and stratified society firmly in the control of a benevolent elite. The Quebec Act of 1774, meant to solve the outstanding constitutional, legal and social issues still left unsettled in the St. Lawrence colony since the later sixties, owed much to Carleton's influence; and it was a major piece of imperial legislation at a critical turning point in Northern American development, at the very outset of the American Revolution.

According to the act, the boundaries of the colony were dramatically enlarged to include the territory east of the Mississippi and north of the Ohio River. The core of the old French western fur empire was reattached to Canada. By this move it was hoped, among other things, to ensure the control of the Quebec entrepreneurs over the "commercial empire of the St. Lawrence." English criminal law was formally established and the "Laws and Customs of Canada" was restored in the area of civil law. The seigneurial system was permitted to continue; the Roman Catholics were left free to worship; but also the payment of their tithes to their Church was enforceable by law. In spite of the shrill complaints of the Anglo-American merchant group, it was decided not to establish an assembly as promised in the Proclamation of 1763 but rather to have the colony administered by a governor and appointed council.

In itself, the Quebec Act appears to have been a piece of unusually enlightened legislation. But when seen beside the official correspondence accompanying the measure, it is virtually certain that the British authorities were determined, after conciliating the French Canadians while there was mounting unrest in the Thirteen Colonies, to assimilate and anglicize them. Even in the short term, to describe the Quebec Act as the "Magna Carta of the French Canadians" is to miss the main thrust of the legislation. The act certainly benefited the traditional leaders of French-Canadian society, the seigneurs and priests, but not the vast majority of residents, the habitants. These people had much to fear from the revitalized Church searching for funds, and from profit-oriented seigneurs.

The rebellious Patriot movement in the American colonies considered the new legislation, which was to come into force on May 1, 1775, as one of the most pernicious of the Intolerable Acts that pointed towards revolution. The Quebec Act had not only cut off the inland west from their expansion, returning it to Canada, it also seemed convincing proof that the British authorities were planing to force Quebec's arbitrary governmental mould and an established Church upon all "liberty-loving" Americans. On hearing of the passage of the act in the autumn of 1774, the newly formed Continental Congress and the rebel Massachusetts government resolved to persuade the Anglo-Americans and French habitants of Quebec to resist "slavery and oppression." Haunted by the memories of devastating Franco-Indian frontier raids during previous wars, the pragmatic Americans wisely wished to dissuade their neighbours from becoming part of any British military thrust against the rebelling colonies. The anti-Quebec Act propaganda struck a responsive chord among some of the two to three thousand Anglo-Americans in the St. Lawrence colony and the more than 75,000 habitants. Those in the former group, who were sympathetic to the revolutionary cause, were particularly bitter because the act not only prohibited an assembly but also made significant concessions to the French-Canadian papists. On the other hand, many of the habitants, for the first time subjected to the heavy bombardment of political propaganda and the persuasive arguments of Congressional agitators, became convinced that the Quebec Act was intended to bind them to "the despotism of their masters." It was indeed noted by one observer that the propaganda offensive had made "a deep impression on the minds of the country people."

Even though there may have been infinite local variation in detail, the habitants, whether they lived in the vicinity of the colony's capital or along the Richelieu River, south of Montreal, nevertheless possessed a certain basic unity of outlook. And this unity was largely based on peculiarly peasant preconceptions. In the context of Quebec in the 1770s, the term peasant refers to a state of mind and not to an economic or a social status. As has been frequently pointed out, the peasant has a tenacious attachment to the soil he cultivates and to the animals he raises. Furthermore, he "delights in the known relationship and is suspicious of any breaches or changes." The anticipated change in their entire life style, resulting from the Quebec Act, was precisely what the habitants vociferously opposed. And the agitators must have realized that this deep-seated fear of change provided the only possible link between the American rebels and the mass of the *Canadiens*.

Governor Carleton, who had returned to Quebec in the late summer of 1774, was certain that the Quebec Act would bring both contentment and unflinching loyalty to his colony. He was so confident of the accuracy of his analysis of the situation that he permitted two of his regiments, in the autumn of 1774, to be sent to reinforce General Gage's beleagured army in Boston. This decision left Carleton with fewer than one thousand regulars and increased his dependency upon the militia. It also meant that the habitants could listen attentively to the Congressional spokesmen without being too concerned about possible military reprisals. The habitants respected force but they had also become skilled in taking full advantage of weakness.

When Carleton and his officials learned of the growing disaffection in the country areas they began a propaganda counter-offensive. But this move, rather than serving to neutralize pro-American

arguments, stirred the agitators to even greater organizational
frenzy in the back country. In the meantime, during the first week
of April 1775, a representative of the Massachusetts Congress, John
Brown, met secretly at Lachine and Montreal with a group of
English-speaking merchants. He unsuccessfully attempted to persuade them to send two delegates to the Continental Congress. The
merchants enjoyed participating in revolutionary events at a safe
distance and vicariously. They were primarily interested in profits,
and the commercial relationship with Britain was a means of maxi-
mizing these. Moreover, against the Quebec Act's debit for failing
to grant an assembly they could set its quite imposing credit, the
restoration of the western fur domain to the colonists of the St.
Lawrence.

Less than two weeks after the Quebec Act became the law of the
land on May 1, the British forts of Ticonderoga and Crown Point,
on Lake Champlain, were captured by American forces. Anticipat-
ing an invasion of his colony, Carleton, almost as a last resort to
keep the habitants in line, persuaded Bishop Briand to issue a *mandement* on May 22. In it the bishop declared to his co-religionists that
"Your oaths, your religion, lay upon you the unavoidable duty of
defending your country and your King with all the strength you
possess." Then on June 9, Carleton proclaimed martial law and
called out the militia. He naively expected that the men of influence
—the clergy and the seigneurs—would, in the final analysis, persuade the rather simple-minded habitants to leave their farms and
their families to defend the interests of the same nation that had
conquered them some fifteen years earlier.

In the Montreal region, especially, there was widespread hostility
to the raising of the militia. But as one moved eastwards towards
Quebec city, the *Canadiens* seemed a little less antagonistic. They
at least went through the motions of being organized into companies
and then they were dismissed to return to their farm work. It was
one thing, however, to have the habitants listed on muster rolls on
the steps of their parish churches. It was quite another, as Carleton
was soon to learn, to move them out of their parishes to fight for
the British.

By early autumn of 1775, Washington and the Continental Congress had reversed themselves and decided that it was now essential for the Americans to strike quickly and boldly at the colony of Quebec. There were at least three major reasons for such a decision. First, it was felt that with fewer than one thousand British regulars in the colony and with many of the habitants seemingly disaffected, the time was propitious for such an invasion. Second, there was a widespread conviction in the Continental Congress that Quebec had to be captured in 1775 in order to prevent a powerful British offensive from the north in the spring of the following year and also to discourage possible Indian raids. Finally, there was, without question, a strong "imperialistic" desire—a desire to absorb the considerable economic potential of the St. Lawrence–Great Lakes system.

Despite the fact that the American army was still poorly organized, by September 1775 a two-pronged offensive was directed against Quebec. One two thousand-man column, under the command of Richard Montgomery, moved up the Lake Champlain–Richelieu River, while the other, consisting of eleven hundred troops under Benedict Arnold, travelled by way of the Kennebec River wilderness route. On December 3, the two prongs converged at the capital of the colony, Quebec. Relatively few *Canadiens* had rushed either to the side of the invaders or to support Carleton. Most had, instead, stuck to their farms and sold supplies, for hard cash, to anyone—American or British. There was a kind of pragmatic neutralism underlying the response of most habitants to the American invasion.

Confronted by the extraordinary weakness of the British military presence and by early decisive American successes, it is not surprising that some *Canadiens* maintained that "if no regular troops could be supplied, they preferred to remain neutral." American propaganda and British military weakness were, without question, critical factors in the development of this pragmatic neutrality. But there were also other factors. As William Hey, the Chief Justice of Quebec, shrewdly observed, the habitants were subject to "a confusion of ignorance, fear, credulity, perversion and prejudices." In the context of their peasant mentality, what seemed to others to be both irrational and inconceivable became the essence of opinions and attitudes commonly held. Some were convinced, for example, that Carleton's attempt to raise the militia was merely the first step in a carefully planned large-scale Acadian-like expulsion of the habitants. There were, moreover, important economic considerations motivating them. The period from 1770 to 1778 was one of unusually good harvests and French-Canadian farmers were eager to reap the rewards of their good fortune. Under the French regime, during the frequent periods of war, they had been compelled to make significant sacrifices only to see various speculators enriching themselves at the expense of the colony. In the early years of the Revolution the war-weary *Canadiens* were determined to share in the profits of warfare and to watch from the sidelines the bloody battle between two groups of Englishmen.

After the Americans, however, failed in an assault on Quebec city during the night of December 30-31, 1775, their position in the colony gradually eroded. They completely destroyed their credibility as enlightened liberators with the habitants by what was described as "scandalous excess." When American troops began to terrorize the countryside and, of greater consequence for the habitants, to offer the despised paper money for provisions, the inhabitants hid their wheat, thus forcing the suddenly created enemy to resort to requisitions. The outbreak of smallpox, and the spread of desertion among the invading forces, their lack of discipline and effective leadership, and finally the arrival in early June 1776 of a British fleet carrying thousands of reinforcements, all resulted in an American withdrawal from the colony on July 2—just two days before the issuing of the Declaration of Independence.

In early July 1776, John Adams maintained that "If a declaration of independence had been declared seven months ago . . . we would be in possession of Canada." Without such a declaration to guide and inspire them, it was contended, the confused *Canadiens* had been incapable of understanding the true motives of the invaders. Consequently, the invasion failed to bring about the kind of popular uprising that Adams felt was possible. But he and other Americans were misinformed concerning the mood of Quebec. A Declaration of Independence would not have transformed the widespread "pragmatic neutrality" into revolutionary agitation—

any more than the Quebec Act could produce ardent loyalty to Britain. Most habitants were obsessed, not with revolutionary or imperial concepts, but with self-preservation and their farms.

During the following year, 1777, the British at Quebec tried to gain the initiative against the Americans by sending a force of seven thousand regulars against Albany, New York. Lieutenant-General John Burgoyne's army, however, met a disastrous end, a humiliating surrender, at Saratoga in October. It is impossible to be certain as to how Burgoyne's capture affected the thinking of the Quebec residents. What may be ascertained, however, is that in 1778, when France entered hostilities on the side of the Americans, the colony was again thrown into a state of confusion and turmoil.

This was the general situation that faced a new governor of Quebec, General Frederick Haldimand, who arrived in late June (Carleton, knighted after his successful defence of Quebec city, had subsequently fallen out with the imperial authorities). When rumours about an imminent French invasion led on land by the Marquis de Lafayette and supported from the sea by Admiral D'Estaing began to sweep the colony in 1778 and 1779, not only the habitants were profoundly affected but many *Canadien* seigneurs and priests as well. An intense pro-French sympathy cut across class lines in sharp contrast to the lack of a unified response to the earlier American invasion. Most British officials, including Haldimand, gloomily predicted that "provided the French would send a fleet into the river they [the French Canadians] would to a man take up arms in favour of the rebels."

The very real possibility of a return to French rule had apparently tapped the large reservoir of racial pride lying near the surface of the collective consciousness of many French Canadians. They wished to have the *fleur-de-lis* of France once again waving over Quebec territory. Since many American leaders had little desire to see France re-established on their northern borders, it was decided in the autumn of 1780 to postpone indefinitely a joint Franco-American assault on Quebec. By this time, after two years of waiting, the early exhilaration of those ardent pro-French supporters was being replaced by a growing incredulity and bitterness as they realized that there was no substance for the rumours about an imminent

French invasion. For the rest of the war—in fact until peace was concluded in 1783—Quebec remained securely in British hands. The colony had, in the 1770s, come to possess a distinctive constitutional and legal structure which *Canadiens* began to view as theirs by right: a bulwark to their own separate identity within North America and the British Empire.

But meanwhile, despite all the alarms and incursions of war, the St. Lawrence fur trade had been growing in the territory west of the Great Lakes. Due in part to wartime dangers and actual fighting, that trade had been spreading towards the northwest, beyond the troubled areas of the Ohio and Great Lakes. "Peddlars" from Canada—as the Hudson's Bay Company saw trading interlopers into its domains—were during the decade increasingly active, from Rainy River and Lake of the Woods to Lake Winnipeg, and from there to the Saskatchewan River. And in 1778 Peter Pond, a Montreal trader originally from Connecticut, established the first post in the Athabasca country, having opened the way from the Saskatchewan to northern, Arctic-flowing waters.

In response to this challenge from the St. Lawrence, the Hudson's Bay Company agents made significant changes in their long-established, non-competitive policy of sitting placidly by Hudson Bay waiting for furs to come to them. As well as sending Samuel Hearne up across the Barren Lands (whereby he reached the Arctic at the mouth of the Coppermine in 1771-2), the Company established its first inland post, Cumberland House, in 1774, to dominate the vital portage route leading northward from the Saskatchewan River. It was the first sign of the old Company's reaction to the expansion of Montreal's far-flung fur trade. And as the decade ended, a whole new era in that trade was taking shape; for in 1779 the North West Company had been organized in Montreal, soon to contend for the mastery of western regions all the way to the Arctic and Pacific. Indeed, here was another theme emerging from the 1770s, to be almost as important for the shaping of a future Canada on the North American continent as was the American Revolution itself.

3: The 1780s

LESLIE UPTON

The decade of the 1780s saw events that not only shaped, but controlled, the future development of Canada. At the end of the American Revolution Britain conceded a boundary line between the United States and the surviving colonies that determined the division of the whole continent between the two powers. Britain's surrender of the Ohio valley to the new republic drew a political barrier for the first time across the geographical extension of the St. Lawrence–Great Lakes waterways. Once the Americans could police their new boundary it would be necessary for traders operating out of Montreal to confine themselves to the northwest, to create those very routes along which political power would one day stretch to the Pacific. The end of the war had more immediate consequences as well, as American Loyalist refugees settled in the western parts of Quebec, confounding the

basic assumption that the province would stay overwhelmingly
Canadien. These settlements represented a leap westward in the
European colonization of America and in strategic terms were both a
safeguard to Britain's claims north of the Great Lakes and a protection for the trade routes that the loss of the Ohio valley had made
more important than ever before. The arrival of large numbers of
Loyalist immigrants in Nova Scotia accelerated the development of
that colony by two generations. The Loyalists who settled along the
Saint John River confirmed British claims to a territory that formed
the land link between Quebec and the Atlantic. When the tide of
emigration from Britain itself began to flow in the 1820s there was a
British America for it to go to. The Loyalists performed a vital holding operation for colonies savagely weakened by the demands of
international diplomacy.

Canada, in fact, barely survived the diplomacy of 1782 that
led to the peace treaty. The whole half-continent, at least in the
view of Benjamin Franklin, was negotiable, for he suggested at the
very first of the preliminary conversations that the British hand it
over to the United States as an earnest of goodwill. Franklin's was
a shrewd move, for the basic aim of the British negotiators was to
gain the friendship, and trade, of their former colonies. Quebec
particularly had played an important part in revolutionary myth-
ology and the Quebec Act remained a symbol of the bad old oppressive laws that the Americans had rebelled against. But the
American negotiators were not in a strong bargaining position:
they had no military claim to any part of the area, and their allies
in France were not ready to support them in further territorial
expansion. In fact, French diplomacy would be best served by
seeing the British remain as a significant force in North America,
strong enough at least to keep the United States dependent on
France for support.

The peace negotiations in Paris took place while a ceasefire was in
effect in North America, but the war between Britain and her
European enemies continued elsewhere. Canada's future lay in the
prowess of British arms against France and Spain. At a bleak
moment in her fortunes, Britain considered surrendering the territory south of Lake Nipissing, including what is now southern On-

tario, to the United States. But when news came of British success at Gibraltar she raised her demands in America to embrace the extensive boundaries of the Quebec Act. The line that emerged in the treaty was a compromise: a composite of traditional demarcations from the Bay of Fundy to the St. Lawrence and a splitting of the difference between the Lake Nipissing and the Ohio valley lines. From the St. Croix River on the Bay of Fundy the boundary followed the 1763 line along unmapped "heights of land" to the St. Lawrence, thence along the middle of the river and lakes to the northwesternmost point of the Lake of the Woods and west along the 45th parallel until it intersected the Mississippi. The treaty was not the final word on the boundary. When it was discovered that the line due west from the Lake of the Woods ran north of the Mississippi, new negotiations were necessary and agreement was only reached in 1818. The line from Lake Superior to the Lake of the Woods was not defined until 1842. Further east, no less than three St. Croix rivers were discovered, and the confusion over this and the unspecified "heights of land" was not ended until the same general settlement of 1842, the Webster-Ashburton treaty.

Another main concern of the negotiators was the future of the Loyalists. These Americans, who had fought for the king or been evicted by the revolutionaries as un-American, had either sailed for Britain, gone to Quebec province or congregated in New York city. They had lost their property, whether it was fifty acres of uncleared land or the investments of a merchant prince; their debtors were released from any obligation to them; and if they were found in their former homes they could be punished even to the point of death. The British hoped that these people would be allowed to go back and resume life where they had left off before the troubles began. This idea was totally unrealistic, for feeling in the United States ran much too high to allow the return of traitors who had prolonged the war by their services and advice to the British. Further, the Loyalists had been driven out by laws in each of the thirteen states, and the Continental Congress had no power to interfere in the internal affairs of the states. Yet the Continental Congress was the only body with which Britain could negotiate for peace. As a result, the British had to drop their insistence that the United States look after the Loyalists and had to undertake the task themselves. All the peace treaty said on the matter was that Congress should "earnestly recommend" the various states to restore the confiscated property of British-born subjects and Americans who had lived in areas under British military control without taking arms against the United States. All others should be allowed to return for twelve months to salvage what they could of their fortunes. No one expected the slightest attention to be paid to this recommendation, and even while the diplomats were haggling over the wording of the treaty, preparations were being made for a mass evacuation of the Loyalists assembled in New York city. The task of evacuation fell to Sir Guy Carleton. He had little stomach for the work, hoping against hope that he would personally conduct peace negotiations with the Americans, and from a position of strength with a reinforced army. But by June 1783, the process of withdrawal was under way. The richest Loyalists, those who could afford to support themselves, went to England to press claims on the government for compensation for their losses. Those less fortunate were moved at public expense to the nearest available British territory, Nova Scotia, where they would be given free grants of land to start life anew. Those already within the British province of Quebec would have to have their position regularized, preferably by moving to Nova Scotia where the laws, language and land tenures were familiar to them.

The British government had many things to consider in the postwar years. It had to decide whether there were any "lessons" to be learned from the American Revolution, and if there were, how to apply them; or if there were not, whether any change at all was needed in imperial policy. Had the Americans rebelled because they lacked an aristocracy or an established church? Because there had been too much control from London, or too little? And did these considerations have any relevance to a British America whose largest constituent element was French-speaking and Roman Catholic? What of the future relations between Britain and the United States? Would a tough line towards the disorganized states be the best approach, or the policy of conciliation that had started at the peace treaty negotiations? How would these alternatives affect decisions on British North America? And, possibly most important of all, how could those distant underdeveloped colonies get a hearing in a House of Commons faced with the Irish problem, the impeachment of Warren Hastings, incipient demands for parliamentary reform, the reconstruction of Britain's position in the world after the loss of a major war?

Despite these distractions, the Loyalist exiles created imperial policy by their very existence as a group with a strong moral claim on Great Britain. It was fortunate that they did; and a brief excursion into the "might-have-beens" shows why. But for their presence, Canada would have been populated from sea to sea by Americans eager to include it in the republican fold. New Yorkers would have moved into the unoccupied area north of Lakes Ontario and Erie in the 1790s and the British would have had neither the resources nor the inclination to protect what was merely the left flank of the Montreal fur trade. Nova Scotia, with the naval base of Halifax, would have been retained as vital to imperial strategy, but there would have been no reason to oppose the influx of American settlers to the western side of the Bay of Fundy when the Maine frontier was ready to send them forth in the 1830s. Quebec, undoubtedly, would have remained loyal to Great Britain as the guarantor of her French distinctiveness, but with the United States west of the Ottawa River and east of Gaspé, Britain would not have risked a land war to keep the St. Lawrence settlements. Quebec would have gone the way of Louisiana, and the route would have lain by Texas-Coahuila, New Mexico and California. With the eastern half of the continent surrendered, Britain would have been in no position to support the vast claims of the antique Hudson's Bay Company, and without that Company there would have been no British presence on the west coast.

II

The two men who had the most important immediate decisions to make about the Loyalists were John Parr and Frederick Haldimand, governors respectively in Nova Scotia and Quebec. Neither man has been given much credit for his part in the establishment of the new arrivals, and in truth they both regarded their new responsibility as an unwelcome chore, something totally unlooked for when they had taken office. Parr was quite rightly afraid there would be feuding between resident Nova Scotians and Loyalists, for while the "old-comers" of the province regarded the new-comers as potential subversives, the Loyalists regarded them as revolutionaries who had never had the courage of their convictions. Haldimand in his turn was concerned over what an influx of English-speaking Protestants would do to a province that was French and Roman Catholic, and he had a free measure of suspicion over the Loyalists' motives as well.

The best solution for both men was to put the Loyalists well away from the existing settlers. Haldimand hoped all his refugees would pack up and go to Nova Scotia, but when they showed no desire to do so he toyed with and dismissed the idea of locating them south of Montreal as a buffer between the *Canadiens* and the United States. Finally he decided they should be located in the wilderness northwest of the Ottawa–St. Lawrence River junction, on lands bought from the Indians. Spotted around Lake Ontario, the Loyalists would be entirely segregated from the French, safely west of the last seigneury, and so less likely to upset the status quo. For Parr the best location was on the mainland side of the Bay of Fundy along the Saint John River valley where the settlers were few and mostly illegal squatters. As this land was still under the jurisdiction of Nova Scotia, the Loyalists could live there apart without crowding the existing residents. Unfortunately for Parr he was not as successful as Haldimand, for about 40 per cent of his Loyalists stayed in peninsula Nova Scotia. The province had to accept them and, in a surprisingly short time, absorbed them.

The Loyalists who went to Nova Scotia moved to a land which in the popular imagination had roughly the same image as Labrador today. Their former fellow countrymen delighted in quips about Nova Scarcity. In order to brace themselves for their future some Loyalists drew up grand schemes for riches in their new homeland. Had not the United States withdrawn itself from the British Empire of trade? And who would now supply the Sugar Islands from the British West Indies and reap the profits of that trade? What better location was there in the whole empire than Nova Scotia? The idea created enthusiasm indeed, but profits never. The province simply could not generate the necessary capital or supply the timber and foodstuffs for the Sugar Islands, whose planters vociferously demanded that they be allowed to trade with their old agents in the United States. But the fact that some of the Loyalists could even think in such terms shows that there was a mercantile element amongst the refugees who would not simply be content with starting life all over again by scratching out a living in the bush. This is not to say, as some have, that all the educated genteel folk of the old colonies migrated northeast in abhorrence of the republic, but it does set the Nova Scotia Loyalists off from those family farmers who went to Quebec and generally refused to see beyond the next harvest. Most of the Nova Scotia Loyalists were also farmers but they came from areas such as New England, southern New York, and Pennsylvania where they had been much exposed to the vigorous sermons and social commentaries of their pastors as well as to the convoluted politics of the colonies. Nova Scotia Loyalists contained a proportion of politically knowledgeable people as high as existed in any group on the Atlantic coastline, much higher than the resident Nova Scotians and phenomenal by contrast with the Loyalists of the Lake Ontario region.

New Brunswick was the result of Loyalist aspirations to form a society uncontaminated by lesser man. As early as 1779, plans had been put forward for the establishment of strong new colonies peopled exclusively by Loyalists. William Knox, undersecretary at the Colonial Office, drew up plans for an ideal Loyalist province between the Penobscot River and Passamaquoddy Bay in the northern half of the district of Maine. "New Ireland," as it was to be called, would be visible proof of the orderliness of British freedom, in sharp contrast to the chaos of runaway democracy. A balanced society would be created with a genuine colonial aristocracy fostered by large land grants, and a labour force of tenants to cultivate them. Each landowner on acquiring his land would have to take a direct oath of allegiance to the king in Parliament. A governor and council would be appointed, but no elected assembly would be called for the time being. Hereditary titles were to be given to those who advised and assisted the government. The Church of England was to be established as the strong right arm of the state. Knox even had a slate of candidates for the first appointments, proven Loyalists to a man. His choice as governor, Thomas Hutchinson, last royal governor of Massachusetts, dismissed the whole plan as "a most preposterous measure." Yet it could be argued that Knox's project was a reasonable extension of the policy behind the Quebec Act. Quebec had an effectively established church and no assembly; its landholders bore titles and took their oaths of fealty; and the seigneurial system appeared, to the distant viewer, to be the embodiment of a landlord and tenant society. New Ireland was never established, for its lands were ceded to the United States, but its ghost was to haunt the Loyalists in their first decade of exile.

The British government was not displeased to receive a petition to establish a new, loyalist, colony around the Saint John River valley. In practical terms, it was very difficult to administer the area from Halifax, as the only communication lay across the treacherous waters of southern Nova Scotia. Perhaps, too, at some future date Britain might profit from the separation, for Nova Scotia was vital to the global strategy of the British Empire and would never be surrendered, while New Brunswick was an expendable piece of the North American mainland. But the immediately useful aspect of creating New Brunswick would be the establishment of a number of government offices which could be used as compensation for deserving individuals. However, most of the best jobs went to those who had been able to go to London to push their own claims, a fact that burdened the new colony with a great deal of resentment from the first. Theoretically, the Loyalists who had suffered so much in common, would now all work together to create the model society that would show how completely wrong-headed the American Revolution had been. New Ireland, shifted northeast of its original location, might yet spring to life, with a properly structured society patterned on rural England, where each man was in his place and an established church reminded him that that was where he should be.

The first question raised by this approach was, who would be the aristocracy? A partial answer could be found by settling the Loyalists in their old regiments, so that the authority of the officers would carry over into peacetime. Even before the evacuation of New York city, fifty-five individuals, civilian and military, had volunteered themselves for the aristocracy by requesting extra large grants of land. But for every Loyalist who thought of social distinctions, there were easily fifty, equally articulate, who denounced the would-be aristocrats. The vast majority of the refugees did not agree that an excess of democracy had brought about their downfall. Bitter recriminations followed, and some Loyalists claimed to be more loyal than the others. As if this did not provide the infant colony of New Brunswick with a sufficiently rich political life at the outset, there were the merchants of the brand-new port of Saint John, the last economic visionaries, who insisted that the emphasis on landed estates was a social and military plot to beggar them. New Brunswick as a haven for the Loyalist consensus was as doomed to failure as the landowner with five thousand acres and no one to work them. The first lieutenant-governor, Thomas Carleton, found it expedient to lock up most of his critics before the first elections were held.

The Loyalists who continued to live in truncated Nova Scotia were not so prone to day-dreaming or to internecine quarrels, for they had the old residents to confront. Pillars of conservatism in the American Revolution, these new arrivals were dangerous radicals in the eyes of their unwilling hosts. At first the Loyalists settled apart. Many hoped to escape the drudgery of farming and live the mercantile life in the instant community of Shelburne. The growth of this settlement on the rocky southern shore was one of the wonders of the day; yet within three years it was a ghost town, its residents moved on elsewhere in the province, or, in unknown numbers, returned home to the United States. There was nothing to trade at Shelburne, and even if there had been, Halifax did not take kindly to competition. Loyalist complaints were frequently aired in the provincial Assembly, which made room for no less than eight members from the new districts. Embarrassing questions were raised for the first time: how much did officials receive from their fees? How exactly was the revenue collected and spent? The administration of justice was attacked as hopelessly inept in a prolonged campaign that reflected Loyalist resentment at being kept out of appointed offices in the province. Yet by 1790, the Nova Scotia Loyalists had ceased to function as a separate group, and the war-borne prosperity that soon followed was a great pacifier. Few Nova Scotians boasted of their Loyalist ancestry in later generations, and they left behind them a folk-memory of a troublesome and hell-raising people, a constant reminder to Nova Scotians of the unfortunate way their neighbours lived in the States.

One group of Nova Scotia Loyalists did not assimilate: the slaves who had been liberated by the British forces during the war, or who had simply attached themselves to the army. Some had fought for the crown; all were subject to enslavement if found in the United States. To the American negotiators at the peace talks, they were so much plundered property for which the British should make restitution, a point that was never conceded. These blacks went to Nova Scotia along with the other Loyalists, but if they thought to find equality of treatment for their services they were mistaken. Was not the fact of their freedom ample reward in itself? The blacks who settled at Shelburne, for example, were allocated the least desirable lots, and on one riotous evening had their flimsy homes burned to the ground by white Loyalists. Henceforth the blacks kept their distance and settled in segregated areas where they were allowed tiny lots of from ten to forty acres on marginal land. Faced with a harsh climate, poor soil, and totally inexperienced in anything but the routine duties of slavery, the black Loyalists faced a miserable future in isolation. They had their freedom, but there was no place for them in Loyalist society.

III

The Loyalists who settled in western Quebec were not distinguished by any of the far-ranging ideas that flitted around their fellows to the east. Most of them were frontier farmers who had never felt themselves to be part of the life of the old colonies; and having always lived on the fringe of society they did not miss its amenities. They had moved north during the war to continue their fight against the Revolution and had not sat out the long idle months of crowded frustration in New York city that gave the eastern Loyalists their occasional touch of paranoia. There was no hope of developing mercantile riches overnight to mislead even the most optimistic. Some attempt was made to carry the discipline of the war over to the new society by locating men in regimental groups with varying amounts of land according to their military rank. But there was no "fifty-five" to make a big issue out of a graded society, and the widespread nature of the settlements defeated any such notion. Quebec had no assembly, no elections where public quarrels could be pursued, and what friction there was remained extremely localized. In any event men were too busy establishing themselves on promising land that contrasted strongly with the penurious soil of Nova Scotia which sent many a defeated farmer to swell the ranks of the discontented. The land of western Quebec was so good in fact that it attracted many Americans who were quite uninterested in matters of political allegiance. Since population was regarded as the measure of success, local land boards cheerfully granted free land to anyone who came before them and swore he had been loyal to George III in the late war. As early as 1787 it was impossible to tell who was a genuine Loyalist and who was just a land-hungry immigrant. The seven thousand Loyalists who had been in the province at war's end proved to be the nucleus of a rapidly growing frontier area, a phenomenon that never overtook the Maritime Loyalists.

The Quebec Loyalists were settled on Indian land in the general area that had been devastated by the Iroquois in the late 1640s. It was still thinly populated, principally by the Mississigua nation, a nomadic people who used it as their hunting grounds. Crown commissioners arranged for the orderly purchase of blocks of land by the government, and no sales were allowed to private parties. This policy at one stroke eliminated the competitive land-grabbing that kept the United States' frontier in turmoil. The first step in negotiations with the Indians was a provisional agreement with tribal representatives, and after the details were worked out a "confirmatory surrender" closed the deal. At each stage the Indians received goods or small sums in cash—half a guinea was the provisional price for the whole tract of land around present-day Toronto. The deeds of surrender, replete with precise legal terminology, were yet vague over such things as the area involved; distances were defined, for example, as "as far as a man can walk in a day." The Indian chiefs, after the translation of each agreement, signed with their totems. Whether or not the procedure was fair, it certainly made for a peaceful transfer of title; and how could vast areas of untouched forest be measured in terms of muskets and cloth, ribbon and kettles, let alone coins?

But not all the Indians were selling land. The Iroquois who had fought as allies of George III had been entirely forgotten in the peace negotiations. The British had handed over their allies' land in the northwest without any consultation, and to atone for this behaviour had promised to settle them on British territory at government expense. Where they had once roamed as conquerors the Iroquois now returned as refugees, receiving land bought from the Mississigua at the Bay of Quinte and along the banks of the Grand River flowing into Lake Erie. These Indian allies were pioneering at the same time as the Loyalists, and a legacy of comradeship in arms served to maintain good relations between the two communities, softening the just resentment of the Iroquois at their treatment. The new settlements in western Quebec were able to enjoy a peaceful existence from the first, an advantage that helped spur their rapid growth.

The success of the new settlements so engrossed the newcomers that they had little time left over for thoughts of the immense significance of their presence in Quebec. Not everyone was satisfied that they should take so apolitical a view of life. In 1789 Governor Lord Dorchester expressed "his wish to put a Marke of Honor upon the families who had adhered to the Unity of the Empire." The attempt to draw up his honour roll, a matter of fascination to later generations, was greeted with massive indifference by the farmers concerned. But the fact that the attempt was made indicated a desire to create something out of this Loyalist experience on an even larger scale than was ever contemplated in New

Brunswick. Once again the impetus came from the top and once again popular support was nonexistent. The idea of identifying families of proven loyalty was but a part of a grand design to weld the whole of British North America into one unit under a viceroy, who would dispense the abundant blessings of British liberty in such a way that the wretched Americans would repent of their folly. They might conceivably apply for readmission to the empire or choose a king from among the British royal family; or at least they would show a healthy respect for the northern colonies and think twice about acts of aggression. These ideas can be traced back to Guy Carleton's army headquarters at New York city in the closing months of the war, for the prospective viceroy was none other than Carleton himself.

The political framework of Quebec was not suited to such grand ideas. The Quebec Act of 1774 had pronounced a French-Canadian status quo for the province, while the accompanying instructions had pointed to an anglicizing drift away from it. Governor Carleton had suppressed his instructions, leaving the act unimpaired, and his francophone successor, Haldimand, had little interest in changing that situation. Moreover, the Revolutionary War imposed its own veto on policy changes in the potentially beleaguered colony. But the ending of that war released a pent-up torrent of discontent amongst the English mercantile minority who felt so discriminated against by the Quebec Act. While profits were high, grievances could be swallowed, but as war contracts ended and financial panic swept the business community the volume of complaints begun to transcend even that which had once driven Governor Murray from the province. Carleton, it may be remembered, had replaced Murray in 1766; could he now replace Haldimand? And would the champion of the Quebec Act be at all sensitive to mercantile complaints? Brook Watson, M.P., principal London agent for all British North American commerce, was convinced that Carleton's wartime experience had changed him, and it was Watson who convinced the British government to authorize the second coming. Carleton's sympathy with the Loyalist refugees in New York city would be translated into favouritism to the Quebec Loyalists, which could only lead to a policy of anglicization healthy for commerce. Newly ennobled as Lord Dorchester, he returned to the province in 1786.

Quebec was the largest colony of settlement in the British Empire and it continued to grow rapidly in population, from 144,000 in 1784 to just over 160,000 in 1790. Even with the coming of the Loyalists the proportion of English-speaking residents rose only from 4 to 14 per cent. The economy that supported these people was overwhelmingly agricultural and the increasing demographic pressure was beginning to show as land values edged upwards in the more desirable seigneuries. Further west, the success of the Loyalists in developing their lands emphasized the agricultural destiny of the province. Yet the promising overseas markets for farm produce failed to develop, and prices remained low as the economy languished in a prolonged postwar depression. There had been a flicker of hope, soon dead, that Quebec too might profit by the exclusion of Americans from the British West Indies, but staple production was too small, and the distance too great. The government, by a clever interpretation of the imperial Acts of Trade and Navigation, had opened trade with the neighbouring independent state of Vermont, although the potential here was not in markets but in the profits from the carrying trade as Vermonters shipped their produce down the St. Lawrence. The inability of Quebec's farmers to provide a steady surplus for export was cruelly underlined in the winter of 1788-89: some 500,000 bushels of wheat had been sent out of the country before it was realized that there would be a poor harvest for the year. The price of bread rose fourfold, and many families, especially in the grain-growing areas around Montreal, were reduced to living on boiled hay. Actual deaths from starvation were reported.

As ever, the fur trade was the principal source of commercial wealth, accounting for 57 per cent of exports in the middle of the decade. The future of the trade had, however, been cast in doubt by the generous concessions made to the United States in 1783. The southwest still provided the bulk of the furs although it was now foreign territory; and it had been preserved for the trade more by accident than design. Governor Haldimand refused to hand over eleven western posts inside the United States as the peace treaty directed, fearing that a British withdrawal would show the

Indians just how completely they had been betrayed and bring their wrath down on their betrayers. A useful side result of this decision was that the area remained open to Montreal traders, but it would stay that way only so long as the illegal occupation of the posts continued. When the United States government protested this foreign presence on their soil, the British came up with the excuse that they were there only because the Americans had not lived up to their commitments to the Loyalists. Obviously, this was a situation that was not going to last for ever, and the fur traders looked increasingly to the northwest for their future development.

The first of the series of partnerships known as the North West Company had appeared in 1779 with the intent of eliminating competition amongst those trading for high quality furs in the distant Athabasca region. The uncertainties of 1783 formed an added reason for cooperation, for it was clear that sooner or later the Montrealers would have to rely exclusively on the northwest for their supplies. The Hudson's Bay Company laid claim to these territories by charter, and the long-standing competition between it and Montreal was sure to increase. But the immediate position of the Hudson's Bay Company was weak, since a French squadron had destroyed its principal base, York Factory, in 1782, carrying off all the staff and several dozen recruits hired to undertake a push inland. Thus the main threat to the Nor'westers came not so much from the Bay Company as from Montreal dissidents who insisted on trying to turn a profit in the fur trade on their own. This competition was often crushed by violence, and the Nor'wester partnership steadily expanded.

In 1784 the annual agreement whereby the member firms shared the costs and profits of the northwest trade was replaced by a five-year combination; and in 1787 a larger, still more lasting agreement among the Montreal partners brought the North West Company to a peak of power. The predominance of Camerons, Grants, McKenzies, McGillivrays and Frasers showed how completely the Scots had taken over the inland Canadian fur trade. In 1789, *Canadiens* supplied only 15 per cent of the trade goods sent into Indian country. The fur trade now demanded capital investment beyond the reach of the surviving *Canadien* merchants; it had ceased to be merely a matter of courage and bargaining skill, and required logistical support of great complexity. At the same time the enterprise and daring of the wintering partners in the interior was vitally necessary to the expansion of the trade. The Nor'westers probed steadily westwards, until one of the winterers, Alexander Mackenzie, in 1789 made his epic canoe voyage from the post at Fort Chipeweyan on Lake Athabasca to the river that would bear his name, and down the Mackenzie to the Arctic shore.

IV

Dorchester failed to meet the challenge of Quebec in his second term of office. His own past placed him in the strange position of being greeted as a saviour by *Canadien* seigneur and English merchant alike. He never resolved that paradox, and, perhaps, held to the notion of a united British America, an ideal that transcended all baser concerns, simply as an escape from his predicament. He proved to be an indecisive governor the second time around, and relied heavily on the activity of his chosen chief justice, William Smith, to cover his own inertia. Smith was a genuine enthusiast, a New York Loyalist convinced that the American disaster had been brought about by a lack of balance in society. However, Smith did not consider the agrarian Loyalists of western Quebec as fit material from which to conjure an aristocracy; nor was he impressed with the hope that the seigneur could fit the part. Smith insisted on the establishment of English forms in Quebec as the basis on which a strong and well-balanced society might grow.

The result of Smith's approach was a head-on clash with the Quebec Act, and an intensification of political strife carried on in the name of "French" and "English" parties inside and outside the Council. The division was not completely along national or linguistic lines, for the ubiquitous Scots provided the majority in both parties. Adam Mabane led the "French" party, which had had a long period of influence under Carleton and Haldimand and was accustomed to the role; while the other party presented the mercantile point of view. The Loyalist immigrants took no part in these affairs, although their principal spokesman and only councillor, Sir John Johnson, could be counted on the "English" side. Nevertheless the few thousand Loyalists were important to the debate: the French saw them as aliens who would "yankify" Canada; while the English claimed them as forerunners of a vast immigration that was the only security for a British Quebec.

Arguments ran high from the first. The survival of Quebec and of the whole of British America was at stake. New France had been conquered, Smith insisted many times, because France had failed to provide enough people to hold the territory; and if the British also failed to do so, they would lose their colonies as surely as France had lost hers. The best possible immigrants came from Britain, but many more were close at hand among the disillusioned citizenry of the new republic. These men should be encouraged to move to Quebec not only by offers of free land, but by creating a social climate attractive to them, where freehold replaced seigneurial tenure, and English laws replaced French. Mabane denied the logic of this argument completely, and broadly hinted that Smith was an American agent working to destroy the very defences that held back a flood of Americans and so preserved the colony for Britain. Rather than encourage such men, the French distinctiveness of Quebec should be enhanced, for concessions to English merchants or Loyalist farmers marked the road to certain ruin.

Chief Justice Smith conducted a vigorous campaign to establish his own point of view. He saw the anglicization of foreigners as an inevitable, if lengthy, process. In his native New York, Dutch had been used in the law courts as late as 1736, and was still heard when farmers came into town on market day; moreover Smith himself was a living testament to the assimilating powers of the English, for his mother had grown up in the French-speaking community of New Rochelle. No process was so inevitable, however, that it did not require assistance, and Smith set about his task with such a degree of self-assurance that many at first feared he was acting on direct orders from London, or at least from Lord Dorchester. But the British government never thanked anybody for stirring up troubled waters in the colonies; and Dorchester was simply incapable of expressing any opinion.

Smith had barely been in the colony three months when he delivered a judgment in the Court of Appeals that shook the Quebec Act to its foundations. He stated that the act required the customary civil laws only for *Canadiens*, while natural-born British subjects retained their right to English laws. This interpretation strongly implied that all those born after the cession in 1763, British subjects by birth, came under English law, and the old French laws would simply wither away with the passing of time. Such a decision aroused the wrath not only of the *Canadiens*, but also of Scottish officials, who saw no logic to the argument that British subjects must have English laws. The judges in the lower courts paid no attention to Smith's interpretation, but it remained as a warning of what could happen unless the French character of the province were vigorously defended. Similarly, Smith tried and failed to allow the conversion of seigneurial tenures to freehold and only succeeded in raising the alarm of English aggression. When he came forward with a well-considered plan for education, making a conscious effort to avoid the clash of nationalities or religious faiths, he ran into stiff opposition from Bishop Hubert, who was convinced that anything that emanated from Smith must be disastrous for the *Canadiens*. And each controversy tailed off into personal vituperation. His decision in the Court of Appeals started a train of events that ended in a general investigation of the administration of justice. Twenty years' accumulation of disappointed litigants publicly criticized the judges for incompetence and prejudice, and many were asked in their turn the barbed question: where were you in the winter of 1775 when the Americans were besieging Quebec city? The attempt to convert seigneurial tenures revolved around the personality of Charles de Lanaudière, a seigneur from a former merchant family, who had petitioned the Council to change his tenure to freehold in the apparent hope of sellings parts of his ancestral estate to Loyalist newcomers; and for that aspiration he was reviled as a vendu. The educational enterprise climaxed in a scathing public ridicule of Hubert's fears by his coadjutor (and hence successor) Bailly, who, it was well known, had long ago made his peace with the English and owed his exalted position to the patronage of Lord Dorchester.

As issues of vast importance dwindled into mere spitefulness those who were still interested in political reform looked elsewhere. After all, Quebec was a colony, and the important decisions about it were made in London. A committee of French and English residents met together in an unusual display of cooperation to send a petition to the House of Commons. There were some disputes, for the French wished the spiritual power of the Pope restored and full recognition given the religious orders, objects of no concern to the English. But the measure of agreement was broad. The final document, presented by the merchant Adam Lymburner to the Commons in 1788, called for an assembly with full control over the amendment of the laws of the province, with membership in the assembly proportioned between French and English as Parliament saw fit. It was at this point that the cracks in the Anglo-French alliance began to show, for as the *Canadiens* comprised 90 per cent of the population there would have to be very special arrangements to avoid the complete annihilation of the English interest in the proposed assembly. The one side gambled that Parliament would protect the minority; the other that it would not.

The participation of *Canadiens* in this petition showed that they were learning some of the techniques of English-style politics. After all, they had listened to the merchants preaching the virtues of English freedom for twenty-five years; and one thing was crystal clear, that the majority controlled an elected assembly. Since the *Canadiens* were so convincingly in the majority, an assembly did not seem to be quite such a sinister device. There were those, particularly in the Council, who insisted that assemblies were yet another tool of Americanization, but their arguments appeared to be those of men unwilling to share their power with elected representatives. The *Canadiens* as a whole were recovering from the shock of the conquest and were regaining their self-confidence. The bourgeoisie, although probably fewer than five hundred families, were far from living in stagnant isolation. The bilingual *Quebec Gazette* and *Montreal Gazette* regularly printed excerpts from the works of *philosophes* such as Voltaire, Rousseau and Diderot. English editions of Voltaire, for example, were on sale in bookstores. French editions of the *philosophes* were more hard to come by because trade with France was forbidden; but copies were held by the Quebec public subscription library, and others came into the province in the baggage of returning travellers. Masonic lodges, with their heavy emphasis on rationalist philosophy, were new arrivals in the province in the 1780s, and attracted members from both the noblesse and bourgeoisie. The *Canadiens* were conscious that as a majority they had great strength: English officials and merchants used the French language, sent their Protestant children to French Roman Catholic schools, while the most prosperous of them bought estates and proudly claimed the title of seigneur. Smith, the standard bearer of the anglicizers, had proved to be an empty threat. Were it not for the distant Loyalists in their forest cantonments, English assimilation to the dominant culture might have seemed reasonably assured.

The British government had revealed some of its own thinking about Quebec when it instructed Lord Dorchester in 1786 to advise on the best line of division within the province. The Loyalist immigration had led to the partition of Nova Scotia, and like conditions in Quebec pointed to a like conclusion. Dorchester was supposed to furnish the imperial government with a variety of information as a basis for deciding policy. He failed to provide anything of substance, and as long as Lord Sydney was the minister responsible for the North American colonies, decisions could be agreeably deferred. But when Sydney was replaced by William Grenville, a young man anxious to make his mark, matters came to a head. In short order, he drafted a constitution that would create two Canadas in Quebec, each equipped with the standard type of colonial government: governor, council, and elected assembly. The Loyalists in the new districts west of Montreal would have their own province where they could enjoy the full blessings of those English liberties for which they had suffered exile; and the *Canadiens* would receive an enlightened constitutional government of the very pattern for which reformers in France itself were contending. Grenville envisaged bolstering these societies with a titled aristocracy to provide the social balance that had been so disastrously lacking in the old colonies.

This plan was sent to Lord Dorchester for his comments. He

contented himself with demolishing the idea of a colonial aristocracy and handed over the task of writing a detailed reply to Chief Justice Smith. Leaning heavily on his experience as a Loyalist, Smith argued that the plan was good but did not go far enough. Since no useful aristocracy could develop in the flux of a new society, Britain would simply be creating additional colonies in the image of the old, with the same inevitable defects that would lead to revolution. What was needed was a framework broad enough to allow for growth without alienation. British America might yet stretch from Hudson Bay to the Gulf of Mexico, for the claims of the United States went no further west than the Mississippi. The only way to grasp the future was to confederate Quebec, New Brunswick, Nova Scotia, Cape Breton Island and Prince Edward Island, so that while each retained its own government, a central government would exist to give coherence to the whole. There would be a governor general, a council of members from each province, and an assembly consisting of members, chosen by the provincial assemblies, meeting every two years. The confederation would enjoy virtual home rule, for the powers of the governor general would severely limit London's intervention in routine matters. This reply simply confirmed Grenville in his suspicion that nothing of use would ever come from Dorchester or his assistant, and, dismissing the plan in a sentence, he pressed on with his own measure. But Dorchester's and Smith's dream of a viceroyalty had finally been put into the official correspondence of Quebec, and there it remained, a forlorn precursor of the act of 1867.

4: The 1790s

S. F. WISE

There were no British North American people in the 1790's, nor even, except in a technical sense, Nova Scotians or Upper Canadians. Although most colonists or *Canadiens* were involved in farming, fishing or the fur trade, economic similarities were less significant than the cultural, religious and geographical isolation that divided colonial groups from each other. For the many little particularisms of British North America, the horizon, intellectual as well as social, extended only to the bounds of a parish, along a stretch of coast, within the limits of a river valley settlement, or to the edge of the ever-present bush.

The network that connected colonial life was the political structure, which together with the lines of trade tied the colonies to London and to a much lesser extent to each other. In each colony, the governor, the civil and military bureaucracies, the members of the legislature and local office-holders constituted the apparatus of government. To a large extent their activities, social as well as political, were confined to the limits of their own group, with the addition of such other members of society who had the wealth, the leisure, the education or some similar qualification of admittance. The official and popular cultures in each colony seldom mingled. It was unusual for popular issues to penetrate the realm of official politics, because colonial societies had not yet reached the state of consciousness for such issues to be defined; naturally it was even more unusual for any fundamental challenge to be levelled at the political system itself.

For the colonial establishments, the French Revolution and the outbreak of war with France in 1793 were the great events of the decade. Britain's preoccupation with France meant that colonial governments could not expect and did not receive much imperial interest in their problems. British leadership of the counter-revolutionary coalition meant that the conservatism of the colonial ruling groups deepened, in harmony with the orthodox response to revolution eloquently voiced in England by Edmund Burke in 1790. But whereas the parliamentary opposition led by Charles Fox kept alive some semblance of debate there about the nature of the Revolution, the politically effective groups in the colonies were at one in their condemnation of republicanism and democracy.

Among the *Canadiens*, there were some stirrings of popular sympathy for the Revolution. In Montreal, clandestine clubs met to discuss French political literature and to circulate French propaganda obtained from such sources as Citizen Genet, the agent of the Republic in the United States. In 1794 and again in 1796, there was popular unrest caused by militia and road acts, but which bore signs of having been influenced by French agents. No echo of this dissent was heard from the French-Canadian elite, however. In 1793, Bishop Hubert declared that the bonds with France had been finally severed by the Revolution; in 1798 Bishop Denaut offered public thanksgiving for Nelson's victory at the Nile, and Abbé Joseph-Octave Plessis contemplated the fate of his compatriots if Canada, "by an unfortunate reverse, should return to its ancient masters." Like their English-speaking counterparts of the Anglican, Presbyterian and Catholic churches, the French-Canadian clergy had made themselves the chief spokesmen for the conservative principles of the colonial establishment.

Conservative principles, too, underlay the Constitutional Act, passed by the British Parliament in 1791. By it Quebec (or rather, Upper and Lower Canada, for the old province was divided by order-in-council) was to receive representative institutions and the blessings of the British constitution. Under that constitution, it was held, a careful balance among its monarchic, aristocratic and democratic parts ensured, through mutual checks, that no unnatural abuse of power occurred. Since in the former Thirteen Colonies the democratic element had clearly proved too powerful, the new colonial legislative assemblies were to be checked by encouraging the emergence of a strong aristocratic element in legislative councils set above them. The forces of order and stability were to be further reinforced by provisions for setting apart a seventh of all lands granted for the support of a Protestant clergy. Although the government left open the question whether the Church of England alone was intended to benefit, the act further provided for the endowment of Church of England rectories out of the clergy sevenths. In instructions which accompanied the act, crown reserves in the same proportion were also provided for, with the intention that revenues from them would guarantee the independence of the executive branch of the colonial governments.

The new province of Upper Canada was dominated in the 1790s by its first lieutenant-governor, John Graves Simcoe. Only here was a deliberate attempt made to integrate the prevailing ideology of Empire with the life and circumstances of the local inhabitants. Simcoe is usually written off as a combination of naive enthusiast and self-interested schemer, most of whose projects were unsuited to an infant colony. Yet he stands in contrast to every other provincial administrator of his time, and to most of his successors as well. He was a man of extraordinary energy, infectious enthusiasm, with an endless flow of ideas on the nurture of colonies, prepared to make exhausting demands upon himself and upon his subordinates in the interests of the province. He was certainly not without ambition, and was quite capable of pettiness, rancor and gross errors in judgment, but he was a warm and vital man with a genuine, if paternalist, regard for the welfare of the inhabitants of the colony.

For Simcoe, Upper Canada was not just a cushy job. He saw himself as a proconsul at the farthest extremity of Empire, fighting the great tide of democratic revolution convulsing Europe and America. He took quite literally the conservative precepts underlying the Constitutional Act, and proposed to erect in North America a model colony with "the very image and transcript" of the British constitution. Should Upper Canada become the beacon of just, stable and free government he intended it to be, perhaps the verdict of the American Revolution could yet be reversed, and inner America, from Vermont to Kentucky, be won back for the crown.

Simcoe's more grandiose plans for Upper Canada failed, as it was inevitable they should. He mistook the surface turbulence of American life and politics for the symptoms of the terminal disease which, in common with his conservative contemporaries, he believed all republics were subject to. The key to all his plans was the peopling of the province with native Americans, who through the influence of British institutions were to be turned into model subjects. Although he had formed an abiding admiration for the Loyalists during his service at the time of the Revolution, he was convinced that many Americans were still loyal to the crown, and that many more could be won back. Six months before he took the oaths of office before his newly assembled Executive Council in Kingston on July 8, 1792, he had issued a proclamation describing the terms under which land was to be granted in Upper Canada, and had contrived to give it some circulation in the United States. The first wave of immigrants to arrive in the province were the so-called "late Loyalists," many of whom had in fact heard of Upper Canada from relatives already there. After 1794, all pretence that persons being granted lands in exchange for an oath of allegiance and the fees of office were Loyalists disappeared; in that year certificates of location were issued to all those "professing the Christian religion, whose past life was respectable and law-abiding and who were capable of manual labour."

Simcoe, moreover, by explicitly appealing to such pacificist religious communities as the Quakers, Mennonites and Dunkards by promising them exemption from militia service, furthered the movement of "plain folk" into the province, a movement already under way before his arrival. These groups, settling in Prince Edward, York and Waterloo counties, gave a distinctive flavour to what was otherwise a quite typical movement of American frontier farmers. By the end of the decade, a thin band of settlement stretched from the Loyalist region around the Bay of Quinte, along the Lake Ontario and Lake Erie shores, north from York and with a sprinkling of settlement in the interior of Western Ontario. For some Loyalists, who did not share Simcoe's optimism about the beneficent influence of British institutions, his open-door policy seemed a betrayal.

Most settlement took place by individual grant. At first, however, Simcoe authorized the grant of over thirty townships on the leader and associate system, hoping thereby to concentrate settlement, and avoid the creation of an unruly, democratic backwoods population. The township grantees, under the impression that the terms of their grants were similar to those obtaining in Lower Canada, engaged in speculative practices and were almost immediately detected. Abruptly the governor ordered further township grants halted; the work of resuming the original grants to the crown was carried out by Peter Russell, his successor. Simcoe's wish to demonstrate the purity of British administration by eliminating any taint of land-jobbing was not to be realized, however. Many individual settlers accepted the initial location tickets, but neglected to take out a final patent for their land because of the fees demanded. A brisk trade in both location tickets and Loyalist rights ensued, with prominent merchants like Richard Cartwright, Robert Hamilton and John Askin being the chief beneficiaries, since they were willing to receive location tickets in lieu of debts owed them.

In this way, and also through generous grants of land made by both Simcoe and Russell to officers of government and members of the Councils in furtherance of the policy of building up a native aristocracy, large blocks of land came into the hands of a few individuals, who held them for speculative purposes. Such tracts would, in the future, impede the settlement process, although their effect was minor compared to the problem of the crown and clergy reserves.

Much depended upon the success of the reserved lands. In the minds of the British government, the function of the crown reserves was to provide an independent resource for government, relieving the British taxpayer of the burden of an expensive colonial establishment. From Simcoe's point of view, revenue from the reserves would not only make the executive government of the province free of the democratic politics that had been the curse of government before the American Revolution, it would also make the lot of the colonist happier by making taxation unnecessary at the crucial early stage of development. Out of this resource, programs of public improvement could be undertaken which would make the province the envy of the neighbouring states.

Similar considerations lay behind the provision of the clergy reserves. To Simcoe, tithes were "most dangerous" because they were "unknown to the American Settler": land endowment, on the other hand, would shield the officially recognized Church from the public obloquy that tithes would bring, especially in a colony in which the overwhelming mass of the people were Protestant dissenters. The role of the Church (and Simcoe was under no doubt that the Church meant by the Constitutional Act was the Church of England) was to act as the handmaiden of government in the inculcation of right principles of order, sobriety and resistance to the subversive levelling ideas of the American state and society.

The reserved land policy in Church and state was founded upon a profound miscalculation of the time in which substantial revenues could be realized from the land resource. Simcoe saw quickly enough that if his plans for the colony were to succeed, interim assistance would have to be provided from Great Britain, but he was unable to persuade either Dundas or Portland, the Secretaries of State during his administration, of that necessity. The same fate attended his project for a provincial educational system and a university. To Henry Dundas, it was self-evident that "the Country must make the University, not the University the Country"; Simcoe's whole approach was based upon the reverse of that pronouncement.

Meanwhile, a line of policy with respect to the land reserves had been decided upon which was to make them a detriment to settlement rather than a benefit to government. D. W. Smith, Simcoe's able and conscientious Surveyor General, had hoped to solve the problem of the location of reserved lands by concentrating them in whole townships at the rear of counties; this was rejected by Dundas on the ground that the value of the reserves would be maximized only if they were distributed throughout the areas in which free grants were being made. The result was the unfortunate "chequered plan," the pattern by which lands were distributed within townships from 1794 on. From the start, this plan prevented continuous and concentrated settlement, and placed special burdens upon the farmer whose land adjoined, or was actually enclosed by, tracts of vacant reserves. What had been intended as a support to government and religion and a boon to the colonists was shortly to become a substantial grievance.

Simcoe's novel attempt to use the military forces at his disposal in his program of colony-building also failed to get much support from the authorities. He and Lord Dorchester, his commander-in-chief, both apprehended danger from the Americans and from the beleaguered Indians of the Ohio lands, but they disagreed acrimoniously over the disposition of forces and the use to be made of troops. Simcoe intended to force settlement and provide protection by establishing garrisons and naval arsenals at such remote points as Toronto, Long Point on Lake Erie, and Chatham, and to connect them with a projected capital at London on the Thames by an interior system of military roads. Troops would be used to alleviate the typical frontier shortage of labour not only by working in public projects such as roads and buildings, but also by acting as hired labour for such pioneering chores as land-clearing. Simcoe was able to use his Queen's Rangers to build Dundas Street from Burlington Bay to the Thames, and Yonge Street from Toronto north to Lake Simcoe, but both his garrison plan and his interior capital went by the boards. Instead, Toronto was promoted from naval arsenal to provincial capital and renamed York. In 1793 Simcoe began clearing its site for blockhouses, guarding the harbour and government buildings. By the end of the decade the last officer of government had protestingly removed to it from the first capital at Niagara on the Lake.

Simcoe's vision of Upper Canada as the magnet by which Britain would regain the continental heartland evaporated with the negotiation of Jay's Treaty in 1794, by which the interior posts south of the Great Lakes held by Britain since the Revolution were to be turned over to the United States in 1796. The idea of an Indian buffer-state which he shared with other British administrators of the period had already been smashed with Anthony Wayne's defeat of the western tribes at Fallen Timbers in 1794, beneath the very noses of the British garrison of Fort Miami.

When Simcoe left Upper Canada in 1796 he was a failure only in terms of the unattainable goals he had set himself. He had established a political and legal structure, which operated with reasonable harmony during the decade. Under his auspices thousands of useful settlers had come in. The beginnings of a road network unmatched in British America had been laid out. The strategy of land use, for good or ill, had been fixed for a generation or more to come. And his grand conception of Upper Canada as a model of British institutions and principles in North America was to become, with some very Canadian variations, the central ideal of a substantial part of the province's people.

II

According to historical convention, the most important development in Lower Canada in this period was the use made of their new representative institutions by the French Canadians, and doubtless this was so. Yet these were matters which affected the mass of the population scarcely at all. About 80 per cent of the French-speaking population farmed the land on the seigneuries, and for most of them it was the ready market for their wheat (due to British demand) that most influenced their activities. A rapid growth in rural population, and the noticeable beginnings of soil exhaustion in some localities, presaged difficult times to come. A number of seigneuries passed into the hands of wealthy Scottish merchants of Montreal, who began to apply to them the improving techniques typical of contemporary British agriculture, without noticeable effect upon the traditional ways of the habitant. Otherwise, affairs in the countryside went on much as they had in the previous decade, with good wheat harvests, good prices, and a substantial degree of rural prosperity.

At the same time, however, developments were taking place at the official level which eventually would end the expansion of the seigneuries, and contribute greatly to the future distress of the rural population. Under the Instructions which accompanied the Constitutional Act, land could be granted in Lower Canada either in seigneurial tenure or in free and common soccage. The rich prize for grantees was the huge expanse of virtually empty land now known as the Eastern Townships. The fateful decision, upheld by imperial authority, was made to grant this land on the leader and associate system familiar in the Thirteen Colonies before the Revolution. Under the regulations adopted in Lower Canada, "associated companies" were to be granted entire townships, and the leader, a man of capital who bore the expenses, legal and otherwise, of settlement would receive compensation from the associates. In 1794 Council decided that a proper compensation would be 1,000 acres of each 1,200-acre grant made to an associate; that is, in exchange for the £500-£600 he expended, a leader would receive 25,000 acres of land. The long delay by the Council in reaching these decisions, and extraordinary confusion and inefficiency on the part of Samuel Holland, the Surveyor General, meant that petitions for grants dragged on for years, many settlers drifted away to Upper Canada or to the United States, and a flourishing speculative commerce in land warrants or "pretensions" commenced. To obtain such warrants from government, prospective leaders who had no supply of Loyalists or quasi-Loyalists ready to hand in Vermont or New Hampshire resorted to shady means to build up impressive lists of associates. The agents for Moses Hart of Trois Rivières, who was interested in the township of Beresford, sent a notary "into the countryside" to sign up associates for five shillings a name; Henry Cull, a Montreal merchant, asked his London agents to ship him out a few hundred "Vagabonds" and "Idlers" in order to secure a warrant for the township of Dunham. Once obtained, a "pretension" became an article of commerce; by the late 1790s pretensions existed for some seventy townships, far more, in fact, than there was land available to grant.

This unsavoury mess was not finally cleared up until 1809, but before it had been settled, it had brought down a governor, Prescott, who was recalled in 1799 for openly accusing his Council of corruption. If the object of the leader and associate system had been to place settlers on the land, it had failed lamentably; with the exception of a number of Loyalists, disbanded soldiers and squatters who were confirmed in their titles, an enormous tract of land, nearly two million acres in extent, wound up in the hands of a few speculators. A very high proportion of this went to Lower Canadian merchants, to add to their holdings of seigneurial land. The proportion granted under the leader and associate system was about 1,100,000 acres; of this amount, executive councillors, assemblymen and other office-holders got a total of just under a quarter of a million acres. Among the principal beneficiaries were Thomas Dunn, Hugh Finlay, Henry Caldwell, Joseph Frobisher, William Grant and John Richardson.

While this gigantic land grab was taking place at one level of the political structure, at another the merchant group found its interests thwarted. In both Executive and Legislative Councils the English were in a majority, but in the Assembly there was no way around the fact that the French population outnumbered the English by 146,000 to 10,000. Even so, adroit constituency juggling gave the English minority sixteen members out of a house of fifty in the elections of 1792. Much to the chagrin of the English members, the advocates, notaries and seigneurs who spoke for the mass of the population did not share their vision of the splendours of commercial empire. From the first, the *Canadiens* exhibited that combination of political agressiveness and social and economic conservatism natural to a people who felt at once politically dominated and culturally threatened. They insisted, therefore, in electing one of their number speaker, and in making French a working language of the Assembly along with English. These victories, immensely important psychologically and symbolically to the French Canadians, were merely irritants to the English. Much more vital was the majority rejection, for obvious reasons, of a tax on land for revenue purposes, and the substitution of duties on imports. This, together with the cold shoulder given by the French to such cherished developmental projects of the merchants as a turnpike road from Montreal to Lachine, and a canal to bypass the Lachine rapids, exasperated them. The representative institutions they had laboured so long to win, and upon which they had placed such high hopes, had, through the division of the old province of Quebec, trapped them instead. John Richardson was bitter. "Nothing can be so irksome as the situation of the English members—without numbers to do any good—doomed to the necessity of combating the absurdities of the majority, without a hope of success."

Donald Creighton's magnificent book, *The Commercial Empire of the St. Lawrence*, has taught us to sympathize with the plight of the merchants. But the righteous indignation of Richardson sounds more like hypocrisy when it is remembered how expertly he and his brethren had used other parts of the 1791 constitution to rape the province, and the bulk of its population, of its great land reserves. And if the rampant acquisitiveness of the merchants had suffered some check in the Assembly, broad prospects were opening up for them in the interior of the continent.

III

The process of settlement in Upper Canada, the production of agricultural surpluses both there and in the newly settled American territories south of the Lakes, and the beginnings of a lumbering industry, brought a profitable diversification of the Montreal trading empire. This hardly meant, however, a diminishing of the great struggle between Montreal and Hudson Bay for the control of the fur trade. In the 1790s that struggle was continued with a steadily rising intensity, for not only did Montreal-based traders push their enterprises more vigorously and efficiently than before, but the Bay Company began to stir itself to meet its rivals.

The North West Company began the decade with a degree of concentration it had never before possessed. Although the Company retained its character as an association of partners who, on the basis of agreements made annually, determined the strategy of the trade, the apportionment of profits and the capital requirements for the coming campaign, in 1790 one firm emerged as the dominant partner. McTavish, Frobisher and Company now controlled a majority of the organization's shares, and in 1790 all the partners agreed that the Montreal end of the fur business would be handled for the Company by the McTavish firm. The latter would take care of the external side of the trade: that is, the procurement of trade goods and credit from England, warehousing and packing services both for goods arriving from England and for the furs being exported, the hiring of labour for the internal trade, and the provision of foodstuffs and other goods required to maintain the internal structure of the Company. For all this McTavish, Frobisher were to receive a commission. The 1790 reorganization gave a significant degree of control over the Company's operations into the hands of Simon McTavish, contributed greatly to the efficiency of the Company, and was successful in the crucial matter of securing capital—that is, credit—for the Company's expanding operations from the London money market. This was emphatically important, because the distance over which the fur route now extended meant that the time gap between the purchase of trade goods in London and the sale of the furs to pay for them was three years or more.

By 1800, the North West Company had established its posts throughout the prairie west, along the Peace River, and on the North Saskatchewan as far as Rocky Mountain House. In its service, Alexander Mackenzie, who had already reached the Arctic Ocean via the river that bears his name, in 1793 ascended the Peace River, and journeyed through the Rockies to Bella Coola inlet on the Pacific, just weeks before Captain George Vancouver reached there by sea in charting the north Pacific coast for the Royal Navy. The next decade would see the Company take advantage of these and further explorations to push its operations to the Pacific slope, thus constructing the first transcontinental economic system in Canadian history.

This extraordinary expansion was spurred on by the peculiar internal structure of the Company. To provide incentive and to give scope to ambition, the Company was forced constantly to enlarge the area of its operations, to create new departments in the interior, to add to the number of its shares, and to promote its clerks to wintering partners. William McGillivray, for example, was promoted to wintering partner in 1791 after serving seven years as a clerk; in 1795 three clerks were promoted, and new shares were added to accommodate Montreal firms which had been Company rivals. The system encouraged sharp and aggressive trading and a relentless search for richer fur regions and ever more guileless Indian suppliers. For the winterers, the rewards were great; it was not only the Montreal merchants who could afford fine houses in Montreal and broad seigneurial acres.

The farther the Company's servants penetrated into the western interior, the more elaborate and costly the logistics of the trade became. The Company was never rich in liquid capital, but during the 1790s it was found necessary to make a series of capital investments on the support side of the trade. The labour force consisted of several hundred men, most of them French Canadians. They manned the large *canôts du maître* which carried goods and provisions up the Ottawa, across the water routes and portages to Georgian Bay, and from thence to Grand Portage at the head of Lake Superior, the site of the Company's interior headquarters. Some two or three hundred more of these *voyageurs* paddled the smaller *canôts du nord* from Grand Portage farther to the west, and there wintered at the posts. To supplement the work of the fur brigades, and also to supply both them and the posts with provisions, the Great Lakes route was exploited. Goods and supplies were sent by batteaux up to Kingston, where they were transshipped to Niagara, carried overland and then by boat to Lake Erie. By 1793 the Company owned vessels of 40 and 45 tons on Lakes Erie, Huron and Michigan, and a 75-ton ship on Lake Superior. In 1797-98 a shallow draft canal was built at Sault Ste. Marie. Food supplies were acquired from the new farming districts of Upper Canada for shipment to the head of the lakes, as well as from older sources like Detroit and Mackinac. In addition, part of the energies of the Company went into the procurement of pemmican from the Plains Indians, a vital element in the diet of the winterers and western *voyageurs*.

Certain permanently operating factors which had always affected the fur trade were accentuated during the decade, and hence pushed the pace of expansion. Exhaustion of the beaver had always been a factor in the steady movement to the west; now that exhaustion took place much more rapidly, for several reasons. Technological development in the European hatting industry with the adoption of mechanized combing techniques meant that both summer and winter skins could be used equally well in the felting process; this, together with the fact that the Northwesters were reaching Indians who had normally used the summer months to travel to the Bay forts for trade, meant that there was no longer a closed season on the trapping of beaver. New trapping techniques, such as the introduction of the steel trap in the 1790s, made it possible to trap out a district within a few years.

Special difficulties were created for the North West Company by the signing of Jay's Treaty. For one thing, their inland headquarters at Grand Portage was within American territory, and the Company was compelled to move to a new base near the site of the old French post of Fort Kaministiquia; this move to what became Fort William was not completed until 1803. Even more important was the shift of Montreal-based traders from the southwest, when the British posts below the Lakes had to be abandoned, into territories where the Nor'westers were operating. By the end of the decade this movement had led to the formation of a rival firm, the New North West Company, made even more formidable by the defection of Alexander Mackenzie to their ranks. This organization, also called the XY Company, Sir Alexander Mackenzie & Company—or simply "the Potties"—appeared just at the time when the North West Company was encountering a serious challenge from its formerly somnolent rival to the north, the much older Hudson's Bay Company.

Two important changes marked the policy of that Company in the 1790s. The first was the recognition by the governing committee in London that the battle with the "Montreal Pedlars" could be directed in only the most general way from London. Beginning in the 1780s, but reaching fruition in the next decade, a substantial delegation of authority took place from the committee to the masters of the Company's posts on the Bay. Company traders were now to move into the interior, locate themselves as close as possible to their Canadian rivals, and compete directly with them for the furs produced by the Indians. The forts on the Bay were to assume the role of factories or supply depots for the inland posts, instead of being trading centres themselves. To make this new policy effective, it was necessary immediately to improve the communications system with the interior. The committee's contribution to this problem was the suggestion that a "Machine" be devised for winter carriage by placing a boat on a sledge, and, with the help of sails, the contraption could then be poled over the snow—an ancestral snowmobile! The answer of the Company's servants was the York boat: a shallow-draft boat some thirty to forty feet in length, capable of carrying five tons of goods and provisions when rowed by a ten-man crew. Experiments with the boats commenced at York and Churchill in the early 1790s; by 1795 a York boat had been launched on the Saskatchewan River. Although much expense was involved in making portage roads and rollers for moving the boats over them, by the end of the decade a system of boat and canoe relays had been developed from York to the interior.

Much, however, depended upon the individual enterprise of the Company's servants. It was difficult for the Hudson's Bay Company, dependent as it was upon the wage system, to match the individual enterprise of the Nor'westers. Daniel Harmon of the North West Company commented in 1800 that since the Bay men "have nothing to expect from the Company but their salaries they seem so far as I can learn to make but little exertion to extend their trade and thereby to benefit their employers," and certainly the failure of the Company adequately to support David Thompson caused this outstanding explorer to leave its service in 1797 for that of men with more "enlarged views." The Company made some attempt to solve this problem with an incentive-pay system; in 1793 "trip-money" was instituted, by which wages were increased proportional to the distance inland from the Bay.

The work of some of the Bay men, and the aggressive new policy, began to pay dividends. As early as 1793 the Nor'westers were challenged in an area crucial to them when the Hudson's Bay Company established a post in the heart of the Red River Department. Brandon House on the Assiniboine was in pemmican country; and without adequate supplies of it, the North West brigades would have to live off the country on their way inland. Even more important were the activities of William Tomison on the Saskatchewan River. As "Inland Chief" he built up a solid transportation and trading organization, culminating in the building of Edmonton House in 1795.

The lines were thus drawn during this decade for the struggle between Montreal and Hudson Bay for the control of the fur trade that was to culminate in the victory of the latter in 1821, when the inherent advantages of geographic location and superior financial structure finally won out. The short-run picture in the 1790s did not reflect that ultimate outcome, however; the North West Company enjoyed by 1800 a share of the trade that was about four times that of its Canadian and Bay rivals combined. The meaning of the fur trade competition has too often been seen merely in terms of the rivalry between the two great companies. Interesting and economically significant though that was, there were other consequences for Canadian development that were very important. The stock of geographical knowledge had been enormously increased in the decade, as a result of the work of fur-trading explorers, in combination with the discoveries and mapping of Captain George Vancouver on the Pacific coast. The experience gained in conducting trade profitably over great distances through combining transportation improvement projects with borrowed capital from the London money market was to be applied to the exploitation of the new staples of the farming and lumbering frontiers. The rich profits of the decade meant the rapid establishment of a number of personal fortunes, and the creation of an English-speaking monied class in Montreal and environs whose influence was to be felt in social and political, as well as economic spheres. Finally, the enormous geographic expansion of the trade during the decade had sucked into the cultural meatgrinder nearly all the remaining Indian groupings of Canada with the exception of the peoples of the Pacific slope, with consequences for them no less demoralizing, and no more remarked by contemporaries, than the earlier impact of European culture upon tribes farther east.

IV

At the beginning of the 1790s, Nova Scotia and New Brunswick were still endeavouring to fill the place of New England in supplying the West Indies. Despite shortages of both labour and capital, the economies of the two provinces had been greatly stimulated by this challenge, especially in the creation of a merchant marine, and optimism ran high in both Halifax and Saint John. Maritime hopes were abruptly dashed by the outbreak of the war with France. Over the protests of the colonial legislatures, the British government issued regulations permitting American vessels direct access to West Indian ports, thus cutting off at a stroke the thriving entrepôt trade by which cheap American produce and timber had been carried to the islands by colonial ships. Maritime carriers could not compete with their American rivals in terms of costs; their sea voyage was longer and their insurance rates were higher because they were prey to French privateers. Shipowners of Saint John and St. Andrews were forced to turn to the coasting trade of the Bay of Fundy; the Liverpool fleet all but disappeared, dropping from sixty ships to one by 1799. The Nova Scotian fisheries, instead of providing a staple for export by colonial merchants to the West Indies, became tributary to the Americans. Outport fishermen found it cheaper to barter their catch for Yankee provisions and East India goods, rather than deal with Halifax merchants who, after 1792, had to pay a duty of 10 per cent on goods imported from Britain. Governor Wentworth, frustrated by his inability to check the flow of smuggled goods, complained that Nova Scotia had become "a fishing colony to the United States instead of to Great Britain."

Nova Scotia also lacked the internal communications needed to enable the farmers of the Annapolis valley, Minas Basin and Chignecto regions to market their surpluses at prices competitive with the cheap foodstuffs from American producers. The only existing roads, connecting Halifax with Annapolis and Truro with Pictou, were not really suitable for wheeled traffic, which meant that the production of beef cattle to be shipped out on the hoof was the most profitable form of farming. Nevertheless, the rising demand from the growing Halifax naval and military establishment, and the higher prices brought by the war, offered some encouragement to the farmer. As early as 1789, an agricultural society was founded in King's County, and its first act was to appoint a marketing agent for beef in Halifax. The society, as it happens, was a most successful one. Its aims were characteristic of a form of communal self-help often found in later Canadian development: "the better improvement of Husbandry, encouragement of Manufactures, cultivation of the Social Virtues, acquirement of Useful Knowledge, and to promote the good order and well being of the Community to which we belong." If the account books of Henry Magee, a Kentville general merchant of the period, are an accurate gauge, the state of agriculture in the area was not nearly so depressed as the complaints of farmers over the importation of American produce would lead one to imagine. In 1795-96 Magee took in almost £3,000 from his customers. (Magee could have used the bank that Halifax merchants were beginning to talk about; he hid "gold in the salt" and "in the apel box in the cellar," and put "silver in the wheat.")

Another settlement which advanced during these years in the face of generally unpromising conditions was the Scottish community of Pictou. Some remarkably enterprising merchants, notably Edward Mortimer from Banffshire in Scotland, built up a thriving trade with Halifax, especially in supplying the naval dockyard, and with Britain, by exploiting the white pine and oak found in the vicinity, and by combining the export of square timber with shipbuilding (including privateers) and the fish trade. The lumbering boom disrupted the original Scottish agricultural settlement; according to the Rev. James McGregor, it introduced "a taste for vanity and expensive living . . . among us"; but by 1800 the foundation for a prosperous, outward-looking community with a strong Scottish flavour had been laid.

Nova Scotian politics of this period registered only imperfectly the social and economic situation of most of the province's people. The most significant development was an adjustment in the official political structure, made necessary by the need to accommodate those Loyalists who laid claim to high office and status by virtue of their loyalty and past position. Because this adjustment was pre-cipitated by a series of direct clashes between the Assembly and the Council from 1787 to 1792, and because the rhetoric employed by Loyalist oppositionists had a distinctly liberal tone, some historians, notably S. D. Clark, convinced themselves that "a distinctive move-ment of political reform" was under way. To the nineteenth-century school of pre-Loyalist historians, however, there was no doubt about what the issues were. For Beamish Murdoch, the struggle was between "native Nova Scotians" who had staunchly defended the province against both Frenchmen and Yankees, and what a colleague of his called "those New York office grabbers."

There was certainly much about these disputes which permits the latter interpretation. For the Loyalists, Nova Scotia had quickly become "Nova Scarcity." As the truth of their situation came home to them, and their proud hopes of reconstituting the life they had formerly led melted away, many of them sought to maintain their position of leadership through government favour. What made them objectionable to the pre-Loyalist inhabitants was that not merely did they plead their loyalty as a cause for special bounty, but they frequently cast disdainful aspersions upon the inferior educational and cultural attainments of the old office-holding class.

It was undoubtedly true, however, that the Loyalists stood for a quite different view of the nature of the colonial constitution. Their Whig principles accorded a role to the Assembly thought radical by the Nova Scotian official class; and they were successful not only in asserting the exclusive right of the Assembly to introduce money bills, but also in challenging the Council's right to amend them. As well, the Loyalist-led Assembly impeached the judges of the Supreme Court for corruption and incompetence, and attacked the union of executive and legislative functions in the Council. One of the Loyalists, Major Barclay, as early as 1789 moved a motion of non-confidence in the Council, assuring his fellow-members that "nothing was more usual than for His Majesty's Commons to move a dismission of his ministers," a constitutional sentiment that a pre-Loyalist member, Alexander Howe, thought "tended to Rebellion."

The Loyalist-led reform movement, such as it was, was deflated shortly after John Wentworth, himself a Loyalist, became governor in 1792. John Parr, his predecessor, had had a low opinion of the Loyalists, "that cursed set of dogs," and believed that they "do not care a damn" for Nova Scotia. Under Wentworth, two of the most outspoken Loyalist politicians, Jonathan Stearns and Barclay, secured good jobs, and that was only the beginning. Although, as Margaret Ells so convincingly showed in a splendid piece of analysis, the Loyalists got only 520 of the 1336 appointments made by Wentworth during his administration, the crucial fact was that they got over 60 per cent of the jobs that carried some remuneration. Moreover, Wentworth's major appointments overwhelmingly favoured the newcomers: seven of the eleven appointments to Council went to Loyalists, and nine of the twelve appointments to major offices under the crown.

The healing balm of patronage, through which the provincial ruling class was enlarged to take in the Loyalists, consolidated the oligarchy for more than a generation, and stilled the reform rhetoric of the Loyalist group. A new ingredient, however, that of American Whiggism, had been added to the values of the governing elite, and was to give provincial politics a distinctive character. There was a less obvious outcome of this period of oligarchic adjustment. There had in fact been no Loyalist "party" in the Sixth Assembly; the Loyalist group in it numbered ten members at most, yet majorities had been won for their motions on a variety of issues, including the winning of the money power for the Assembly. It thus is probable that the Loyalists were joined on such issues by members representing the outports, who wished not only to strike a constitutional blow at conciliar control, but also to wrest financial power from the Halifax mercantile group, and through such legislation as the revenue duties provide the money for roads, schools, and other public improvements much needed by their isolated communities. This was clearly the significance of the overturning of the sitting members for Halifax County during the election of 1799. The four members were all Halifax merchants, yet the constituency they sat for also included Colchester and Pictou. A country coalition, led by William Cottnam Tonge, turned three of them out on a platform of maintenance of the revenue duties and the use of the revenues for road-building and education. Tonge was to provide, on behalf of the people of the outports, the first real challenge to the new oligarchy that Wentworth had so smoothly created.

For the people of New Brunswick, the time was one of blighted hopes, economic distress, and embittered politics. The outlook seemed bright enough to begin with. Up the St. Croix and along the Fundy coast, sawmills sprang up during the late 1780s and early 1790s, a good deal of shipbuilding was carried on both at St. Andrews and Saint John, and the Fundy and Atlantic fisheries based on these ports seemed to augur well for the commercial prospects of the province. The Fundy region was connected with the settlements up the St. John by the internal highway of the river itself, and so the elements for a regional exchange of products existed. But lumbering flagged once the stands of timber near the water's edge had been cut off. Timber operators lacked the capital to build lumbering roads; a survey of 1802 found less than ten miles of road suitable for wheeled traffic in the whole province. Shortage of labour meant high wages and inability to compete with more cheaply produced American timber, which a proclamation by Governor Thomas Carleton admitted to the province in 1791. Only in the far-off Miramichi settlements did naval masting contracts bring some degree of local prosperity.

New Brunswick agriculture also suffered from a labour shortage. After the outbreak of the French wars, no immigrants could be expected from England in any event, but a 1790 regulation of the Secretary of State (unobserved in other colonies) forbade temporarily the further granting of lands. This order, which outlasted the decade, locked up 90 per cent of the province. Although Carleton permitted squatting, there was little inducement for Americans to settle in the province when title to good land was readily available in New York state and Upper Canada. In consequence, there was a net emigration from New Brunswick during the 1790s, including several hundred Loyalists who re-settled in Upper Canada.

Lack of labour for land-clearing meant that the farming region of the St. John valley failed to produce reliable surpluses to feed Fredericton, let alone Saint John and the other communities of the Fundy shore. The small stimulus of the garrison market disappeared in 1792 when the two regiments stationed in the province were withdrawn. Food imports from the United States ensured that local agriculture would continue in a depressed state. Such prominent Loyalist landowners as Ward Chipman, Edward Winslow and Stair Agnew, who had hoped to establish country estates and themselves as New Brunswick gentry, had no means to transform the hard laws of frontier economics. The letters Chipman and Winslow exchanged over a period of more than twenty years portray the progressive abandonment of their social ambitions. Chipman had sent his son to Harvard, and hoped unavailingly to give him a professional education at one of the Inns of Court. "I cannot bear the thought of him burying himelf in this country, and it is not in my power to educate him in and for any other." In 1797, Winslow, looking back on the enthusiasm with which he and others of his class had braved the first rigorous of settlement, saw "the whole society gradually sinking into a sort of lethargy." What was the point of being "loaded with titles, overwhelmed with honours," of owning a beautiful estate on a magnificent river, with prodigious stands of pine, when "I had hardly credit to buy an axe"? "I have dashed at every opening," he wrote, "but a wife, ten children and the gout have held me fast."

Men like Chipman and Winslow, who at least had a few crumbs from the official table through various minor offices, remained pillars of the establishment, but other members of their class, who would normally have been staunch supporters of the existing order, expressed their disappointment in political opposition. Stair Agnew actually advocated annexation to the United States as a solution for agricultural distress, and found plenty of Loyalists to vote for him. Governor Carleton had neither the means nor the dexterity to placate such resentment, nor, unlike Simcoe, did he have the drive and imagination to keep bright the vision of a better future.

A whole set of frictions arose around the now-familiar antithesis of New Brunswick life, that between south and north, Saint John

and Fredericton. Instead of complementarity, the regions represented by the two towns developed antagonisms. Most of the business activity of the province centred on Saint John; compared to
it, Fredericton was a rural village. Yet Fredericton was the capital,
the place where the legislature met, where government offices were
situated, and where the Supreme Court sat. Its outlook was bureaucratic, Anglican and rural, a mingling of the values of the Loyalist
gentry and the official class. The counties of St. John, Charlotte and
Westmoreland were more outward looking, commercially oriented,
and the centres of Protestant dissent. Strong feelings were generated
in these counties by such issues as the failure of the Supreme Court
to hold sittings elsewhere than in the capital, the special position
accorded the Anglican Church, and the proposal to establish, with
public money, an academy at Fredericton which quite obviously
would be intended for the sons of gentlemen.

Had economic difficulties not brought out regional, social and
religious disparities, it is doubtful whether such issues would have
penetrated the normal decorum of official politics. But stagnation
and lack of imaginative leadership split the province's natural ruling
class, and brought the formation of a temporarily formidable political opposition, led by a brilliant and erratic Scot, James Glenie.

Glenie was a graduate of St. Andrew's University and Woolwich
Academy, who had been elected a fellow of the Royal Society for
papers on mathematics while serving in the army during the American Revolution. His military career was studded with incidents
of insubordination, and although reinstated after being cashiered
by a court martial (on which Thomas Carleton sat), he left the
army in 1787 and settled in New Brunswick. He got into the timber
business, and was elected to the Assembly in 1789 for Sunbury, the
only county with a substantial pre-Loyalist population of New
Englanders.

By skilfully exploiting the various grievances of New Brunswickers, Glenie built within a relatively short time a coalition that could
command majorities in the Assembly. He attacked the privileged
status of the Church of England, criticized the raising of a fencible
(home defence) regiment in New Brunswick in 1793 because it
would contribute to the labour shortage that "renders Agricultural

improvements almost impracticable," blocked the establishment of Fredericton Academy and attempted to establish a province-wide system of education based on the parish unit. The activities of the coalition produced a four-year deadlock over appropriations, during which time (1795-99) the administration got no money votes from the Assembly, and Assembly members got no salaries.

The Glenie coalition, although it rested in part upon a regional base that was to remain a fact of life in provincial politics, was essentially a temporary one. Glenie had a special talent for alienating as well as for attracting support. Conscious of his own abilities, he had a blistering contempt for those of others, especially if they happened to be colonials. The Chief Justice was "illiterate" and "strutting," another judge was "an ignorant, uncouth Dutch boor whom no Gentleman is ever seen to associate with," and the Council was made up entirely of "Americans," without one "European" of liberal education on it, "though there ought always to be at least a Majority." Moreover, although discontent was deep enough to win majorities for specific causes in the Assembly, it did not really extend to challenges to the political system itself. When in 1797 Glenie moved a resolution censuring Governor Carleton himself, most of his supporters deserted him, and he was defeated by a large majority. Higher prices for farm products and timber brought about by the war, and the feeling that direct opposition to the representative of the crown was not only radical but revolutionary, and unpatriotic during a war crisis, may have helped to destroy his authority; certainly he was deserted by erstwhile "country" supporters like Agnew.

V

The history of Prince Edward Island in this decade is a history apart. In no colony except Newfoundland does British colonial administration appear in a worse light. The root of the problem was still the manner in which the island had been divided among great land proprietors in 1767. None of the conditions by which the grantees were to settle tenants on their 20,000-acre lots within ten years had been adhered to. In 1797, twenty-three of the lots were still completely empty of settlers, but since the majority of proprietors lived in Great Britain, some of their lands were already being pre-empted by squatters whose occupancy had no standing in law. Because the proprietors had been permitted to escape their quit-rent obligations, the little island government had virtually no revenue for improvement projects. Charlottetown itself had no more than seventy dwellings, and the total population of the province was some 4,400, of whom well over half were Catholic Scots and Acadians. Except for the small official class, a few merchants and those proprietors who had established themselves in Charlottetown, the people were dispersed on isolated holdings throughout the island, pursuing "a catch as catch can" agriculture, and combining it with spring herring fishing, and fishing for cod in small boats off the north shore.

Isolation, tenantry, farming little above the subsistence level, and absentee landlordism were ingredients for real discontent. It is probably significant that Lieutenant-Governor Fanning discovered in 1793 "a general opposition to a militia" among the inhabitants, an opposition that was surely symptomatic of deeper grievances. The tenantry put their faith in the confiscation of the land of absentee landlords for non-fulfilment of the terms of the original grants. In 1781, Lieutenant-Governor Patterson had taken legal action in the Island courts against a number of grantees for non-payment of quit-rents, and as a consequence, a number of townships had been resumed by the crown and later sold. In 1797, the Assembly was encouraged by Fanning and his officials to pass a quit-rent bill, which allowed judgments against a number of grants to be obtained. The lands thus freed, however, were purchased by a small group of residents who had the favour of the lieutenant-governor.

Neglected by Britain and exploited shamelessly by their own government, there was little left to the inhabitants of the Island but to help themselves. There is a fascinating document from 1795 which shows how two of the Island groups went about the matter of survival and self-help. It is a letter from "the Committee of the General Meeting of the Roman Catholics" living on the eastern half of the Island to "the Acadians, Inhabitants of the Bay of Fortune." For some years past the religious needs of the Scottish Catholics had been met by priests from their homeland, who had also served the Acadian population of the Island. Because the settlements of the Acadians were dispersed in remote parts, the priest had spent most of his time in travel. "Such fluctuation and deficiency of the ordinary means of Instruction and practice," observed the Scots, "tend to make people degenerate, and by want of schooling the rising generation becomes ignorant and less fit even for the purpose of Civil Society." They therefore proposed that two priests be obtained, and that the families of both groups commit themselves to an annual subscription for their maintenance and for the purchase of two farms upon which the priests could settle. The amount they proposed was no more than the price of a barrel of pork, surely a small sum "for a People, none of whom will hesitate to expend very improperly three or four times the amount upon riotous funerals and marriage feasts."

What is interesting about this letter is not only what it shows about the Scottish capacity to organize themselves for community action in a cause "laudable, decent, useful, necessary and even Economical," but also what it reveals about the Acadians, at least through Scottish eyes. It is clear from the letter that the Acadians had been less than co-operative in their response to the plan, but more than that, from the beginning they had not "thought proper to assimilate" with the Scots, but instead had kept to themselves. "Some of our own people," said the Scots, "are more distantly situated, but instead of litigating they are preparing to bring themselves in effect nearer by cutting a road through the woods: you alone seem disposed to dispute every inch." To the Scot, the Acadian was a light-minded person, "shifting about, as incidental impulses lead you."

VI

Two cultures, two histories touched here but failed to mingle. If the Island's history was a history apart, the Acadians were a people apart. Made homeless by their tragic dispersion, "they still preserve," said a contemporary, "an Idea which they deliver down to their children that they shall repossess their lands again and be restored to the enjoyment of that happy age which they formerly experienced under a patriarchal government." The Acadian's sustaining myth of that primitive age of "Arcadian innocence and simplicity" had taken firm hold, and given this people an unmatched degree of self-consciousness and will to survive on their own terms. If the Acadians of Prince Edward Island were still in a semi-nomadic state in the 1790s, their brethren elsewhere were beginning the creation of stable, inward-looking little communities. In 1793, for example, those Acadians who had left Cape Breton a generation earlier for Miquelon and the Magdalen Islands returned, took the oath of allegiance and settled down on Isle Madame and Little Bras d'Or. As early as the late 1760s the Acadians had returned to Yarmouth County in Nova Scotia; by the 1790s shipowners and captains with names like D'Entremont, Surette and Doucette were operating from the little fishing villages of the south shore of the Bay of Fundy. Perhaps their outport location alone would have permitted the people of this community to survive as a distinct group, but in 1799 that possibility was reinforced by the arrival of the Abbé Jean-Mande Sigogne, a French emigré priest who was to provide religious and secular leadership for the next forty-five years. Three months after he had established himself on St. Mary's Bay he had all the heads of families of the several Acadian outports sign, under oath, a set of regulations of twenty-eight articles which effectively laid the foundation for a semi-autonomous, Catholic and French-speaking society on the south shore. The regulations set up an informal system of law and self-government, similar to that which had existed before the dispersion, under which the priest assisted by "arbitrators" and "assessors" oversaw the morals of the community and settled disputes among its members in order that no Acadian should have to resort to the Nova Scotian courts in a suit against his brethren, but only in cases involving "strangers to the Catholic faith."

It is obvious that the Acadians, for good reason, had a decided mistrust of English justice. Little that happened to the Acadians of New Brunswick after the arrival of the Loyalists was calculated to lessen their suspicions. Those at the head of the Bay of Fundy or the Gulf of St. Lawrence Shore who had been lucky enough to have obtained land grants already were not disturbed, and some of the squatters at Memramcook managed to buy land from the Loyalist grantees. But the Acadians who had squatted on the fertile intervale at Hammond River and St. Anne's got summary treatment. As Winslow put it, "a number of Frenchmen . . . have been most unjustly ousted from their land"; according to Acadian tradition, the Loyalists tore down and burnt their fences. Governor Carleton deplored the situation, but refused to act, since the Acadians' land had been granted to the 2nd Battalion of New Jersey Volunteers.

And so the Acadians made their last migration. During the next quarter of a century, they spread up the Gulf or North Shore from Memramcook, the villages of Buctouche, Tracadie, Richibucto, Pokemouche, Kouchibouguacsis, Shippegan, Miscou and Barachois marking the path of their movement up to 1800. The Acadians displaced from the Saint John settlements were seated by Thomas Carleton about the mouth of the Madawaska River, and up the Madawaska valley. Had their new lands not been in a region in which the boundary between New Brunswick and Lower Canada had not been determined, little of their life in this period would be known. They themselves were illiterate, the New Brunswick government, after performing its act of elementary justice in resettling them, took not the slightest interest in their welfare, and a priest from Quebec resided among them for only a brief period during the decade. Carleton did appoint a justice of the peace, Thomas Costin, who was selected because he could read and write, after a fashion, and because he was the only person in the community whose religion did not prevent him from taking the oaths of office. Lord Dorchester, exerting the Quebec claim to jurisdiction, appointed two officers of militia. When their authority was challenged by the Acadians, Carleton, at his brother's tart suggestion, also issued them commissions. There was in fact little formal government in the community. The Acadians went on as they had for generations, making verbal contracts, settling disputes by using itinerant priests and local "assessors" as adjudicators, and

having the same priests perform retroactive marriages and wholesale baptisms whenever they chanced to visit. The boundary dispute brought some disorders, however. As Costin pointed out,
Madawaska became "a place of retirance" for fugitives from
Quebec justice. "Whenever these gentlemen hear the judges of
the court of Quebec is a coming down in the lower parishes of
Canada they desert to this place . . . and whenever they get in
debt they return to Canada." As for the Acadians, the situation
was a familiar one: once more they were history's catspaws, the
subject of dispute between two governments, and they exploited
the situation as best they could.

VII

The history of Newfoundland in the 1790s is characterized by exploitation and absurdity. Exploitation seemed a permanent feature
of the island's history: exploitation of the humble cod, upon which
rested not only the economy of the island but also that of a good
part of the North Atlantic trading system, and exploitation of the
island's people by the merchants and shipowners of Britain, New
England and St. John's itself. Absurdity had been a part of Newfoundland's story from the early seventeenth century onwards, because of the conflict between the local reality of settlement and the
imperial mercantilist theory, that treated the island as an economic
and naval resource and not as a "plantation"—a resort for the
fishing fleets of the English West Country, whose interests must
not be shaken. Thus settlement on the island had been expressly
forbidden, and "government" for the fishery still consisted of the
senior naval officer on station at St. John's during the fishing season.
Before the 1790s, reality had forced only minor alterations in Newfoundland's "floating government." In 1728, the naval governor
had been empowered to appoint justices of the peace, resident on
the island throughout the year (the "winter justices"). In 1765,
because New Englanders, with their native aptitude for resource-
fully exploiting the realities of the Atlantic economy, had been
making a good thing out of the exchange of goods from the French
West Indies for Newfoundland fish, the Board of Trade had es-

tablished a customs house at St. John's, seeing "no reason to doubt" that Newfoundland, at least for the purpose of His Majesty's Navigation Laws, was "a part of His Majesty's plantations."

As late as 1789, Lord Grenville could pronounce for the British government that "Newfoundland is in no respect a British colony and is never so considered in our laws," and that it was the prime object of government "to restrain the subjects of Great Britain from colonising that Island." Even as he wrote, there were at least 12,000 people who had no home but Newfoundland; by 1800 it was estimated that the island's population was 20,000. It is an odd aspect of this absurd situation that there were many more people in a territory in which settlement was expressly forbidden than on the much kinder island of Prince Edward Island where the imperial arrangements supposedly had been designed to encourage settlement, and not much fewer than in Upper Canada. As the most acute critic of British policy towards Newfoundland in the 1790s, John Reeves, said, "Newfoundland has been peopled behind your Back; you have abandoned it to be inhabited by any one who chooses, because you thought appointing a Governor would constitute a Colony and encourage Population."

The West Country merchants and shipowners had themselves been primarily responsible for Newfoundland settlement. It had been good business for them to encourage the English, and later Irish labourers who came out in the spring fleet to winter on the island, to build small boats, and in exchange for food and wages, to provide fish. Palliser's Act of 1775, which had been intended to ensure that seamen returned to Europe at the end of the season by providing that forty shillings was to be held back from their wages for the return passage, simply opened up a new source of revenue for the West Countrymen. Why not pocket the forty shillings, leave the men behind, and fill the ship's cabins with dried fish for the return voyage? By the 1790s, this process had gone so far that the island population had thrown up its own merchant class, go-between for the resident fishermen and the West Countrymen, whose role had become increasingly confined to the supply of provisions and goods in exchange for fish. It was the period of the French wars that finally ensured that the fisheries, if not the trade arising from them, were primarily a Newfoundland, not a British pursuit. High insurance rates and the danger from French commerce raiders, the wartime difficulty of finding seamen to man the ships, and the fact that Newfoundlanders could produce fish more cheaply than the transatlantic fishing fleet, meant that by 1800 or shortly thereafter the era of the West Country Bankers was over.

This hardly meant the dawn of a new day for the people of Newfoundland. Their life continued hard in the extreme. For most of them, a bare livelihood depended upon unceasing activity during the season. In their struggle to survive, they could look for no helping hand from a government, or much in the way of relieving balm from organized religion. What we know of their life comes almost entirely from official sources, filled out by the reports of travellers and of itinerant priests and missionaries. A visiting missionary said in 1790 that the islanders were "a people distracted about property." Small wonder. Since the islanders as a people could not, according to British law, exist, it followed that there could be no legal title whatever to the land on which they lived. The only form of property that the naval governors were permitted to recognize was the annual occupancy of fishing rooms, that is, space along the shore for sheds, flakes, wharves and other structures necessary for carrying on the making of fish for export. The sharp drop in the size of the English fishing fleet in the 1790s (from 330 ships in 1788 to 30 in 1803), meant that vacant ship-rooms were occupied, illegally, by islanders who built houses and outbuildings on them. St. John's, which by the end of the decade was a relatively large town as colonial towns went, with a population of perhaps five thousand, had been built planlessly and confusedly, of the most impermanent and makeshift of materials. Mingled in its crazy jumble were hundreds of tiny wooden sheds inhabited by fishermen and their families, together with the more substantial establishments of the resident merchant group, whose shops, "factories" and houses took up most of the town's waterfront. A succession of distracted governors, caught between the absurdity of their instructions and the rapidity with which the ramshackle towns were growing, tried as best they could to curb development. Admiral Waldegrave, in 1797, reproved one of his officials who had permitted new building to take place: "Your having suffered Thomas Nevan to put up what you are pleased to call a few sheds, is clearly an infraction of my orders; you will therefore direct him to remove them immediately"; "You will take good care that Jeremiah Marroty and John Fitzgerald do not erect chimneys to their sheds, or even light fires in them of any kind"; and so on. Around every settled cove and harbour on the island, Richard Routh noted in 1797, there were "little farms and gardens"—again quite illegal— which the people cultivated for themselves in order to supplement their diet. Every governor reported that despite the absence of legal title to property, lands and houses were bought and sold, and disputes occurred over rights and boundaries, just as if rights existed in the land.

Disputes inevitably arose, not only about land and buildings, but about all manner of civil causes. These, plus the fact that the quarter-sessions of the justices of the peace were held in contempt by the islanders, brought the first significant breach in long-standing British policy towards Newfoundland in the 1790s. On the advice of Governor Milbanke, and over the vehement protests of the West Country interests, who only wanted, said the governor, the kind of courts that enabled them "to tear to pieces the boatmen and other poor people with impunity," a court of civil jurisdiction was established in 1791 by act of Parliament. Although the court functioned only during the governor's period of residence, its first chief justice, John Reeves, learned enough during his brief stay to recommend that a court of civil and criminal justice be established, and also that surrogate courts of civil justice be set up throughout the island. This reform was effected in 1792.

John Reeves was certainly the ablest man to be associated with Newfoundland during these years. His *History of the Government of Newfoundland*, published in 1793, remained until this century the best-documented and most incisive record of British policy towards that unfortunate island. It was distinguished not only for the quality of his analysis of that policy, but for the great sympathy Reeves displayed for the people of Newfoundland. His sympathy emerged strongly as well during the parliamentary inquiry into the Newfoundland fishery set up in 1793 to investigate complaints by

English merchants that the fishery was declining, among other reasons because of the courts which had been instituted. He dismissed out of hand the "fears about colonization" that still affected politicians. From the imperial point of view, "Newfoundland is still nothing but a great ship, dependent upon the mother country for everything they eat, drink, and wear, or for the funds to procure them"; the more people there are, the more their dependence increases. The testimony of Reeves and others was sufficient to persuade the parliamentary committee to recommend that the new legal system be retained. But aside from this single advance, nothing further was done by the home government to bring to the scattered population of the island some of the elementary benefits of civil society enjoyed nearly everywhere else in settled British North America. It is manifestly impossible to relate the experience of the people of Newfoundland to that of other colonists or *Canadiens* in the 1790s, just as it is impossible not to believe that this experience continued to mark Newfoundland society in a special way.

No other colonial group, not even the Acadians, was left so completely to fend for itself as were the Newfoundlanders. But most colonists and *Canadiens*, except the few who lived in towns and villages, were scarcely aware of the presence of government. It is misleading, therefore, to take a politics-centred view of life in the 1790s, even though a measure like the Constitutional Act, or procedural victories like the winning of the money-power by the Nova Scotian Assembly, or the assertion of the place of the French language by the Assembly majority in Lower Canada were to have important long-run consequences. British North America was not two solitudes but many. Only Simcoe had made the attempt to fuse the culture of the political realm with that of the people; given the instruments available to government and the realities of colonial existence, that attempt was bound to fail. Ultimately, politics would have a part to play in forming the many particularisms of the colonies into larger communities, but before that could happen, a much higher degree of economic and social integration than that existing in 1800 would be needed. In the new century, in most of the colonies, such a development was to begin.

5: The 1800s

JEAN-PIERRE WALLOT

Americanism, development, democracy, nationalism. These four words convey most of the excitement, hopes, frustrations and outright clashes of the 1800s throughout British North America. These were key years for all the colonies. The Maritimes benefited, like the Canadas, from economic expansion, but faced sharp American competition as well. American trade and imperialism also penetrated the western parts of the fur empire. In both Canadas many lasting features of later Canadian growth appeared. They would experience, in a kaleidoscopic fashion, the first development of a hope-inspiring but largely unworkable colonial parliamentary system, at the same time democratic and aristocratic; the unnerving pressures of the United States, both military and economic; the growing strain between conflicting nationalisms and classes; and an economic restructuring of considerable importance. The future, however, still looked open to British North America. It was possible to visualize the maturing of a French-Canadian nation in Lower Canada, an increasingly Americanized Upper Canada, a prosperous market for the Maritimes' fisheries in the British West Indies, and the successful competition of the St. Lawrence system with the then more difficult route between Lake Ontario and New York. Such a mixture of great expectations, exasperation at the harsh unyielding realities, and conflicting objectives, characterizes the 1800s.

I

The all-out struggle between Great Britain and France on the one hand, and the strained relations between the British Empire and the United States on the other, stamped the economic, political and even social outlooks in all the British North American colonies during those ten years. With the fortifications at Halifax and the British fleet off their shores, the Maritimes could feel reasonably secure, although a resolute attack by a strong French squadron would have inflicted heavy damage to their ports and military installations. In Upper Canada American settlers soon outnumbered the Loyalists, while the Indians continued to press claims to their lands. In Lower Canada francophobia flourished. The British officials and merchants distrusted the *Canadiens'* loyalty and suspected that French (and American) agents were infiltrating the province and the Indian territories to stage an overthrow of the British government. In fact, they uncovered very few plots and agents; and these were mostly Americans who were enraged at being left out of the land-granting spree, particularly in Upper Canada. In 1801, for instance, the Montreal militia enthusiastically mustered to protect the town against an expected assault by a bunch of Vermontese pillagers. During the decade, Upper Canadian authorities, too, felt threatened by the Americans and regularly called for strengthening of the western garrisons.

Tension built up between the British Empire and the United States all through the 1800s. By 1805-7 the European belligerents had entered a phase of total economic war. Through escalating orders-in-council in England and similar decrees in France neutral trade with continental Europe was being crushed. The blockade enforced by the British navy, because of its mastery of the seas, was inflicting the heaviest damage on the Americans, who were the most important neutral traders. Moreover, the British exercised their traditional right of stopping and boarding foreign merchant vessels on the high seas to impress British sailors and deserters who might be on them. Again, the Americans were the worst sufferers, for English captains were more interested in filling their manpower needs than in distinguishing between a British subject and a *bona fide* American. For years the United States vainly asserted the relatively new theory of national sovereignty on the high seas. "The pretension that the American flag should protect every individual sailing under it on board of a merchant-ship," exclaimed Lord Harrowby, "is too extravagant to require any serious refutation." Finally, in the interior of the continent, Americans always suspected the British of arming and inciting the Indians against their settlers in the Middle West. "In the event of hostilities," expostulated a New England newspaper in October 1808, the Canadas "will pay liberally for the scalps of our warriors and their wives and children." These conflicts on the high seas and on land lent some justification to American plans for taking over the British colonies and their resources.

Anglo-American strains first reached a climax in 1807. In June the British warship *Leopard* fired upon and heavily damaged the American warship *Chesapeake,* killing and wounding many men. Four British so-called deserters were taken from the humiliated ship. Emotion ran high all through the United States. War cries were frequent, and inevitably, they turned against the Canadas: "Nearly half of the inhabitants of Canada," proclaimed one newspaper at the peak of the crisis, "are friendly to the United States, and only wait a favorable opportunity to tear asunder the shackles of English tyranny . . . [Let us] make ourselves and posterity forever secure, by the expulsion of the English from North America." In Lower Canada and in Nova Scotia, the militia was called out. A loyal spirit seemed to unite the British North Americans against the possible invaders. Upper Canadian authorities looked nervously at any movement of men on the American side. But the United States was not prepared to go to war at this time, possibly because it had as much reason to fight France as it had to strike at England. At the end of 1807 the American government imposed an embargo on all trade with foreign countries: President Jefferson hoped that economic pressures would compel one or both belligerents to come to terms. He failed miserably in this and only succeeded in paralysing American maritime trade, while English and British North Americans inherited what American smugglers left them. This entailed a significant rise in the colonies' exports and imports. In fact, the northeastern states systematically evaded the embargo. Vermont and New York, for instance, used the Richelieu–St. Lawrence system to export their surpluses through all kinds of methods, including when necessary the killing of border guards. Early in 1809 public pressure forced the American government to repeal the embargo and to replace it by the Non-Intercourse Act, which legalized commerce with all ports other than those under belligerent control; and even this was relaxed in 1810. The beneficial side effect of this commercial war was clearly perceived by the whole of British North America, even by the habitants. As one of them commented to another in 1809, "the *non-intercourse* pleased him fairly, for it brought a raise in wheat prices, a war did not frighten him just so he had a good market for his produce."

It was at this critical juncture, in late 1807, that England sent an experienced and trusted military leader as governor of both Canadas: Sir James Henry Craig. As soon as he arrived at Quebec, and although he was afflicted by a near-fatal illness, Craig energetically prepared the colony for a possible American invasion. In the following four years, he spent hundreds of thousands of pounds on fortifications in both provinces, but mainly around Quebec. He repeatedly asked for and obtained reinforcements. One of his main preoccupations was rekindling the long-neglected Indian alliance without actually encouraging the Indians to war. This was an extremely delicate policy, for the Indians would have been quite happy to drag the "red coats" into a war with the Americans just to recoup their lost territories. Finally, although the French-

Canadian militia had clearly demonstrated its loyalty and zeal in 1801 and 1807, Craig would not trust it, particularly in the event of an alliance between France and the United States. The British merchants, officials and newspapers generally concurred, although they muted their disapproving comments of French Canadians with the approach of war in late 1810 and 1811-12. Then, they suddenly started to celebrate newly found qualities in the latter. "The Pious and loyal Canadian will never abandon his fields, his religion and his king, to the licentiousness of republican governments."

II

In the 1800s, the economic development of the British North American colonies was closely linked to outside stimuli, themselves the result of the continental blockade, the self-defeating American commercial embargo and opportunistic policies of Great Britain responding to wartime needs.

At the turn of the century the Maritime provinces faced some difficult problems, although they were generally prosperous. Because of the commercial privileges derived from Jay's Treaty of 1794, the Americans had nearly taken over the carrying trade between the British colonies and the West Indies. Not only did American fish, wheat, wood and other products enter quite freely on the latter market, but the produce of the British colonies, even fish, would generally filter there through American channels. The return trade, of course, followed the same route. Like the Canadians, the merchants of Nova Scotia and Newfoundland would complain bitterly against the unfair American competition on imperial markets.

This situation, however, was modified to a large extent after 1803, when war between Britain and Napoleonic France, briefly halted, broke out again. Imperial bounties to Maritimers and partial withdrawal of privileges to the Americans sparked a vigorous growth in the international trade of the British colonies. Newfoundland fisheries rose again to some affluence. The American embargo was compounded by the British decision to make Halifax, Shelburne, Saint John and St. Andrews free ports, in 1808 and 1809.

Not only did British bottoms recapture a large part of the West Indies and other imperial trades, but large (and illegal) American exports and imports used the Maritimes' free ports, so that these became so many distributing centres for North Atlantic commerce. When Jefferson's embargo was lifted, British trade between the Maritimes and the West Indies had picked up enough momentum to continue to grow of its own accord. Furthermore, there was the rising trade of great square-hewn timbers for the British market, now that war had cut off Baltic wood supplies from Britain. Although this timber trade was less important than in the Canadas, it further buoyed the economy of the eastern provinces, and more particularly of New Brunswick where, after 1807, it became the main source of prosperity. On the whole, then, the 1800s witnessed an impressive leap of the Maritimes' economy from mere prosperity to real boom.

In both Canadas and their western fur trade dependencies, the 1800s nearly completed the economic restructuring begun in 1783 by the amputation of large chunks of the old fur empire and the arrival of the Loyalists, then continued in the 1790s with a sporadic (and at times intense) rise of agricultural exports, and finally directed on a new course by the timber boom of the 1800s. In fact, the Canadian economy was not only restructured; it was

Table I

EXPORTS FROM THE PORT OF QUEBEC

Year	Number of ships	Tonnage
1800	153	20,725
1801	188	27,986
1802	211	35,754
1803	175	30,483
1804	173	26,883
1805	170	26,506
1806	193	33,996
1807	239	42,293
1808	334	70,275
1809	435	87,964
1810	661	143,893

modernized, as the power of the market imposed itself. The pulse
of the international trade of both Canadas can be crudely measured
by the tonnage of exports from the port of Quebec. While from
1793 to 1800, the level had averaged 17,000 tons, it climbed to a
level of 30,000 tons between 1801 and 1806, then doubled between
1806 and 1808, and doubled again between 1808 and 1810 (Table
I). In value, Canadian exports jumped from £120,000 in 1763, to
£300,000 in 1793, and finally to £1,220,963 in 1810. The first
two levels (till 1806) were clearly dominated by furs, then by furs
and wheat. The explosion of tonnage after that was due to the
lumber boom (Table II). If the demand was artificially stimulated

Table II

COMMODITIES EXPORTED FROM THE
PORT OF QUEBEC

Year	Beaver pelts	Wheat (bushels)	Oak and pine pieces	Pine planks
1800	135,043	217,125	1,645	34,863
1801	119,965	472,723	2,329	60,033
1802	144,189	1,010,033	2,642	104,735
1803	93,778	360,892	6,972	124,197
1804	111,448	201,543	5,102	78,391
1805	92,003	22,016	5,431	42,820
1806	119,708	96,908	10,308	66,116
1807	114,363	231,543	14,528	106,363
1808	126,927	186,708	26,888	194,467
1809	105,032	198,221	33,842	262,280
1810	98,523	170,860	103,069	312,423

by wartime circumstances and new imperial tariff preferences, it
still propelled a fantastic economic growth based on wood that
would last till the 1850s and remain, throughout, the mainstay of
Canadian international trade.

Thus wood was the key-good or staple, fertilizing the whole
economy. In the Canadas the dominating power of lumber was
immensely stronger than that of furs, or even wheat. In 1810, wood
accounted for nearly 70 per cent of exports; of the 661 ships that

left Quebec that year, about 500 of them were involved in the lumber trade. More than £150,000 was invested in a very few years, and a large demand for labour was created. This extraordinary upsurge radically readjusted the Canadian economy and initiated a series of adaptations; the impact, for instance, was felt in the technology of maritime traffic. A comparison of the average tonnage of ships entering the port of Quebec between 1793 and 1800 and between 1804 and 1810, shows an increase of 25 per cent. Transportation productivity per sailor also rose by 14 per cent. These growths are clearly tied to the growth in the lumber trade.

Even social technology was altered. More and more, during the period, the Canadas were drawn into the "signal" system of the international market, with all its risks and vagaries, particularly if one remembers that ships—and letters—often took months to get to their destination. Each autumn or in early winter, English importers made their expected needs known to their colonial partners and exporters. Price and market information were thus stimuli but they were sometimes dangerously out of date by the time they arrived at their destination. This signal system, ever-present with its market values, affected the *Canadien* mentality. Contrary to popular legend, they showed remarkable power of adaptation, be it to war, to the demands stemming from the lumber trade or to the expanded local markets and opportunities. For instance, the habitants near Quebec city stopped cultivating wheat around 1807-8, and let hay grow by itself while they worked as labourers, getting high wages for themselves and for the use of their horses, and also payments for hay bought by their employers for the horses. When distilleries opened, they cultivated barley. In the words of the economist Polanyi, a "chain-reaction was started—what before were merely isolated markets was transmuted into a self-regulating system of markets. And with the new economy, a new society sprang into being."

The domestic private sector of economic life was also shaped, of course, by the internal dynamics of the Canadian economy, which stemmed from the nature of the staple. An economy succeeds when and if the restructuring process has started an enlargement of the matrix of development, which was assuredly the case in the Canadas. First, in this regard, one must note the great expansion of their population: it doubled between 1785 and 1815, growing from 150,000 to approximately 350,000, out of which more than 75,000 lived in Upper Canada. If this advance of settlement was forcing the fur trade and the Indians further west, it also produced new staples (wheat, flour, salted meats, wood, potash) in growing quantity. Upper Canada, in particular, benefited from the establishment of nearby British or American garrisons, followed by local villages as rising markets. Later on, the upper province carved itself an increasing share of the external trade with lumber and agricultural products. In both Canadas, the expansion of population also required the building of mills, villages, small industries, while the settlements needed tools and imported commodities. The new staples took their place beside the fur trade and would eventually replace it.

During the 1800s, the fur trade through the St. Lawrence system lost much of its importance, both in relative and absolute terms, particularly when the returns are compared to the increasing distances to be traversed and the consequent mounting costs of transportation. By 1808-10, moreover, American impediments of all kinds (such as taxes, closing of the Missouri area to non-Americans, and seizures of British trade goods) relentlessly pushed Montreal's South-West Company to amalgamate with the New York-based Astor empire. In the northwest, the Montreal-based traders repeatedly failed to interest the British government in their need for cheaper supply routes and in the economic and imperial competition of the Americans, more costly to them yet than that of the Hudson's Bay Company. And yet, despite these problems, North West Company enterprise continued to expand across the continent as discoverers like David Thompson and Simon Fraser opened vast new territories to it in this decade—for example, through Fraser's arduous voyage down the river that bears his name to the Pacific in 1808. His route would ultimately lay the basis for a transcontinental Canadian traffic system.

But far from the wilderness fur trade, in the changing Canadas there now began to develop a small industrial sector tied to internal consumption and sometimes exports, but largely independent of either lumber or agriculture; for example, the St. Maurice Iron Works, the Batiscan Iron Works, and also manufactures of candles, soap, or hats. Another industrial development participated much more closely in the frenetic economic boom started by the lumber explosion. For instance, shipbuilding became very prosperous in Quebec, Montreal and even William-Henry (Sorel). Till 1806-8, these shipyards launched six to eight vessels a year (of 200 to 500 tons each), a number that rose to twenty-six in 1810 and went on growing. However, if the size and quantity of shipbuilding tended to increase, no corresponding improvement was made to the hopelessly outdated and inadequate canal and lock system along the St. Lawrence waterway. Tolls did not raise sufficient amounts (£600 a year) to even repair the existing facilities at a cost estimated, in the early 1800s, at more than £6,000. The imperial government itself balked at such investments; and the local legislatures of Upper and Lower Canadas did not collect enough revenues before 1809-10, to be induced to embark on a costly program of transportation improvements. Roads were generally bad in both provinces, especially between Kingston and Montreal. In 1810, however, Governor Craig used the army and some unlawfully borrowed money from the provincial treasury to build a road from Quebec to the American border through the Eastern Townships, so as to insure better communications with that part of the colony and cheaper provisions for the Quebec markets.

Finally, as for the agricultural sector, it was independent of the wood staple, but still linked with it in numerous direct and indirect ways. The lumber boom created additional revenues and great prosperity which in conjunction with the prodigious increase of the population, activated local demand for agricultural products. On the other hand, lumber contested with agriculture for much of the labour force. The habitants were sensitive to the fluctuations of the international markets, despite the fact that the demand for wheat and flour greatly varied in England from year to year. The more so were they to the opportunities of the enlarged local markets. On the whole, it would be misleading to talk of a decline or a crisis in agriculture in these years. Rather, it responded to a series of forces which changed it while bringing more prosperity: for instance, the lumber boom, and the large military expenditures in the late

1800s, the demand for a labour force in certain urban centres, the growth of more diversified and enlarged local markets, the variations of international markets, the penetration of the market mentality among habitants, and the high wages offered. Land was not yet scarce. Nor were there signs of peasants' indebtedness. But, wrote a contemporary observer, "since the immense increase of commerce in this province, agriculture has been much neglected."

It is not surprising that at the end of the period, Montreal, Quebec and Upper Canadian towns celebrated the new prosperity, even while fearing an eventual slump might come. Many indicators of well-being confirm this general assessment. While new social groups had appeared or been reinforced (entrepreneurs, small industrialists, professional men, skilled and unskilled labourers), studies of prices and revenues reveal that all groups significantly benefited from the general prosperity, including the farmers and even the civil servants. The common labourers, for instance, saw their wages soar from 2s.6d. a day in 1800 to six shillings in 1809 and 1810: the carpenters, from five to fifteen shillings. Active and competent notaries and lawyers in Lower Canada could earn between £350 to £900 a year. In the agricultural sector, the sharp rise in prices favoured the farmers, particularly those of the Quebec area, while prices were more stable and lower in Montreal, probably because of the larger agricultural base in the latter area. The evidence even suggests a more dynamic and prosperous Quebec district than the Montreal one. The significant growth in the size of the market, of population and of commerce made profitable the establishment of new institutional arrangements. The land-granting business, in the Canadas, produced in fact an embryonic form of corporations. The creation of banks suddenly became a high priority as well, leading to the establishment of the Bank of Montreal in the next decade. Only the civil government, handicapped by annual deficits till 1809 and by clashes in the Assembly, did not participate fully in the modernization process of the economy. The military side of government, on the other hand, had to invest heavily.

In Lower Canada, the restructuring of the economy took place completely outside the French Canadians' control or efforts. True, the habitants sold more wheat, most of the time at a better price, and many of them were hired as paid labourers. But French Canadians had been out of international commerce since the 1780s. British entrepreneurs and exporters, often helped by contracts from the Admiralty, exploited the forest as they had the fur trade and presided over the exports of wheat and flour. They were the ones who accumulated commercial capital and diversified investments, a preliminary step indispensable to the start of industrialization. Even the artisans often came from the British Isles or the United States, for British capitalists were loath to train the *Canadiens*.

III

On the political level, circumstances varied considerably from one colony to another. Although they shared some common traits, particularly in the struggles over financial matters, the degree of unrest seemed linked to the extent of the development of the colony. Newfoundland, of course, wholly lacked representative government. But merchants had some brushes with officials and at the end of the period, were asking for a House of Assembly. In New Brunswick, early theoretical discussions dissolved, after 1803, before the necessity of coping with local improvements. No great issue dominated politics, nor was the mood of the settlers favourable to dissertations on constitutional matters. Quite naturally, however, the House of Assembly picked up the American practice of initiating money grants. In Nova Scotia, sharper issues and conflicts existed. The country interests which dominated the Assembly opposed the town interests entrenched in the Council, while the House of Assembly was determined to maintain its control of money appropriations against conciliar encroachments. There was even some talk of establishing an elective Legislative Council; the administration and the leaders in the Assembly fought for domination over patronage, with some repression against the "democrats."

In Upper Canada, difficulties thrived on such questions as immigration and settlement, land-granting, internal improvements, and the rivalries and jealousies of a small political community which had few spoils to share. The original Loyalist population was soon outnumbered, but it held the majority of offices. It felt threatened by the influx of American settlers, most of whom were little concerned with the British characteristics of the government and institutions. The land-granting procedure and the speculation that ensued, the clergy and crown reserves, the favoured position of the Church of England, all these problems, although not yet acute, engendered frictions. Anti-government feelings were strong among the population, at least in elections. And the House of Assembly angrily fought the Legislative Council's attempts to amend money bills. A few agitators (Joseph Willcocks, William Weekes, Charles Wyatt, Thomas Thorpe) exploited the grievances, real or imaginary, felt by the Loyalists in the administration of justice and government patronage. Thorpe even appealed to the "common people" against the Executive—a most dangerous practice, thought Lieutenant-Governor Gore, "in this Province, where Republican Principles prevail so much." An opposition newspaper, *The Upper Canadian Guardian or Freeman's Journal*, was published for a short while, but its editor was imprisoned for libel by the House of Assembly, not the Executive! Gore must have agreed with the house, for he considered the newspaper very dangerous: "Our Revolutionary Press," he admitted to Craig in March 1808, "continues its operations, and I have reason to fear, received support from New York." But on the whole, it is hard to consider this incipient agitation as an organized struggle for authentic political reform. The detractors of government shared little political program and doctrine among themselves, if indeed they had any at all. In the house, no coherent movement along party lines could be detected during the 1800s, although many of the issues would worsen and poison the province's political life later on.

The situation was very different in Lower Canada, the oldest and most heavily populated colony in British North America. The general disaffection from the government, clearly visible during the early part of the American Revolution and in the 1790s, was now channelled into a political war that was fought in elections and in the House of Assembly between clear-cut parties. These largely corresponded to ethnic and social lines. From 1793, the first session, till 1812, the recorded votes in the Assembly followed the lines of those parties in the nearly unvarying ratio of 80 per cent.

First, there was the British party. It had been bitterly disappointed by the division of the former Province of Quebec in two colonies, and by its unsuccessful attempts to influence the electors or the House of Assembly by virtue of its assumed superior qualifications. It comprised strange bedfellows, running the full range of social classes, but all united in a common front against French Canada and what it represented. The group included British aristocrats and officials, their ranks singularly reinforced in the 1790s by the arrival of such brilliant new members as Bishop Jacob Mountain, Secretary Herman W. Ryland, and Attorney-General (and later Chief Justice) Jonathan Sewell. It included the British merchants, who were in fact its most vocal members in newspapers, pamphlets, political campaigns and in Parliament. Finally, in the 1800s, leaders from the British colonists in the Eastern Townships were brought into the fold.

The British party was mostly interested in the commercial and demographic development of the English part of the population, and also in places, patronage and money. It was not content with running the economy, the executive branch of government and even controlling the Legislative Council. It needed the active support of the House of Assembly to vote laws that would further its interests. Extremely loyal to the government, to Anglo-Saxon institutions and laws, and most of all to themselves as British colonists, intolerant of the laws, religion and customs of the *Canadiens* and even more so of their collective survival as an homogeneous "body politic," its members compensated for their minority position in the Assembly by their economic, social and even political supremacy, which provoked the French-Canadian leaders to accuse the government of allowing the existence of a "ministry in the opposition." After the quarrel in 1805 over taxation to build jails, indeed the British party would find it more and more difficult to have more than twelve members elected, as compared to sixteen previously.

In constitutional and political matters, the British party and *The Quebec Mercury*, its newspaper, found themselves in the awkward position of denying to the French-Canadian dominated Assembly the normal rights and prerogatives of such a representative body in the English system. They naturally fought for the progress of commerce, of colonization and of immigration, particularly by Americans. On this subject, they vehemently responded to the *Canadiens'* strong criticism of the Americans as "strangers" or even barbarous "Goths and Visigoths": did the French Canadians "imagine Canada was only created to be established by papists?", demanded the *Quebec Mercury*, in early 1807. Along with social and economic reforms, in fact inherently bound up with them, the British party desired the assimilation of French Canadians for a multitude of reasons. It was necessary to "unfrenchify" the colony, asserted the *Mercury*: "after forty-seven years possession of Quebec, it is time the province should be english." Assimilation would have been just and reasonable after the conquest. Now, it was imperative. The French Canadians' secret allegiance to France was dreaded: how could a French education bring up British subjects? Homogeneity of language and manners was preferable in a nation. Moreover, the British were already the salient force in the really important activities in the colony, notably commerce. The province was vast, nearly empty, destined to receive a large influx of British and American population. Could French Canadians ever hope to become a distinct nation in a continent forever English? Worse, they were ignorant, and it had been a dangerous mistake to grant them an assembly. In fact, this backward and inert people would benefit from assimilation, for only thus could they catch the British incentive and share in the fruits of an expanding economy. Thus John Henry (who had served as an agent for Governor Craig in the United States), wrote in 1810 that only demagogues "interested in keeping the people ignorant" were preventing assimilation,

> . . . which opposition however can be referred to no reasonable or justifiable motive; since if it be consistent with the true interests of the Canadians and English, that should be *in reality as they are nominally, one people*; those who oppose their assimilation are enemies to both. They can only become one people by similarity of language, laws, education, manners and habits. . . .
>
> If the Canadians would seriously reflect on the benefits which would result to themselves from their entire incorporation into the English population, the candid and intelligent part of them would find stronger motives to become the advocates of the proposed alteration . . . than any Englishman can possibly feel.

The means suggested to bring about assimilation varied from the suppression of the Assembly and the withdrawal of "privileges" to the conquered, to the union of the Canadas and the multiplying of counties in the Eastern Townships; to American immigration, English education and control of the Catholic Church (accused of "silently" opposing assimilation); or to the exclusive use of English in Parliament and in the courts after a fixed and short delay—and so on. Some moderate Britishers found these policies unpalatable; although in sympathy with their aim, they feared an ethnic battle. A very small number even challenged these views, accused the Americans of being the real threat in the colony, and asserted that to guard against this danger the British colonists should ally themselves with French-Canadian particularism.

French Canadians had also grouped together in a party that was the natural outgrowth of the "democratic party" in the 1780s and early 1790s. This *parti canadien* became naturally more tight and organized through the years. It comprised members of the new elite—notaries, lawyers, doctors, surveyors, some artisans and shopkeepers, well-to-do farmers. It was thus much more intimately connected with the great mass of the people than the seigneurs, whose social, economic and political decline was nearly completed. For the members of the *parti canadien*, there was only one organized ethnic group in Lower Canada, the *nation canadienne*, by the will of England itself. The other inhabitants were considered by them as transients who had come to make a quick profit and would move on, or as immigrants who should assimilate themselves to the great majority of French Canadians. Because of the preceding thirty years, the latter thought of themselves as a collectivity protected by England, destined to become a *nation* inside the British Empire precisely because of this British protection against the United States and the internal threat from the *Anti-Canadiens*. They extolled the marvels of the British constitution. But they wanted to extract from it all the possible advantages. This in turn explains their mounting anger at the officials of the Chateau Clique around the governor and at the British party who contradicted what appeared to them the explicit intentions of England and their own plans for the future—who granted under the English laws and tenure lands that should be reserved for the future generation of French Canadians, and worse, distributed those lands as so many gifts to *Yankeys* so they would flood the province and assimilate the *Canadiens*—who were misinterpreting and corrupting the French laws in the courts of justice—who were closing commerce, places and the Councils to most French Canadians; who had taken over the means necessary to finance a French educational system (the Jesuits' estates) and so on.

In November 1806, the *parti canadien* launched its newspaper, *Le Canadien*, which would express their objectives and constitutional theories till its seizure by government, in March 1810. The newspaper tried to refute the *Mercury*'s and Britishers' accusations against French Canadians. Not only did it exalt *Canadien* laws, customs, religion, education, but it developed the national feelings and ambitions of the French Canadians. It accused the British party of spreading a "civil war between the races in Lower Canada," and the merchants of trying to hide behind their necessary role the establishment of their tyranny. It even reversed the arguments about loyalty: while the French Canadians were loyal by religious principle, necessity and interest, the British and the immigrants in the colony were much closer to the *Yankeys*. In effect, assimilation of French Canadians would spell the Americanization of the province, while the maintenance of their customs, language and cohesiveness would act as a shield against it. It was in the interest of Great Britain to nurture the French-Canadian nationality so as to keep the province in the Empire. The government, argued Denis-Benjamin Viger, should strive towards "consolidating in this country isolated by nature, an homogeneous population . . . susceptible of acquiring great vigour without extending itself . . . and to insure help without giving any reason of fear. . . . Moreover, the establishment of Canada . . . is even complete in all its most important parts."

The most important contribution of *Le Canadien*—and of the *parti canadien*—was constitutional and political. At the end of 1806 and in early 1807, it was the first in the British Empire after the American Revolution to expound the essential aspects of the system of responsible government; that is, that the governor should choose his advisers from amongst the leaders of the elected majority in the Assembly, while the house should also control expenditures and patronage. The French-Canadian leaders, particularly Pierre

Bédard, Jean-Antoine Panet, François Blanchet, Jean-Thomas Taschereau and a few others, borrowed their arguments not from the
radicals but from such great British liberal parliamentarians and
theoreticians as Fox, Burke, Locke, Blackstone; from French philo-
sophers like Montesquieu and from the precedents and rules of the
Parliament of Great Britain, which they sprung on their unwary
opponents on specific cases. Their tactics were essentially to identify
as closely as possible the constitution of Lower Canada to that of
Great Britain, and to try to apply to the Assembly the same
privileges and powers as those enjoyed by the House of Commons
in England. They insisted on the notion of equilibrium and independence between the "different branches of the legislature." The pres-
ervation of this equilibrium required the House of Assembly to fight
all encroachments of its privileges—and of course those of the
people, since it was the "popular branch"—by the Executive. The
French-Canadian leaders also proposed to provide part at least of
the advisers or "ministers" surrounding the governor, and to render
these ministers and other officials responsible for their advice, threatening the use of "impeachment" if necessary. They did not venture,
however, into the realm of the collective responsibility of the ministry.
They thus greatly admired the British constitution. But they believed
it was malfunctioning in Lower Canada, for it allowed for secret
and non-representative ministers, for the intervention of officials in
the elections and the like.

French Canadians did not constitute one solid bloc. A small
minority, mostly placemen and members of the seigneural elite,
formed some sort of "moderate" or government party. Of the 40
per cent of jobs and pensions given to French Canadians they controlled at least half—and always the better ones. Until 1807-8, because of the general absenteeism in the House of Assembly, their few
elected members would sometimes hold the balance of power. They
were the only French Canadians admitted to the Legislative and
Executive Councils. With few exceptions, they were not the "traitors"
harshly condemned by *Le Canadien*. Essentially, they were of the
opinion that things were going as well as could be expected, that the
inevitable and small injustices here and there would eventually dis-
appear. They also dreamed of *la nation canadienne*, but of one that

would be some kind of reincarnated *ancien régime* under their en-lightened leadership. They despised the leaders of the House of Assembly, mostly professional men, as a bunch of hungry demagogues clamouring to take their own place. They thus viewed the conflicts along social rather than ethnic lines, although they did recognize and even criticize the avowed intentions of many Britishers to assimilate the French Canadians. They expressed themselves in *Le Courier de Quebec*, established in 1808, and later on, in *Le Vrai-Canadien*. They were profiting from the status quo. They could see no urgent necessity to change it.

IV

Chronologically, in the crucial struggle of people and ideas in Lower Canada, the new century opened with the first serious questioning of the Constitution of 1791 from the British point of view. In a long dispatch of November 1800, newly arrived Lieutenant-Governor Robert Milnes stated his profound sense of uneasiness at the fact that French Canadians had not assimilated, but continued to be French, independent, and to dislike the British. He attributed this situation to the influence of the Catholic Church, which had to be curtailed, to the democratic character of the Canadian society and to the lack of a strong landed aristocracy thanks to the seigneurial regime. Out of this reappraisal was born the first serious plan of correction. Milnes, helped by Attorney-General Sewell, tried to sub-mit the clergy to the royal prerogative, using slow and devious manoeuvres and pressures. In 1801, with Sewell again, he tried to initiate a movement for the abolition of the system of seigneurial tenure in order to mix British settlers and French-Canadian farmers and thus assimilate the latter. Bishop Mountain's plan of assimila-tion by education was embodied in the Royal Institution of 1801, which the few French-Canadian members present in the house opposed very strongly. Milnes also encouraged the most important English merchants to become candidates in elections and even secretly initiated petitions by the Eastern Townships for the creation of new counties, which would have had the effect of raising the number of British members in the house.

These slow, veiled and cautious moves could not cope with the rising tide of French-Canadian nationalism. The British party exploded in bitter denunciation of *Canadiens* in 1805, when the French-Canadian majority in the Assembly passed a bill allowing taxes on commerce—not on lands, as the merchants had requested—for the building of new jails in Quebec and Montreal. It also failed to have a bill adopted which would have permitted the voluntary abolition of the seigneurial system. As in some previous and following sessions, it also attacked the French language and laws.

These conflicts, particularly on the taxation issue, simply pitted the two main parties against each other more strongly than ever. In the next five years, the *parti canadien* followed a clear strategy of aiming at the complete control of the internal matters in the colony. They tried to maintain their majority in the house by an unsuccessful attempt to vote a sum of money to defray the expenses of members of the Assembly coming from outside Quebec—the reason for the absenteeism. The placemen in the house allied themselves to the British party to veto the bill. This explains the growing bitterness of the *parti canadien* against the "Chouayens" or French-Canadian "traitors." In another bid for control the *parti canadien* tried to exclude judges and a Jew named Hart, all of whom allied themselves with the British party. This atmosphere of crisis brought about two dissolutions, in 1809 and 1810, by the stern governor, who had clearly turned against the *parti canadien* after the elections of May 1808. He even questioned their loyalty.

In the elections, however, the *parti canadien* greatly improved their position. In the house their whole approach was constantly to oppose the interests of the governor, councillors and placemen (whom they dubbed "rich landowners," "aristocrats" who "have a lot to preserve"), and represented themselves as the champions of "the people." The people therefore had the duty to elect members not committed to the Executive or the British party, members who had only the interests of the ordinary *Canadien* at heart. The popular leaders, indeed, preached the sovereignty of the people, the necessity of controlling the finances of the province so as to submit officials to the will of the Assembly and of the people and asserted the existence of a ministry. In the session of 1810, the house went so far as to vote resolutions to the king and British Parliament declaring its determination to pay all the civil expenditures in the future: a gesture which, as Craig, who rebuked it, understood very well, would give to the house absolute control over the local government. There were many instances, also, of direct ethnic appeals. For example, a British citizen was scandalized when, in the elections of 1808, a French-Canadian candidate exclaimed that the people were being chained and invited the electors to vote for a French Canadian. The British candidate, who was in advance, was beaten:

> I suppose the annals of the late Revolution in France cannot furnish two speeches that had a more diabolical effect upon the minds of the people than these above mentioned——It seemed to have electrified them and gained ground like wild fire . . . and I am informed one could hear . . . here and there amongst the people, *point d'Anglais, point d'Anglais*! In a short time the dye seemed to be cast and the Inhabitants were apparently soon united, as if in the defence of a common Enemy . . . I was sorry to see . . . several honest men, upon whom I could depend . . . vote . . . against *les Anglais*.

The British party did not bear very patiently these nationalist designs. Their newspapers, pamphlets and petitions recommended strong action from the government and assimilation of the *Canadiens* as rapidly as possible. But more important still, the British party could now count on the energetic backing of the governor. Craig fought and dissolved the Assembly twice (1809, 1810) over political matters. He also indulged in an electoral tour of the province, in 1809. And in his despatches, he lost no opportunity to describe the leaders of the *parti canadien* as demagogues and desperadoes, ready to try anything for personal gain. In March 1810, in the middle of the electoral campaign, the governor took advantage of some daring articles printed in *Le Canadien* to seize its press and imprison its editors and some of its distributors throughout the province (more than twenty persons in all). As the governor had foreseen, it did not change the results of the election: the *parti canadien* was reelected stronger than ever. However, with its chief leaders in jail, it would be quiet for some time, enough to hopefully bring about some important and urgent reforms.

For by 1810, the governor, his advisers and the merchants were convinced that nothing short of radical changes in the constitution would quash the two great dangers looming over the colony: the nationalist aspirations of the French-Canadian leaders, and their dangerous democratic tendencies. As Craig explained to London on the second point, he was more concerned with a state of mind than an immediate apprehended insurrection or plot:

> . . . it has not been my intention to represent the leaders of the popular party here, as being in an actual intercourse with France or, that an attempt at Revolution is to be immediately apprehended. . . . What I mean is, that such is the state of the People's mind that, sooner or later, Revolution may be looked for, and that perhaps, without any view to an immediate occurrence of such an event, the proceedings of the party all tend to facilitate and prepare the way for it.

But the other aspect of the problem was much clearer and more dangerous. And the British party's views, explained before, became sharper, more focused on specific evils and remedies. In a long memorandum in 1810, for instance, Chief Justice Sewell stated that French Canadians were "still French; their habits, religion and laws are still those of Frenchmen and absolutely opposed to the habits of our people." He thus recommended the assimilation of French Canadians by favouring a large immigration from the United States, by uniting both Canadas so as to artificially place the French Canadians in a minority position in the Assembly, and by implementing a close control over the Catholic clergy and over education. Craig agreed with most of Sewell's diagnosis and proposals, although he personally preferred the suppression of the Assembly to union. He also proposed the carving of new counties in the Townships, a sharp increase in the property qualifications for candidates and the submission of the Catholic Church to the royal prerogative. Merchants in the colony and in London also transmitted petitions to much the same effect.

Governor Craig sent his secretary Ryland to England so as to give more detailed information to the ministers and to press the proposed plans on them. But Ryland walked from office to office without visible result during more than two years (1810-1812). And the flood of memoranda, petitions, dispatches on assimilation, religious matters and constitutional change swelled without producing any visible result. True, some British ministers recognized the apparent error of 1791, as did Lord Liverpool, in guarded words in September 1810. But the British government did not dare to introduce new legislation less than twenty years after the adoption of the Constitutional Act—particularly at a time when the ministry was weak, the king sick, the war in Europe in its most critical phase, the officials of Lower Canada divided among themselves on the practical measures to be pursued, and the Americans ever more threatening.

V

Understandably, in these colonial societies, religious, cultural and social problems abounded. In Newfoundland, the Church of England maintained its strong position. But elsewhere in the Maritimes, although it could count on some help from England, it continued to lose ground to the "dissenters," the majority of the Protestant population—Presbyterians, Baptists, Methodists—and to Catholics also. In Nova Scotia, the House of Assembly refused to collect quit-rents for the support of the Church of England, or any other denomination. The religious rivalries carried over into education. There was some real concern, notably in Nova Scotia and New Brunswick, for elementary education, but although progress was made in the towns it did not reach the rural population at this early date. As for Nova Scotia's King's College, it largely failed to grow because of its strictly Anglican religious adherence.

In Upper Canada, the plight of the Anglican and the Presbyterian Churches was not enviable: the combined number of their ministers varied between six and eight during the 1800s. However, an extraordinary number of dissenting sects flourished, often under the care of transient ministers from the United States: for example Methodists, the largest group, Quakers, Baptist or Mennonites. Some ministers, particularly those of the Church of England, opened private schools. Teachers also appeared in the towns and in some townships, offering their services to the local population. The mores and social habits of the population, in York and throughout the province, appear to have been robust, but not exceedingly turbulent, considering the circumstances.

It is often assumed that the people of Lower Canada were devout, obedient, pastoral and God-fearing, under the strong authority of the Catholic Church. In effect, during the 1800s particularly, the Church was under the immediate threat of being taken over by the state, which would have meant stringent governmental control over the property of the Church, its general "policy" and the choice of bishops and priests and their appointments, as well as close supervision of the seminaries, the cutting off of relations with Rome and the devolving of the final authority to the king's representative. The government officials used pressure and legal actions to bring the Catholic Church to terms. Since the Church and its bishop did not exist legally, they could hardly fight in the courts or hold to some of their properties if their existence was challenged. Moreover, all the parishes created after 1722 had never been civilly recognized. With the immense growth in population, this created compounding problems. Sewell thus summed up the officials' doctrine in a suit that the Catholic Church lost, in 1805-6: "There is no Catholic Bishop of Quebec by law. His office became extinct at the Conquest, and the patronage of the benefices . . . and the Edict of the Bishop, is devolved to His Majesty." After his arrival, Craig also tried to bully the bishop into submission, in which he failed. The same factors that ground the political offensive to a halt in 1810-12, however, played in favour of the Catholic Church.

Internal problems also plagued the Catholic Church: the lack of priests and vocations, the poor quality of the theological training of those ordained in Canada and the fact that these were often sent into parishes too young and not well enough prepared. After 1800, the government objected to the immigration of refugee French priests on the ground that they made French Canadians recall their French origin, and that they meddled into political matters. The lack of priests was extremely critical, with no more than 165 priests in 1805 for a diocese of more than 200,000 faithful spread out over an immense territory (the Maritimes and both Canadas from the Atlantic to the western plains). This matter comes into better perspective when it is remembered that there were 170 priests at the time of the conquest for 60,000 adherents. Overworked priests fell ill easily, others exploited the circumstances to challenge the bishop or misbehave, "thinking they can do so with impunity," explained the bishop.

The relations between the Church and French-Canadian laymen were also difficult. To safeguard what it considered a necessary religious independence, the Church had to maintain good relations with the civil authority without being subservient to it. But the *parti canadien* which drew its power in the Assembly from the large mass of the people who were also the faithful, was waging a bitter war against the Executive. The Church could not side politically with the Executive without sacrificing its autonomy and jeopardizing its influence over its adherents. On the other hand, it could not back the *parti canadien* because of the Catholic doctrine of submission to the lawful government, Mgr. Plessis's suspicious dislike of "democratic principles," and the ever-present threat of the application of the royal prerogative. This loyal neutrality, impossible in times of acute crisis (for example, in 1810), could not really satisfy the government, while it widened the breach between the Catholic hierarchy and the French-Canadian political leaders in the Assembly. These two elites were both nationalist in different ways, though the Church's mission was of another nature. The ordinary priests were closer to the people's political beliefs, however. Moreover, the divorce between the Church and the lay elite was not yet completed, even though the bishop admitted that the Church could not count on seigneurs and placemen, subservient to the British officials, or on the members of the legal profession, most of whom did not practice because of the Church's rigid stand on loans and interests.

The Church's lack of legal status and other problems could not but influence greatly the relations between the Church and the faithful laymen in general. Many of these refused to pay their tithes and other dues on all kinds of pretexts. The habitants' traditional independence from the Church could only thrive on such circumstances. Although the *Canadiens* were religious to a certain extent, they were superstitious, hard-hearted, like peasants elsewhere, disobedient and very close with their cash as far as religion was concerned, always trying to evade, in an incredible number of ways, the payment of the tithe and necessary repairs to the churches and presbyteries. One must add to that secular and religious ignorance. It did not bother the *habitants* near the border to go and get married in the United States, if they could not get a dispensation from the Church. Order in the churches during religious ceremonies had often to be maintained by physical force. The picture comes more clearly into focus by adding the French Canadians' undeniable propensity for drinking, dancing, and the rest, in part because of their relative affluence and the long inactive months in winter. Those who had sojourned in the western territories seemed the wildest. Naturally there were good, pious and exemplary families. But the point is they did not seem to be very numerous.

The bishops' letters and mandements, the annual charges of the grand juries, the reports of the governor, of the judges and justices of the peace, all concur in suggesting a picture of easy debauchery, charivaris and merriments of all kinds, particularly in the cities, where prosperity (wrote Craig in 1810) brought moral havoc and a higher rate of crime. Prostitution was at a peak in Quebec city; estimates in 1808-10 ranged from 600 to 800 for a town of 12,000 to 14,000 inhabitants! Illegitimate children were numerous. The habitants in the countryside, of course, usually led a more quiet and virtuous life. Their debaucheries were more occasional, coinciding with local or family festivals, feasts and holidays. The higher classes' conduct met with this harsh judgment by John Lambert, in 1810:

> There is nothing to boast of in the morals of the higher classes of the people in Canada. The little blackening accounts of scandal are sought for, promulgated, and listened to with avidity; while good actions are often mangled, distorted, and heard with secret envy . . . The female parties compose a school for scandal . . . For a small society like that of Canada, the number of unfaithful wives, kept mistresses, and girls of easy virtue, exceed in proportion those of the old country; and it is supposed, that in the towns, more children are born *illegitimately* than in wedlock . . . Trials for *criminal conduct* are however, unknown; neither are duels ever resorted to by the Canadian gentry, to avenge their injured honour. The husbands general'y wink at the frailties of their wives, and either content themselves with increasing the number of their *horned* brethren, or fly for comfort into the arms of a *fille de chambre*.

Americanism, development, democracy, nationalism. These themes strongly pervade the whole decade, but in varying degrees depending on the regions. Economically, the strong surge of Upper Canada was a sign of the future importance of that area. In the older colonies, Nova Scotia and Lower Canada, the constitutional or political struggles were the more articulate. Particularly in the latter, they led to the demand by the House of Assembly of control over local matters. But Lower Canada also presented a distinctive case, as it always would do so in the future evolution of Canada. For here two social structures ethnically differentiated (the *Canadiens*, the Britishers) were pitted against each other through political, economic, social, cultural and religious conflicts—points of friction between the two societies. The ethnic factor did not suppress, but it intensified, polarized and distorted the other levels of confrontation. For instance, while Britishers of all classes allied themselves on many issues, the French-Canadian bourgeoisie, mostly professional, had come to defend values and institutions (for example, the seigneurial regime) that many of them had condemned earlier. This was because those *Canadien* institutions came to constitute, for them, a sort of armour, hampering but necessary to insure the survival of French Canada and defeat the assimilation plans of the British colonists. An aberration, also, was this suicidal division of the Lower Canadian bourgeoisie against itself—merchants against professionals, ordinarily natural allies, condemning all efforts for reform to failure. The British merchants would favour economic and social progress but political conservatism; the French professionals would veto economic and social change, but fight for political reform. The ethnic struggle, then, did not suppress other levels of conflict, some quite normal, whether constitutional or social; it rather distorted them and prevented a normal evolution as in other more homogeneous colonies. But ultimately, as Craig and the Montreal merchants had understood, Lower Canada held the key to the success of the whole string of British North American colonies based on the St. Lawrence system.

6: The 1810s

ALAN WILSON

For most of Britain's North American colonies the 1810s were a décade of transition rather than of fulfilment. Dominated by Britain's wars—first, the great struggle against France that did not end till 1815, and, second, the War of 1812 against the United States—the period assumed a character responsive to circumstance, military exigency and regional interest. In some colonies the wars merely accelerated or intensified problems and promises that were already present. The American war of 1812-14, which was a late development in Britain's long conflict with Revolutionary and Napoleonic France, affected Upper Canada most deeply. Several other colonies responded largely to indigenous factors and to the French war. The latter, indeed, more directly affected the colonists of the Atlantic region, though commanding British sea power generally kept them safe from serious danger. Yet safe or not, both Newfoundland and Prince Edward Island shared continuing problems of absentee interference and primitive conditions of insularity. Each was moved by its own frustrations, and in each there were significant popular stirrings.

For Newfoundland, war had continued to bring development to its staple cod fishing. The French had not been competitors since their fishing bases of Miquelon and St. Pierre and their fishing rights on Newfoundland's western shore had been seized. The consequent monopoly of the Mediterranean market brought huge profits, and after Jefferson's embargo, the West Indies trade had also assumed great importance. Until the War of 1812, food prices remained moderate and a fair prosperity prevailed. The real beneficiaries were the St. John's native fishing proprietors and merchants. Their self-conscious rise to economic power had been reflected in a program of public improvements; yet in 1810 even St. John's had no municipal institutions and the island was still administered by the Admiralty. The new confidence and prosperity, however, were bound to stimulate reform demands.

With the War of 1812 and heavy increases in Irish immigration prompted by the good times in the fisheries, a specific issue arose. In a forceful pamphlet, *Letter to Members of Parliament,* the district surgeon, William Carson, attacked the old prohibition of 1699 against agriculture in Newfoundland. Shortages brought on by the new war and Irish immigration would lead to starvation and public disorder unless the ban was lifted. "War gardens" and farm squatting near St. John's had already proved their worth; it was a matter of legitimizing and extending them. Backed by the merchants, for whom property rights held as much attraction as agriculture, Carson also gained the support of the Irish. By June 1813 London had granted the request in view of the circumstances: the ban remained in force, but cultivation was condoned for individuals accepting small plots and large quit-rents. The concession, although less than adequate, was a singular achievement, and in 1813 Carson confidently produced another pamphlet, *Reasons for Colonizing the Island of Newfoundland.*

For the merchants Carson's new campaign was more controversial than the war gardens issue, for he now demanded civil government and a local legislature. Other issues seemed more important, however, when the end of war brought depression and social unrest. In 1815 French and American fishermen were again competing in the fisheries. Despite urgent pleas for Newfoundlanders' fishing rights within the old French limits, peace brought the restoration to France of St. Pierre, Miquelon and the French Shore, and closed out facilities and settlements built up over a period of twenty years. It also shut off valuable agricultural land from a rapidly growing population. Postwar diplomatic settlement in Europe had disregarded a generation of civil growth in Newfoundland.

Diplomatic setbacks and depression exposed the evils of the "truck" system by which the merchants kept most fishermen in bondage. With renewed competition, dwindling catches, and the collapse of a hundred trading firms in two years, the island had lost virtually every gain since 1793. Three years of depression and famine, climaxed by the extraordinary cold of the winter of 1817-18, saw tempers frayed and suspicions easily aroused. Methodist missionary activity gave rise to Irish fears of an anti-papist campaign, and even the Anglican merchant clique resented their success. By 1817 fear was endemic among the Irish while disease and overcrowding in St. John's went unchecked. In November three hundred houses were destroyed by fire, and rumours were common that incendiaries were responsible.

With a population of forty thousand, one-quarter of them crowded into St. John's, the island in its troubles could no longer be regarded as a transient outpost. A British parliamentary enquiry in 1817 recommended that the admiral governors should henceforth remain in residence throughout the winter, and that the governor be instructed to recommend means by which the administration might be improved. The reformers could also take heart from the activities of the new chief justice, Francis Forbes, who confronted the justices and the naval surrogates with a more humane interpretation of the law. Carson's old issues had reappeared, and Carson himself was joined by a demagogic St. John's merchant, Patrick Morris. Each stimulating the other's impetuosity, they pushed forward their "final solution": a local assembly based on a wide franchise. Discounting the lack of an educational system and of a moderating middle class, passing over the growing religious strife, and ignoring the outports' isolation, they encouraged at St. John's a popular demand for representative government. This movement would have large repercussions in the island in years ahead.

Unlike Newfoundland, Prince Edward Island's chief activity was farming, and the fisheries were neglected. Its population was scarcely larger than St. John's by 1820, mostly Scots and one-tenth Acadian; immigration was intermittent. Although all but three townships were open to the sea, the settlement of the middle and eastern areas was only beginning. Travel was on horseback or by foot, there being no four-wheeled carriage on the island before 1820. Roads were tracks, beach-paths being the most dependable. A new barracks and courthouse stood in Charlottetown, but there were virtually no church buildings in the colony. Religious activity depended largely upon itinerant ministers and missionaries. No provision having been made for public schools, instruction was by private tutoring, although in 1815 the first Acadian parish school was begun at Rustico. By 1820, however, the Methodists had established a chapel in the capital, the Scots were organizing a presbytery, and the French and Scotch Catholics had joined to erect a new cathedral.

The decade's politics were promising but anomalous. The octagenarian governor, J. F. W. Des Barres, had encouraged an independent course by supporting a reforming Irish lawyer, James B. Palmer. Palmer's chief allies were Loyalists claiming clear title to their lands under the government's promise of 1784 to the supporters of United Empire; seeking, in short, to contest the grip of the absentee proprietors in England over their island estates. Their American background also taught them to value a strong assembly. Forming a society, the "Loyal Electors," they soon won important offices, a strong position in the Council, and ascendancy in the Assembly. Their goals were clear: to meet the Loyalists' claims, to insist upon better administration, and to seek more liberal land laws. By 1812, however, Des Barres' faith in Palmer was wavering.

For two years, despite worsening relations with the Americans, the Assembly dominated by the Electors had failed to meet Des Barres' request for a large militia grant. They trusted in the Royal Navy. By stirring up opinion on other issues at public meetings and by extending their membership, however, they had put their loyalty into question. The chief justice, Caesar Colclough, for whom Des Barres held no brief, labelled them "Jacobins," warning that "Democracy is making such strides here that without some man of firmness and sense is sent or the Island is annexed to Nova Scotia I really trouble for its safety should there be war with America." Des Barres hesitated, and the initiative slipped to the absentee interests in London. The result was his own recall, Palmer's dismissal from all offices, and the conversion of the Electors to an underground movement subject throughout the American war to charges of sedition and worse.

The war prompted a modest prosperity for those who could engage in naval and military provisioning, but by 1815 the island's political problems were paramount. The Electors' disappearance had led to the substitution of official tyranny for moderate dissent, in the person of Governor Charles Douglas Smith. Favouritism had brought Smith his post, to which he added nepotism. The Assembly met infrequently and clashed regularly with Smith and his corps of incompetents. The governor did nothing to shake the absentee proprietors, and he created his own faction to frustrate the reappearance of a reform party. By his own admission, however, the Electors were still secretly at work, and the Assembly gained purpose from his outrageous assaults upon its competence. On one occasion after their refusal to prorogue, the governor's son, a boy whom Smith had named Acting Provost Marshall and naval liaison officer, vented his rage by smashing the Assembly's windows during a session. Called before the house for contempt, he recalled, "I ups with my fist and slashed through the windows," but proffered no explantation before being ordered to pay costs and be jailed at the Assembly's pleasure.

Despite such comic-opera confrontations, by 1818 the Assembly's goals were firmly expressed: the demand for regular meetings, insistence on judicial and other appointees who would not interfere in elections or grab escheated lands, and a plea for general land reform. So great was the Assembly's frustration, however, that early in 1819 it prayed the crown for "the same control and power . . . as the Houses of other colonies, or . . . meet the ardent wishes of their constituents by re-annexing this Island to the envied and flourishing province of Nova Scotia." Later that year, although refusing to recall Smith, the Colonial Secretary, Lord Bathurst, acknowledged the weakness of his constitutional position. With the annexation movement thus discouraged for the moment, the island looked in the 1820s for a constitutional governor who would undertake the badly needed reforms in education, agriculture and landholding.

There was still another island colony in this period, Cape Breton —though its status had remained uncertain ever since it had been set up separately from Nova Scotia in 1784. With haphazard arrivals of Scots from Skye and the Highlands, the western harbours and glens and the Bras d'Or shores had begun to fill. The newcomers' outlook was local, their tongue Gaelic, and their culture clannish. In their isolation the French or American wars had made little difference. Through these years Catholic and Protestant Scots had lived in segregated antipathy while French refugees from Miquelon at Arichat sadly faced the former French fisheries at Canso. Sydney's tiny, self-seeking bureaucracy was less lonely, sharing its despair with a rabble of coal smugglers evading the official coal mine monopoly, seasonal fishermen and anxious merchants. An ineffectual government-by-council, petty administration and economic discord prevailed. Sydney lacked even the crumbling dignity of her fore-runner, the nearby old French base of Louisbourg. Maintaining such a colonial anachronism after 1815 was a burden for postwar Britain, and six thousand scattered colonists at subsistence level hardly valued a government offering no benefit and inviting no participation. In 1819, when Nova Scotia again raised a recurrent cry for reunion Bathurst moved willingly to end a minor imperial headache. On January 1, 1821, Cape Breton was re-annexed to Nova Scotia. She looked now for sound administration, investment, and heavy immigration—preferably Scots.

II

In the first half of the 1810s the two mainland Maritime colonies responded similarly to corresponding conditions; after 1815 their paths diverged. The historian Beamish Murdoch might have been describing both his own province and New Brunswick in 1810: "While war raged elsewhere, Nova Scotia was peaceful, busy and prosperous (on a limited scale), and free from disturbance, agitation, or crime." New England's trading losses under the embargo had greatly benefited both Maritime provinces. Nova Scotia doubled her exports to the West Indies and began a modest shipbuilding industry. New Brunswick preferred the British square timber market, but shared the ambition to become a entrepôt centre for American trade. Both sought continued recognition of their free ports, where Yankees could trade without customs imposts, and the Free Ports Act of 1811 was passed in anticipation of the coming American war. Halifax, Shelburne, Saint John and St. Andrews were thus confirmed as major North Atlantic ports. The opening of direct colonial trade with the Mediterranean thrust Maritime shippers into prominence and ambition in the international carrying trade. But these events had serious domestic repercussions.

In New Brunswick the wartime timber boom led to neglect of both fisheries and farming. The dominance of timber in New Brunswick prompted a fundamental shift in the old Loyalist plan for compact and largely self-sufficient communities. The people were becoming scattered; immigration complicated the situation; and the timber and land administration was confused. Sir John Wentworth, the aging Surveyor General of the King's Woods, lived in Halifax. An imperial appointee, Wentworth operated in an uncharted bureaucratic wilderness, without reference to governor or Council. In her urgent need for ship timber, London ignored reports of forest depredations and the evils of economic over-concentration. Meanwhile, in 1812, the Scottish Baltic timber supplier, Alexander Rankin, brought his capital and experience to the Miramichi; others followed, and a vigorous shipbuilding industry developed to serve the export trade. The American war simply intensified a pattern apparent since 1808.

In Nova Scotia the effects of war were equally promising and less alarming. Shipbuilding flourished, the fisheries thrived, and a more experienced commercial community avoided the rush to a single staple. Instead, in 1811 imperial permission was sought to undertake coal mining and joint-stock banking. Road-building continued, and the economic boom was matched by other developments. An Education Act of 1811 greatly extended grammer school facilities; in Pictou Thomas McCulloch founded his remarkable Academy. At Halifax the Assembly agreed to construction of an imposing stone "Province Building" and a mansion for the naval commander. The *Acadian Recorder* made its appearance and immediately elevated journalism and stimulated public debate. On the eve of a further war with the United States, the old church of St. Paul's in Halifax, resplendent with a new tower and steeple, symbolized the expansiveness of the province, assured of naval protection for new trade, prosperity and patriotism.

Even before the American war Saint John and Halifax had seen its foreshadowing. In May 1811, the British sloop *Little Belt* had limped into Halifax with her dead and damages after encountering the U.S. frigate *President*. A wave of anti-American feeling ensued, paralleling feelings in Saint John where Yankee shipwrights driven north by the embargo were resented by native labourers but welcomed by merchants and shipbuilders. In New Brunswick the Revolutionary War veterans, the Fencibles, were reorganized as the 104th Regiment. In Nova Scotia, Governor Sir John Coape Sherbrooke reduced the number of regulars rotated to Bermuda and ordered the strengthening of the colony's principal military works. Both provinces anticipated the threats and promises of war. By July 1812, it was evident that the promises would take precedence. From Eastport, eastern Maine declared its preference for commerce, not conflict, and, as the historian of New Brunswick remarks, "it became clear that the chief patriotic role New Brunswickers should play was that of trading with the enemy." Nova Scotians would not be left out, however, for Sherbrooke recognized the value of licensed trading with New England to attract specie, in view of the large amounts of capital, arms and supplies being called to Canada by the commander-in-chief, Governor Prevost. In 1813 Sherbrooke assured London that the Yankee trade diverted many Americans from the war and was worth several thousand soldiers.

Increased trade was one avenue to wealth; privateering was another. The early success of American privateers along Nova Scotia's coast caused alarm. The Royal Navy lost five ships and was forced to admit the superiority of American naval gunnery. With the Navy diverted to blockading the middle and southern American coasts, there arose new fears for Maritime shipping. Sherbrooke now gave his support to several aggressive Halifax shippers asking for "letters of marque" to authorize them to act as privateersmen. Despite the appearance of American vessels in Saint John's outer harbour, however, some New Brunswick shippers were uneasy over the effect of privateering upon the licensed American trade. Thus privateering gained greater support in Nova Scotia, where the success of vessels such as the *Liverpool Packet* left tales and legends for the province's history. In November 1813, permission to export American prize goods to American markets heightened the irony of the bizarre wartime trade. Cheaper imports of food appeared when Sherbrooke also agreed to the transport of Nova Scotia timber to the Indies in American vessels. In Halifax French and American prisoners were boarded and employed by local residents seeking cheap labour. War was a profitable industry.

Amidst such good times, the news of Napoleon's fall in 1814 might almost have brought dismay, but in Halifax there were public celebrations, and in Saint John an ox was roasted in the King's Square. After all, the American war was not yet over, and new inflows of British ships, troops and capital might be expected. Meanwhile, Sherbrooke was preparing to consolidate the brisk trade along the New Brunswick border, and with the first arrivals of veteran forces from the war in Europe there developed an offensive strategy new to the Maritimes. A series of successful combined operations in mid-summer 1814 sent British regulars and sailors against the New England towns of Eastport, Castine and Bangor, thereby establishing the British as masters of the northeastern coastal trade. Occupation and increased commerce might lead to enlarged authority for New Brunswick and a favourable clarification of her boundary with Maine. The opening of this second front thus raised hopes widely. At the end of 1814, however, the American war ended in the Treaty of Ghent. It simply restored the "status quo ante bellum," Britain being ready to accept a virtual stalemate since Napoleon had returned to power in France. It was not till after his final defeat at Waterloo in June 1815, therefore, that peacetime conditions fully began for the British American colonies.

Important differences soon arose in the postwar development of the two mainland Atlantic provinces. In New Brunswick there was dissatisfaction with old ties persisting with Nova Scotia, particularly among the religious denominations. By 1820 Baptists, Presbyterians and Anglicans in the former colony were all seeking provincial organization. Only the Acadians of New Brunswick remained content with their isolated temporal existence under the spiritual province of Quebec. Demobilization and immigration also differed between the two Maritime colonies. New Brunswick's 104th Regiment, which had fought in Canada at Stoney Creek, Lundy's Lane and Fort Erie, was disbanded in Upper Canada, and many of its veterans did not return home. No program of systematic British immigration was undertaken, newcomers arriving casually with the timberships and frequently drifting to the United States. Saint John merchants and timbermen opposed immigration and agriculture as incipient threats to their exploitation of the forest. New Brunswick agriculture thus continued to reflect a dangerous dependence upon the Americans and upon other colonies.

Neglect of the fisheries, at the same time, gave a hollow ring to the cries of alarm over American pretensions. A sounder resentment arose over American manoeuvring and British wavering on the problem of the disputed boundary between New Brunswick and New England; and when the issue finally went unresolved public criticism was intense. In any case, timber and its oligarchs remained paramount in the province, though they could not remain insulated indefinitely against economic hazards and public concern. With the end of her war needs, it was Britain that first abandoned the indifference to conditions in the timber industry and Governor Smith was ordered to demand full fees and respect for tighter land and timber regulations. As the governor and Council obeyed their instructions, the Assembly denounced the financial strengthening of the Executive and demanded a voice in framing new regulations affecting the colony's greatest asset. Commercial figures in Saint John looked to their interest in the matter, and a coalition appeared likely with the dissidents in the Assembly. In the election of 1820, therefore, Ward Chipman's emergence as the leader of this new group signalled a decade of fresh conflict over the colony's growth and direction.

As for Nova Scotia, despite a one-third drop in revenue in 1815, no postwar slump occurred. Returns were still three times their prewar level, and Governor Sherbrooke recommended a program of public improvement. There ensued a general economic development and much public and private activity. Road-building showed the most obvious results, with annual expenditures of nearly £25,000 to 1818. One-quarter was assigned to improvement of the "great roads," the rest to local contracts. The new governor, Lord Dalhousie, expressed satisfaction with this program, but in 1819 he proposed a major overhaul of the system which would have the effect of reducing the local opportunities for pork-barrel politics and enlarge the Council's powers over the important trunk roads. The issue remained unresolved in 1820. Meanwhile, Samuel Cunard and colleagues in the Halifax shipping world had pressed for additions to the lighthouse service; the Halifax-Dartmouth ferry service had accepted the principle of steam; a stage-coach service to Windsor was initiated at $6 for "inside passengers." Feasibility studies and preliminary clearing for the Shubenacadie canal to link Atlantic and Bay of Fundy waters also received firm support. In Halifax a night watch and the proposal for street lighting indicated the growing interest in public improvements in a more mature society.

Nova Scotia's development was reflected in other fields as well: the first Catholic bishop was appointed and St. Mary's Cathedral founded in Halifax. A second controversial journal, the *Free Press,* appeared, and in 1818 newspaper coverage of the Assembly's proceedings was initiated. Professional theatricals were common at the wharf theatres of Halifax; in Pictou McCulloch's Pictou Academy added a museum and science exhibit. In higher education Dalhousie sought the secularization of Anglican King's College at Windsor, its removal to Halifax, and promised £11,000, already earmarked from the customs revenue of occupied Castine, to its support. Failing to overcome the objections of King's College he assisted happily in the founding in 1820 of Dalhousie College at Halifax. The problem of higher education, however, diverted attention from the lack of rural elementary school facilities in many parts of the province.

In the midst of general prosperity, too, Nova Scotia had its problems. Although the Convention of 1818 between Britain and the United States, settling old fishing issues between them, actually reduced claims in the inshore fishery, it was feared that the fishing facilities it gave them in Newfoundland must increase their competition in distant markets. The Nova Scotia Assembly thus sought to encourage diversification by offering to subsidize a whale fishery, but Britain's relaxation of the prohibitions against American traders in the Indies added to their basic alarm. The sea had its limitations, and so had the forest. Unlike New Brunswick, Nova Scotia did not have even an imperfect forest reservation system, and the war years had mixed pillage with profit. Only a few commercial operators could be indefinitely supported on existing stands without regulation.

Shipbuilding and a first paper mill were operating well at the end of the decade, but Nova Scotia's primary industry and the export trade had to depend, as in New England at its height, upon a foundation of agriculture. Two bad crop years in 1815-16 reinforced this conclusion, and Dalhousie proposed to encourage a general improvement in agricultural methods and stock. His principal allies were the publisher of the *Acadian Recorder*, A. J. Holland, and the local Scottish agricultural authority, John Young. The publication in the *Recorder* in 1818 of Young's pseudonymous "Letters of Agricola" swept aside the indifference of merchants and shippers and gave to the agricultural campaign a splendid beginning. Within a year a flourishing Provincial Agricultural Society was spawning branches across the province; from ploughing matches to technical correspondence, the shared experience promised improved yields and better stock. The pioneering aspect of the colony's farming was finally being displaced.

For many recent arrivals, however, even primitive cultivation was a major challenge. At Bathurst's suggestion Dalhousie had initiated an examination of settlers' difficulties, and in 1817 the Assembly reported that large-scale absenteeism, high fees, lack of local labour, and the scarcity of wilderness roads were the greatest evils. The house proposed remedies in which Dalhousie heartily concurred. The results in increased immigration bore no comparison to Upper Canada, but they were encouraging. Several groups, however, encountered serious problems of assimilation and settlement. In 1814 nearly two thousand Negroes brought back from the Chesapeake expedition were deposited isolated and unprepared at Hammonds Plains, Preston and other points in Halifax County. Together with hundreds of indigent Irish from Newfoundland they reaped an undeserved and sadly understandable resentment. In the same period, Dalhousie asked the Assembly's support in assisting the Indians "in their disposition to fix their abode and cultivate the land." Rural ghettoes for Indian and Negro, in fact, were really begun in the 1810s.

As Lord Dalhousie prepared to take his leave of Nova Scotia in 1819, he rejoiced that "this happy country is yet ignorant of the influence of party or faction." Talented, substantial men of the calibre of Simon Robie, Brenton Halliburton and Samuel Archibald had arisen in legislative circles and leadership seemed secure. Dalhousie's satisfaction was premature, however, for before his departure he differed sharply with the Assembly over roads and militia policies. In the same months there arose a new fear over imperial intentions in regard to the fisheries and the Indies trade. In a mixture of expansionism and commercial uncertainty, the Assembly demanded the re-unification of Cape Breton and Prince Edward Island with Nova Scotia. The re-annexation of Cape Breton promised some improvement, but the new governor, Sir James Kempt, faced the difficult task of mending fences and restoring confidence.

III

For Lower Canada, too, the Napoleonic and American wars offered economic opportunity to merchants and shippers. After 1811 Britain's favourable differential duties encouraged the continued growth

of a huge square timber trade, exceeding even New Brunswick's, and
sparked by experienced British timber firms with agencies in the
colony. Although most seigneurs were only marginally concerned with
the timber trade, some responded by building sawmills and reserving
timber lands. The effect was to slow the popular movement to new
lands and unsettled parts of older seigneuries. Despite economic and
psychological hardships, however, the heavy population increase
continued. Consequently, over-population was becoming critical and
the habitant faced the prospect of old age without the comfort of
being surrounded by three generations.

This cultural threat to the integrity of the French-Canadian
family added a deeper dimension to the so-called "Reign of Terror,"
when Governor Craig had dissolved the Assembly in 1810, seized
the press of *Le Canadien*, and arrested its closest associates—men
like Pierre Bédard. Nevertheless, in the ensuing elections Bédard and
his supporters were returned, while Craig, in grotesque fears of a
Napoleonic plot linked with dangerous *Canadien* democracy, even
sought to press for the revocation of the Constitutional Act of 1791.

Meanwhile, the tide of prosperity in Lower Canada since 1807
had not greatly favoured the French-Canadian merchant, but the
English welcomed improvements in furs, agriculture and imports—
and the rise in prices. By 1811 their energies were increasingly being
directed toward the ownership and commercial development of the
seigneuries, so that a new crisis developed. This trend must threaten
the primarily social nature of the French seigneury, and the alarm
was sounded by those in the professions. These men—lawyers and
doctors, principally—had long been on the increase, but their
chances of employment had regularly lagged behind the colony's
economic growth. Many came from rural areas and remained there
in frustration, thus amplifying their sense of grievance and broadening their influence. In many respects they were as elitist as the
higher clergy and the merchants of whom they were so critical, but
they were conscious of the obstacles to prominence in their professions. The grander role as social and racial defenders of the French-
Canadian nation was a fit substitute, and politics through the
Assembly was the vehicle closest to hand. Their concern, then, lay
with the evils of rampant capitalism, official patronage and threats

to the social values of the seigneury. The recent socio-economic improvements gained by the merchants, and Craig's repressive tactics, added to the intensity of their concern and confirmed their struggle along racial lines. Many English only broadened their antipathy to all *Canadiens* for resisting agricultural change and profit-directed commercialism.

On the eve of the American war these tensions alarmed the imperial authorities, and Craig's strong antidotes were summarily rejected. In June 1811, although his enemies were in disarray, Craig was recalled. His successor was a cautious, conciliatory, bilingual Swiss, Sir George Prevost, with a mandate to moderate at home and mobilize abroad. Prevost's strategy was to disarm the extremists. In disowning the combination of church, bureaucrat and merchant, represented by such anglophiles as Bishop Mountain and Herman Ryland, officers were not removed but their functions were limited and their benefits reduced. Toward the French extremists the governor showed greater sympathy, but his way was eased by confusion of their leaders. Bédard's health and temperament prevented his continued militance, and a judgeship eased his security. Others received lesser honours cheerfully, for the patronage issue had been paramount in Craig's regime. Militia appointments were also attractive in the prospect of war. For young members of the *parti canadien*, like the rising Louis-Joseph Papineau, a period of moderation would permit re-grouping under fresh leadership. Prevost's sure touch is undeniable, although circumstances favoured him greatly. A common enemy is a great unifier, and the anglophiles rallied against the Americans despite their rage at Prevost. Moreover, a defensive war against the Americans attracted the *Canadiens*, for pre-Jacksonian America seemed a blatant example of the Anglo-Saxon materialism and capitalism threatening Quebec's traditional values.

In mobilizing the colony Prevost was instructed to move slowly and quietly to avoid alarming the Americans. He wisely confirmed General Isaac Brock, temporary administrator of Upper Canada, as commander in that area. In Lower Canada he himself succeeded in rallying and organizing the militia as an effective military force. The record of the famed Voltigeurs under Colonel Charles de Salaberry, himself a regular British army officer, added to the legends of the war, especially in repulsing American invading forces at Lacolle and Chateauguay. Although Lower Canadian forces were not often employed directly in a war staged mainly in Upper Canada, their reserve strength allowed the regulars' decisive concentration at the front. Moreover, the Assembly out-stripped those of all the other colonies in providing financial support for the war. There could be no question of Lower Canada's commitment to the prosecution of the conflict nor of her contribution to military successes.

With the peace, internal unrest returned. Prevost's controversial military conduct of the unsuccessful British thrust into the Lake Champlain region in 1814 weakened his authority. But in any case, a revival of discord had been predictable in Lower Canada. The Assembly, strengthened in morale by its wartime loyalty, generosity and cohesion, confronted the English party centred in the Legislative and Executive Councils, who had cause for concern over their reduced strength. These alarms came to a head when the house adopted a resolution to "impeach" two notable office-holders, the chief justices, Jonathan Sewell and James Monk. The main issue was certain arbitrary changes that had been made in the rules for practice of law. Prevost refused to suspend the judges, but Sewell was permitted to plead his case in London. The Assembly voted £5,000 to despatch spokesmen; their action was peremptorily rejected by the Legislative Council. Thus, a constitutional confrontation developed as a counterpoint to the central issue. Other factors heightened tensions further. Wartime interruptions in the fur trade merged with an intensified struggle against the Hudson's Bay Company that tested the Montreal-based operations severely. Agricultural conditions in Lower Canada, bad enough during the war, grew steadily worse. Wheat production and farm prices fell. Only timber persisted profitably, but seigneurial reservations increased and large timber profits were returned to England. At best, timber tempered the otherwise depressed economy of the province.

Prevost's recall in 1815, because of criticisms of his military judgment, gave the signal for fresh strife. The locum tenens, Sir Gordon Drummond, inherited the unpleasant duty of reporting to the Assembly the failure of the case against Sewell in England.

Under its new speaker, the fiery, eloquent Papineau, the Assembly insisted upon an appeal, and Drummond, under orders, thereupon proclaimed its dissolution. Hopes rose once more, however, when in 1816 the new governor, Sir John Sherbrooke, arrived after an exceptionally successful administration in Nova Scotia. Sherbrooke was already an aged and ailing man, but he began vigorously and shrewdly by seeking Papineau's opinions and by inviting mutual confidence and moderation. By 1818 he had overhauled the composition of the two appointive councils in a bid to assuage the Assembly. Even his elevation of Plessis to the Legislative Council and to full episcopal recognition passed the anglophiles and the radical liberals. Simultaneously, he reassured the whole community of his sense of justice and concern for a comprehensive recovery from their economic ills. The confidence now given the governor served him to initiate negotiations with Assembly and imperial leaders over the public debt, the civil list and budgetary review. By the end of 1817 significant constitutional progress seemed possible through Papineau's moderation and Sherbrooke's patience. But tragically, on February 5, 1818, the governor suffered a paralytic stroke.

Although Sherbrooke had been able to depend upon the Assembly's understanding to grant supplies and to skirt the issue of budgetary review for the moment, the matter now passed to his successor. In July 1818, the Duke of Richmond, Bathurst's brother-in-law, landed in Quebec, and within a year Sherbrooke's patiently built edifice of confidence was toppled. Richmond's experience as Viceroy of Ireland had taught him little, for he moved thoughtlessly into the arms of the English party. His first budget virtually ignored Sherbrooke's earlier negotiations, and his response to the house's objections was petulance and dissolution.

As the 1810s closed, the issues of the control of land, agricultural conditions and over-population had become critical in Lower Canada. The governor seemed the symbol of Anglo-Saxon indifference, and as well the English were bestirring themselves, urging British immigration, improved commercial facilities for the St. Lawrence, and closer relations with Anglo-Saxon Upper Canada to solve the colony's troubles. In the *Canadien* back parishes alarm grew among the dispossessed, and the racial cleavage seemed more awesome than ever to those of the liberal professions. Suddenly, in the summer of 1819, Richmond's brief career in Canada, which had arisen at Sherbrooke's tragic collapse, came to its own disastrous end. As the Duke lay dying from the bite of a rabid pet fox, Lord Dalhousie prepared to follow his predecessor from Nova Scotia to Quebec. But amid the warmth of ceremonious leave-taking, it seemed ominous that so bitterly had Dalhousie quarrelled with his own Assembly in Halifax that he had refused even to accept their proffered address and final gift of esteem.

IV

The question of the fate of the northwest in the 1810s was a constant irritant to the British element in Lower Canada. Montreal's deteriorating position in the fur trade helps to explain some of the aggressive and insensitive attitude of the British commercial class in the city toward the French Canadians, as they saw themselves in danger of losing a vast empire in the West.

The decade began with American invasion of the Columbia region of the Pacific northwest in 1811, when John Jacob Astor, powerful master of the American Fur Company, engaged numbers of dissident Montreal traders and established Fort Astoria at the mouth of the Columbia River to safeguard his projected Pacific fur empire. The splendid discoveries of David Thompson, that had disclosed the Columbia route from the interior to Canadian traders, would be nullified if the Nor'Westers could not dislodge the Americans. With the War of 1812, release seemed possible, and H.M.S. *Racoon* was despatched to the Columbia to bolster the Canadians' thrust. Astor's empire, however, was already crumbling from its own internal stresses. The comic-opera "seizure" of the American posts merely paved the way for handing them back at the peace, on its principle of restoration to the status quo ante bellum. The far west remained a largely profitless headache for Canadian fur traders throughout the decade.

Astor's Pacific venture had forced the Montrealers in 1811 to conclude a hasty agreement for an international operation in the old fur empire southwest of the Lakes. Again, however, the Americans' extraordinary peacetime diplomatic successes humiliated the Canadians, and the westward extension of the international boundary compelled their withdrawal from the South West Fur Company in 1817. Increasingly, the value of the vast fur-rich Athabasca region in the northwest mounted; yet in that area they were faced with two threats to their old hegemony of the western interior. In 1810, in a sudden takeover, the Hudson's Bay Company had fallen under the direction of several Scottish investors led by Thomas Douglas, Earl of Selkirk. The new directors saw the value of adopting the transportation and trading techniques, and the personnel incentives of the Nor'Westers. Under the direction of Selkirk's brother-in-law, Andrew Wedderburn Colville, their counter-attack was carried forward swiftly and successfully. Throughout the decade heavy competition, increased transportation costs and high taxes were consuming the Montrealers' slender capital and morale.

Throughout this struggle, moreover, the Nor'Westers also had to contend with the settlement which Selkirk founded deep in the continent, and from which modern Manitoba would arise. Pursuing a dream of making a haven for Scots and Irish poor (that had already led him to plant a settlement in Prince Edward Island in the previous decade), this wealthy philanthropist obtained a grant of forty-five million acres in the Red River valley, ceded out of Rupert's Land by the Hudson's Bay Company in 1811. In this vast patriarchy, Assiniboia, a tiny farming colony emerged below the junction of the Red and Assiniboine, as settlers were sent in by way of Hudson Bay. Yet this Red River colony sat astride the vital fur trade route to the Athabasca country, and also commanded the Nor'Wester's equally vital pemmican supplies. These were chiefly obtained through the Métis, skilled buffalo hunters, the product of generations of marriage "by custom of the country" of fur traders and Indian women. They saw themselves as a proud new people of the plains. Métis desires to protect their own free hunting existence could readily be worked upon by Nor'Wester allies, fearful themselves of the aims of Selkirk's colony.

The colony's tenuous relations with the rival Bay Company were both suspect and inflammatory, as were ill-judged, high-handed actions by the colony's successive governors, Miles Macdonell and Robert Semple. In the angry disputes that arose the Nor'Westers used intimidation and the threat of the Métis, and for a time completely dispersed the colony. A Hudson's Bay counterforce helped re-establish it; but in 1816 Robert Semple and twenty colonists were killed at Seven Oaks in a disastrous skirmish with the Métis. In response, Selkirk engaged veterans from the War of 1812 as mercenaries. Moving west from Montreal, he seized Fort William, the North West Company's great inland headquarters, arrested that company's chief leader, William McGillivray, and went on to restore his colony. Strengthened by Selkirk's efforts, it gradually began to grow. By 1820 the Red River colony was lastingly rooted as the first farming settlement in the northwest of British America, though it long remained small and isolated. Meanwhile, however, the whole pattern of the fur trade West had changed.

The long, expensive struggle had exhausted both fur companies. Besides, there was a costly series of suits and counter suits over the depredations at Red River and the seizure of Fort William, that led to Selkirk's death, worn out, and to the near-ruin of the Montreal company, whose finances had been the more severely strained for years. Accordingly, in 1820, when it was evident that the Montrealers had lost the confidence of their wintering partners in the interior, while the Bay Company was ready to receive her enemies into her ranks, William McGillivray strove to negotiate a union of the two organizations. It took effect in 1821. The newly amalgamated Hudson's Bay Company thereafter ruled unchallenged to the Arctic and Pacific; but Montreal and Canada had witnessed the defeat of their first great transcontinental commercial system. The West had fallen from their grip, and in the east the effects of that loss would go far beyond mere sentiment for lost glory.

V

Unlike the other colonies, Upper Canada had been little affected by the French wars, except through the virtual exclusion of British immigrants that ensued. Set off from the rest of British North America, she appeared like a long defiant arm thrust deep into the

Americans' continental migration route. As a consequence she was bound to attract American travellers and settlers, and to tempt militant American expansionists. Her widely scattered population of 75,000 fronted a nation of seven million; perhaps three-fifths of her inhabitants had their roots in pre- or post-revolutionary America, a third of these being land-hungry frontiersmen from more recent migrations. Her only towns of any size, York and Kingston, failed as rallying points, for they were surrounded by immense tracts of wilderness. Her principal roads were few and indifferently maintained, and her main settled areas were readily accessible to attack from water, or in the distinctly "American" western half to combined assaults by land and water. No other colony was so little protected by regular forces, and none therefore invited so readily an American attack in the event of war with Britain. Moreover, none would be so deeply affected by the war both materially and in her public consciousness and memory.

On the eve of the War of 1812, Upper Canada still lacked a sense of community. Not even the awareness of inefficiency in government, favouritism in land-granting, and shortcomings in communication had stirred the populace to accept the ministrations of demagogues who had thrust themselves forward in the preceding years. If no one was very active, there could be no complaint of a tyrannous oligarchy. The new American settlers were not yet Britons, but in their indifference to politics and to the regime's languid activity they none the less remained in Canada, preoccupied with getting on in their own world of stumps, seed and sows. Although isolation was a source of discontent, it was not yet a political issue, and it might even be a safeguard against sedition in time of war.

Fortunately the Americans were as ill-prepared for war as Upper Canada. The enthusiasm of those elements in the United States who urged war had outdistanced their prudence. Strategically the upper province could have been written off if Montreal, and preferably Quebec, could be taken. The wasteful American campaign to occupy Upper Canada by way of its western extremity instead could never have been so satisfactory as tying it off at its base. Indeed, the Americans' early failure to act upon the latter principle proved one of Britain's greatest assets, for Major-General Isaac

Brock had only sound military insight, professional skill, and a corporal's guard of sixteen hundred regulars to defend Upper Canada. The man who could channel the powerful influence of Tecumseh and the Indians of the region to the British cause, however, could defeat even the maudlin over-celebration of his talents that has followed since his dramatic death at the battle of Queenston Heights in 1812.

British naval command of the Great Lakes was of inestimable value, but Brock's earliest problems were psychological: "My situation is most critical, not from anything the enemy can do, but from the disposition of the people. . . . A full belief possesses them that this Province must inevitably succumb." A successful strike might shock them from their apathy, and Brock undertook two. The swift seizure of Fort Mackinac in Lake Michigan brought a flood of Tecumseh's Indians to the British, while Brock's dogged intimidation that brought an American army to surrender at Detroit in August 1812 struck with chagrin at many Upper Canadians who had withheld their loyalty and support from the war. His heroic death two months later set the seal on Upper Canada's dedication to the man and the cause. Thenceforth, sedition, when it appeared, was isolated, and neutrality, though it was common, was countered by the legend of Brock when the war reached its worst moments. Leadership emerged; the Glengarry Highland veterans matched the reputation of the Voltigeurs; the few regulars generally received the civilian support necessary for the conduct of the war; and a board of war claims, a widows' and disabled pension fund, and the private relief of a Loyal and Patriotic Society at York reassured and bandaged the afflicted. Even some neutral settlers took up arms, if only to discourage further American invasion and expedite the return to peaceful pursuits.

In 1813 the early British naval strength was briefly challenged by the Americans in Lake Ontario, and the capital at York was raided. When the Americans also advanced from the Niagara frontier, confidence wavered and disaffection and militia desertions reappeared until the American thrust was stopped at Stoney Creek by the regulars under Lieutenant-Colonel John Harvey, and turned back by the Indians at Beaver Dam. Although the centre of the province now was secure, in October 1813 an improved American western army at Detroit succeeded in penetrating the Thames valley and defeating a small force of regulars and Indians at Moravian-town. Fortunately, the quality of American military leadership had not improved, and the Americans were withdrawn to Detroit. In the east, American leadership also contributed to the British and Canadian victories at Chateauguay and Crysler's Farm. As plans were laid for the 1814 campaigns it had become problematical whether the steadily improving American forces might soon triumph over their generals, and before Britain could send reinforcements of skilled French war veterans to match their strength.

In July 1814, the bloody battle of Lundy's Lane near Niagara Falls put an end to these speculations when the Americans exhausted their final effort in Upper Canada. The British offensives in Maine, and at Washington, Lake Champlain, and New Orleans brought the fighting war to an inconclusive halt. The Treaty of Ghent of Christmas Eve, 1814, proved an unwelcome holiday greeting to British North America. It was in effect an armistice. And the round of diplomacy that followed fired the spirit of Upper Canada and helped preserve the flame of nationalism kindled by war. Upper Canadians shared with the lower province the sense of achievement in the war, and their legends of glory. With the Maritimers and the Montreal fur traders they nursed a postwar resentment of the extent to which America's diplomats managed to out-general her wartime commanders. The Rush-Bagot Agreement of 1817—limiting naval armament on the Lakes, and committing Britain to its maintenance—offered a positive foundation, however, for the security and growth of the new nationalism among British North Americans.

The war had effected some damage—at York, on the Erie shore, and in the western half of the province—but on balance the militia's improvement of strategic roads, the regulars' specie and paper issue, the provisioning, and the high farm prices had brought a general prosperity to Upper Canada's inhabitants who numbered about 90,000 in 1815. The tenuous nature of the province's growth in 1812 had now been replaced by a feeling of character, ambition and permanence.

York had suffered heavily from invasion, and remained a village capital of fewer than a thousand persons—one-tenth the size of St. John's. Even her political future remained in doubt in the 1810s, and the centres of power and dissent seemed to be growing elsewhere. Nonetheless, together with Sandwich and Amherstburg, she set an early model for the colony in introducing municipal reforms in keeping with her new ambitions. Firefighting equipment, street lighting and maintenance, market regulations, slaughterhouse standards, bread price controls and other details of a more sophisticated municipal life were being brought under magistrates' supervision.

York's chief rival, Kingston, had thrived on naval construction and her strategic location during the war, and by 1817 had a population of nearly three thousand. In peace she became the armed fulcrum of Britain's Lake strategy: construction, fortifications, garrison troops, shipbuilding and immigration contributed to her impressive growth. While York fell once more into economic dependence upon Montreal, Kingston flourished as the go-between in their mutual commerce. Stagecoach and steamship facilities between the two Canadian colonies came into service at Kingston in 1817. The opening of the Lachine canal in 1816 and the advance of the Rideau canal survey steadily amplified Kingston's prospects. The urban community of Ontario was coming into being in this decade.

The war had also hastened the displacement of many of the executive officers and judicial advisers who had so complacently watched over the province's public life in the past. Vigorous new men had been brought into prominence—Reverend John Strachan, Rector of York, the most prominent Anglican clergyman in the province, John Beverley Robinson, Christopher Hagerman, William Allan, the Boultons—many of them building their reputation and their special brand of loyalty during the war. Some were Loyalists or, more often, their sons; others were British-born and saw themselves as imperial citizens. They could dine or quarrel with Whitehall and its representatives, for they assumed a role as consuls of a common British confession. A society still lacking developed talent seemed to bolster the inclination of these men toward aristocracy and their assumptions of the essential fitness of British constitutional monarchy and the established churches. Such an outlook found expression in aggressive leadership against the incorrigible republicanism and common democracy of America. The concept of loyalty was sharpened, and legitimate dissent was held to be presumptively close to sedition.

Some Upper Canadians of American background might be nettled, or even threatened, by such a point of view as this, but to many it was not an offensive doctrine. Although it was the particular expression of the assumptions of relatively few men, in many respects it was only an extension of the basic tory and monarchical nature of Upper Canada as it had been forged in the two American wars. Differences might arise over details—or even over vital features, such as the right of establishment of the Church of England or the Church of Scotland—but there was a core of firm agreement that lay at the heart of developing Ontario.

Anti-Americanism was one of the most contentious and difficult strains in this emergent public philosophy. In the enthusiasm of the new leaders they willingly accepted Lord Bathurst's conclusion that the war had demonstrated the need to increase the British element in the province's population. This was to be accomplished by offering inducements to the regulars to accept demobilization and lands, and to encourage selected immigration from Britain itself. The Perth military settlement was one result of this policy. Its obverse was the exclusion of American frontiersmen from purchase of lands in the province and the firm application of dormant laws governing resident aliens. Simcoe's anglophile dreams had reappeared, but their effect threatened serious divisions if, in their new form, they excluded Americans as aliens.

When the new men at York failed to meet the threat of postwar depression, opposition from elsewhere in the province developed swiftly. Moreover, these early dissidents were no wild-eyed radicals stirred by envy of America's progress and moved by the example of republican democracy. Instead, like Colonel Robert Nichol, William Dickson and Thomas Clark, they were loyal, uncompensated war sufferers in the old, war-ravaged Niagara district. Their large landholdings, when sold to American frontier-jumpers, were designed to be the means of recouping their fortunes. Bathurst's orders against American immigration, and York's complicity, threatened their security and their prospects. Their alienation was significant, for Nichol was a prominent assemblyman, and Dickson and Clark were legislative councillors.

In 1816 the Assembly first elected in 1812 was dissolved. Although early in the war Brock had experienced difficulty with the Assembly over militia and mobilization arrangements, the war Assembly had generally complied with the Executive. Even in 1816 it had made an unprecedented permanent contribution to the support of the civil government without demanding in return such powers as were being called for by the Lower Canadian house. And despite certain limitations introduced into its Common School Bill in the same session, the Assembly accepted the amended measure. But the elections of that year produced a house of different character, managed by the aggrieved Robert Nichol. In March 1817, the Assembly moved to establish an extraordinary committee to investigate the state of the province.

Dickson's representation to the Council and Nichol's Assembly resolutions of April 5 ushered in an era of postwar dissent. Although there was no evidence of a developed party system within the Assembly, Nichol's persistence served notice to the York elite that other regional oligarchies, if not the masses of Upper Canada, were prepared to oppose them. The leading issues were matters of land policy, communications and administrative efficiency; resentment of American exclusion, the alien question, and poor roads were at the root of this first expression of dissent. In reply, the governor, Sir Francis Gore, resorted to prorogation before a third of the projected resolutions had been put to the house. Two months later, Robert Gourlay arrived in the province, an energetic and officious Scot, with grand ideas and enthusiasms for promoting more effective British settlement in Upper Canada.

Gourlay was a radical's radical, pathologically sensitive and with a genius for shrewd insights and half-truths. In the following months he travelled throughout the province gathering material for his studies of immigration and settlement, and becoming steadily more alarmed with what he encountered in Upper Canada. Through pamphlets and addresses he began to galvanize the Niagara district and the west to voice their legitimate complaints against York and

Whitehall. A comprehensive questionnaire on provincial grievances prompted organized meetings, often under respectable local auspices; Gourlay then proposed a provincial convention to be assembled in York in July 1818, to coordinate these statesments of grievance and their remedies. There was little doubt at York that such activities had prompted the agitated spirit evident in the Assembly in 1818: a major conflict with the Legislative Council had arisen over financial powers, and the house had once again been swiftly prorogued, without voting supply.

Although a new governor, Sir Peregrine Maitland, now attempted land reforms from real conviction, his efforts were not appreciated in the circumstances. Agitation was general, and the regulars had virtually been withdrawn from the province after the war. Maitland had little choice, if he had wished to exercise it, than to accept his councillors' advice to attempt Gourlay's removal by quasi-legal means. Stretching the definitions of libel and of sedition, the authorities succeeded in imprisoning and ultimately in banishing Robert Gourlay, but his martyrdom would serve his supporters well.

As the decade closed there was little unanimity among Upper Canada's dissidents—Gourlay had divided as well as goaded them —but there was a universal and growing discontent. York had entered a three-year depression, and the effects of the American financial panic of 1819 were being felt. Provincial bankruptcy was a serious possibility, for want of customs revenues through a workable arrangement with Lower Canada. In Niagara, certain Presbyterians asked, and were denied, a share of the clergy reserves. In the following year, 1820, John Strachan was appointed to the Legislative Council, and another irascible Scot, William Lyon Mackenzie, migrated to the province. Assuredly, the 1820s promised to provide an atmosphere of lively controversy here and elsewhere throughout British North America. From the 1810s, however, most of the colonies had emerged with a basic loyalty, a clearer character and a high ambition for colonial progress stemming from the crises of war, depression and public debate that had marked this crowded decade.

7: The 1820s

MICHAEL CROSS

The eighteenth century was a lusty, playful old aristocrat. The reports of his death in anno domini 1800 were greatly exaggerated, for he was alive and apparently well in British North America in 1820. In the decade which followed, however, he was challenged and by 1830 he was finally yielding to the nineteenth century.

The 1820s saw the first great waves of British immigration which would sweep away the narrow little colonial society of the past. They saw the rise of reform movements in all the colonies and with them increasingly successful challenges to the old political order. They saw growing sophistication in the economy, a change symbolized by the passing of the Montreal fur trade in 1821. Yet this was the decade, deceptively enough, of the oligarchies, local and provincial —the Family Compact of Upper Canada, the Chateau Clique of

Lower Canada, the Council of Twelve in Nova Scotia, and their like—all apparently at the height of their power. The tensions between the old and the new were everywhere in these provincial societies in flux.

The great folk movement that was British migration after the Napoleonic Wars began to transform British North America in the 1820s. While the total was modest by the standards of the flood which would follow in the two decades ahead, over 125,000 Britons left their homes for the North American colonies in these ten years. They filled in the settled areas, they pushed back the frontier, they brought large amounts of cash into an economy chronically short of specie. Their skills built Canadian businesses, from Nova Scotia's Albion coalmines to York's wholesale houses. Above all, they strengthened British customs, and ways of thought, and values, in colonies previously dominated by an American population.

Immigration alone could not assure prosperity in a British North America dependent upon unstable export trades. Timber, wheat and fish remained the key factors in the Canadian economy. Throughout the 1820s the colonists suffered the effects of the end of the artificial wartime markets in Britain and of British disenchantment with the imperial trading system. The British Corn Laws of 1815, which prohibited the import of colonial wheat when the British price for wheat fell below 67 shillings per quarter, punished Canada between 1820 and 1823, when low prices in Britain cut off British North American wheat. Reduction of the preference for colonial timber in 1821 dealt another blow. Petitioning the British Parliament in 1822, the Lower Canadian House of Assembly claimed that these imperial policies had destroyed the province's export trade, reduced the value of the land by 50 per cent and slashed provincial revenues by one-fifth. Suggestions in Britain to further reduce preferences in 1825 and 1826, coinciding with a financial depression in Britain and North America, sent more tremors through the economy.

The impact of the economic uncertainties varied from province to province. Upper Canada, with its vigorous agricultural establishment and its trade links across the lakes with the United States, grew rapidly and steadily throughout the decade. Lower Canada had a more stuttering development, its trade problems complicated by difficulties in the decaying seigneurial agricultural system; the 1820s were nevertheless a time of growth in the Lower Canadian economy. Relatively unaffected was Prince Edward Island, a substantially self-sufficient farm country. The other Maritime provinces, however, did not fare so well.

Nova Scotia was faced by American competition in the fisheries, facilitated by the Convention of 1818. The result was a steady drop in the price of fish on the American market, from a best price of $6.00 per quintal (a hundredweight) of cod in 1815 to $2.23 per quintal in 1829. Nova Scotia and New Brunswick (which was also trying to build a strong fishery), attempted to improve their trade by offering bounties to fish exporters, but with only moderate success. Nova Scotia also sought other expedients. After considerable pressure on Britain the Assembly won the abolition of customs fees, a serious discouragement to trade, although the high salary of the collector of customs at Halifax remained a point of great dispute. A further concession from Britain was the passing of legislation in 1825 to make Halifax a free warehousing port, joined later by Pictou and Sydney. Nova Scotia was also aided by the failure of Anglo-American diplomacy. Britain's inability to achieve an agreement with the United States for reciprocal opening of ports reserved for Nova Scotia a large share of the trade of the British West Indies, which otherwise would have fallen to American vessels. By decade's end, these measures had helped to revive the Nova Scotian economy. To assure prosperity would continue Halifax was busy improving the transportation facilities upon which that prosperity depended. The Nova Scotia Assembly granted £1500 toward the launching of a steamer service between Quebec and Halifax, a service which would prove uneconomic when established in 1831. The other major project was the Shubenacadie Canal, begun in 1826 to link Halifax with the farming areas on the Bay of Fundy. Halifax had high hopes for the canal. Some other areas, which resented more money being spent for the capital's advantage, were less enthusiastic. Nathaniel White, a community leader in Shelburne, denounced the Shubenacadie Canal as the "humbug of the day," describing it as running "through a country on whose surface not enough is grown to give a wholesome meal to a grasshopper. . . ." White's judgment was sounder than the sanguine hopes of Halifax; when the canal was finally completed thirty years later it was obsolete, an economic disaster.

New Brunswick had ample reason in the 1820s to reflect upon the dangers of its staple trade. The 74,000 people recorded in the provincial census of 1824 were almost totally dependent upon the timber trade for their economic well-being. Agriculture, indeed all other occupations, languished in New Brunswick's single-minded commitment to timbering. That had been safe enough in the prosperous Napoleonic War period. It was not now. The first blow was the Miramichi fire. In October 1825, fire broke out in the forests along the Miramichi River, then the leading timbering area in New Brunswick. Fanned by high winds it swept through the tinder-dry woods. By the time it had run its course, the conflagration had burned over six thousand square miles, devastated the towns of Newcastle, Douglastown and Fredericton, and taken one hundred and sixty lives. The timber trade was ruined and many inhabitants were forced to migrate to the United States. The agony of Miramichi was soon shared in some measure by the rest of the province. On April 3, 1826, the ship *Jane* arrived at Saint John, bringing the news of bank collapses in Britain and the resultant depression of the market for timber. "Black Monday," it was called, and combined with the Miramichi fire it left the provincial economy in a debilitated state from which it would not fully recover within the decade.

It was, nevertheless, a time of important economic development in all the colonies. The staple trades were being reinforced, in Nova Scotia, New Brunswick and Lower Canada, by shipbuilding, important not only because of the cash it produced but also because of the skills in craftsmanship and entrepreneurship it developed. At Montreal the fur trade began to evaporate, with the merger of the Hudson's Bay and North West Companies in 1821 and the shift of the trade to Hudson Bay which followed. But this represented no serious loss to the city. The business leaders now were the merchants, the wholesalers and the côterie of businessmen who had founded the Bank of Montreal in 1817 and saw it firmly established by the time of its incorporation in 1822. A further stimulus to Montreal was the construction of the Lachine Canal between 1817 and 1825, at a cost of some £115,000. As well as providing jobs and pouring a good deal of cash into the city's economy during construction, the canal eased Montreal's access to the interior of the Canadas and consolidated its dominance over the trade of the west.

II

York followed a similar pattern. Although with 2,800 people in 1830 it was a mere village in comparison to Montreal, a city of over 40,000, York was also developing its metropolitan influence in central Upper Canada. The major business of the town was retail trade, supplying the needs of the Home District up Yonge Street. The rapidly growing population in that hinterland allowed the development of larger, more specialized businesses in York. By the end of the 1820s the leading firms in the town were the wholesalers who supplied country merchants. Many were buying their goods directly from Britain, rather than from Montreal, as had been the pattern in 1820. To compensate, some Montreal firms were establishing branch operations in York. Further strengthening the town's position was its role as provincial capital, which centred the courts and government, with their civil servants, at York. It also meant that York had a powerful establishment to work for its interests. How advantageous this could be was demonstrated when York's rival Kingston attempted to charter the first bank in the province. After considerable chicanery by government officials, the bewildered Kingstonians found that when the Bank of Upper Canada was incorporated in 1821, it was located at York, not Kingston. Nor did the favouritism to the capital stop there. Unable to raise sufficient funds for the bank privately, the York group induced the government to become the largest shareholder and, in 1824, to pass a law banning outside banks from competing with their institution within Upper Canada. The Bank of Upper Canada, in fact, had become indistinguishable in the public mind from the executive. In 1830, of the fourteen men who held more than one hundred shares in the bank, ten were senior officials in the government or their relatives.

Upper Canadians were bitten by the canal-building bug in the 1820s as were Nova Scotians and English-speaking Lower Canadians. The canal was one of a series of panaceas which took the imagination of British North Americans—canals in the 1820s, macadamized roads in the 1830s and 1840s, railroads in the 1850s— each one seen in its time as the rose-petal path to prosperity. That none fulfilled their promise did not discourage the eternally optimistic North American developmentalism. Upper Canada was the deepest bitten of the provinces: it was the most Americanized colony, the most likely to absorb the ideology of progress; it was also competing for trade with the neighbouring American states, and with New York state's Erie Canal. Upper Canada was stirring with canal projects. In the east, the imperial government financed the Rideau Canal from Kingston to the new village of Bytown, a work begun in 1826 primarily for military reasons. It would prove unnecessary for defence, of marginal value economically, and its soaring construction costs would ruin the career of its brilliant commandant, Lieutenant-Colonel John By. No more successful was the other canal commenced in 1826, the Desjardins, from Burlington Bay to Dundas. As the decade ended it was still seven years from completion and impossibly far from financial solvency.

The great project of the time, however, was the Welland Canal. The brain-child of a St. Catharines businessman, William Hamilton Merritt, it linked Lakes Erie and Ontario, and was promoted as the definitive answer to the Erie Canal. Merritt, who was to follow a shifting, highly pragmatic course in Canadian life—jumping nimbly from toryism to reformism when it was to his advantage—proved his entrepreneurial talents in guiding his scheme to fruition. Incorporated as a purely private venture in 1824, the Welland Canal almost immediately ran into financial troubles. To obtain funds at least to start construction, Merritt turned to American financiers who eagerly agreed to back the canal, which they hoped to use as a feeder line for the Erie. This was a master-stroke, for it frightened the anti-American government of Upper Canada and stirred it to resist this Yankee influence. In 1825 the Welland Canal Company received a land grant, in 1826 it gained its first government loan. By the time the first ship passed through the still-unfinished canal in 1829, it had become a government-financed project, and eventual public ownership was inevitable. Soon it was also clear that the Welland Canal would not outstrip the Erie, that it would not pour the riches of the American West through Canada. But it did greatly appreciate the value of the land along the canal route— much of it owned by William Hamilton Merritt.

Whatever their success, the canals were symbols of the growth of British North America, of its increasing economic sophistication, and of its belief in its future. The development was far from easy, however. More important than the projects which failed, or the ups and downs of the economy, was the difficulty of knitting together the polyglot populations of the colonies. Social dislocation was inevitable in societies undergoing large-scale immigration. It was especially so when many carried with them both traditions of social disorder and ancient animosities, as the Irish did—the Irish who could not forget the torments of their agonized homeland. Nor was the task made easier by the class distribution of the migration. British North America received the poorest immigrants, those who could not afford the higher rates to the United States and therefore rode the timberships, with their cheap steerage, to the New World; it also received the few upper middle-class people who left Britain, and who wished to stay within the Empire; it received substantially fewer middle-class immigrants than the United States, the people who could supply leadership and more significantly the social cement required for functioning communities.

The most balanced, the most successful society in British North America was that of Nova Scotia. Halifax was the centre and the image of this community. A city of fifteen thousand by decade's end, Halifax presented a picture of bustling urban life to the visitor. From the harbour, three structures dominated the scene. To the south was Government House, residence of the lieutenant-governor, a sombre but impressive stone building. The best building in the city, traveller John McGregor called it "the most splendid edifice in North America . . . ," was the Province Building, an enormous structure 140 feet long, adorned with classic Ionic columns, which housed the legislature, the supreme court, the executive offices and the public library. Above all the visitor was struck by the Citadel and its massive earthworks, a heritage of Halifax's position as a naval centre. The military presence was still strong in the city. The garrison paraded every summer Sunday at three p.m. Every morning the military band played for the trooping of the colours on the parade square, while at dusk fife and drum paraded from the barracks to Government House. There was even a macabre parody of the military presence in the pathetic Negro population. Blacks who fled the United States during the War of 1812 were settled in the Halifax area at Hammond Plains and Prescott. Many were supplied with uniforms captured from the Americans and were to be seen lounging about the town in the ill-fitting, ragged blue coats with tattered red facings. Reared in slavery, despised and segregated in their new home, the blacks formed one of Halifax's least attractive heritages from its military history.

Like the rest of the province, the capital was a curious combination of the traditions which had joined to create it: the military and naval power of the Empire; Puritan New England; the liberal North American environment. The restraints of the British and New England backgrounds coexisted with North American licence. Halifax was a bawdy town, often filled with roistering sailors. Liquor flowed freely, especially at the centre of town, where the main market was flanked by two busy grog shops. Here the truckmen lined up their carts and played football and quarrelled while they waited for business, always well-supplied from convenient liquor stores. Yet they did not smoke, for the magistrates had prohibited smoking in the streets. As the twenties wore on, Halifax moved more in the direction of restraint. Perhaps it was the economic recession of early years of the decade which wiped away the sybaritic prosperity of the war period. Certainly the style set by the governors had an influence, as Sir James Kempt, lieutenant-governor from 1820 to 1828, was replaced by Sir Peregrine Maitland. Sternly moral, Maitland was a champion of the closed Sabbath. He ended the major social event in the city, the Sunday garrison parades, and publicly denounced the open Sunday market. The town fathers followed his lead, adding their own touch of North American puritan morality. Displeased by the cheerful chaos in the streets which had always marked this busy port, the commissioners of streets cleared the sidewalks of all obstructions in 1829 and in the process cut down all the stately willows and poplars that had shaded the streets.

The sensible austerity of Halifax characterized most of the province. In a sense Halifax represented part of a closed frontier; the military significance of the site had meant that the imperial presence was strongly maintained, that the links to Britain were tight, a situation only strengthened by the Loyalist migration. The people moving out on to the frontier under such circumstances were insulated from its influence, they retained the sense of community and order of the Old World. In Nova Scotia the same was true of those who moved within other traditions. The Scots who joined the Highland communities of northeast Nova Scotia bore little resemblance to Haligonians; they formed a unique society. But, bonded by clan ties and by the Gaelic, they too moved in a closed frontier. The wilderness impact was weakened, in many respects neutralized, by these bonds and by their often painful longing for their homeland. The leading Gaelic poet, the bard MacLean who migrated to Barney's River in Pictou County in 1819, spoke for many when he sang of the "hidden grief" of their exile. They responded to this grief by emphasizing their native customs, their Scottishness. Some went further to creative totally closed Highland communities. Norman McLeod, a fire-and-brimstone evangelist, came to Nova Scotia with some of his fanatical followers in 1817. Finding Pictou too wordly a place, he and his disciples sailed to St. Ann's, Cape Breton, in 1820. Joined there by more recruits from Scotland, they formed a theocratic, puritanical community with McLeod as priest-king. His was the wrath of the righteous, exercising arbitrary justice to maintain the purity of his community; one boy, accused of stealing, had his ears clipped in punishment. When advancing settlement threatened their isolation, Norman McLeod and his faithful fled to a new Arcadia in New Zealand.

Prince Edward Island, travellers agreed, had the most homogeneous population of all the colonies. It was normally peaceful, even placid, lacking the turmoil found in other provinces, but also lacking the sophistication and spark of Nova Scotia. A vast garden occupied by yeoman farmers, the island was too pleasant an environment. Agriculture was so easy that the inhabitants were not impelled to improve their methods. Their farming techniques, and even more their livestock, horrified visitors. John McGregor described the swine as "tall, long-snouted animals, resembling greyhounds nearly as much as they do the better kinds of hogs. . . ."

No such peaceful image was projected by New Brunswick. There agriculture was ignored by much of the population which preferred instead to risk their future in pursuit of the adventure and potential riches of the timber trade. The society was unsettled and often violent as a result. The timber trade not only produced uncertainty by its unpredictable "booms and busts," but it weakened the restraints of society—taking men away from authority and from families for extended periods, exposing them to the violent turmoil of spring river-drives, depositing them after the timber was marketed in large towns, with substantial sums of money, there to be preyed upon by thieves and prostitutes. This general unsteadiness could burst into large-scale disorder. Along the Miramichi the riotous behaviour of sailors from the timberships and roving bands of Irish lumberers forced the government to despatch troops to the area in 1822. It was not possible to withdraw the soldiers until six years later, when the Miramichi fire had greatly reduced the timber trade and driven away some of the disorderly population.

Newfoundland suffered similar problems. As at Halifax, St. John's spoke of the nature of its province. The ships in the harbour, the batteries looming over it, showed that Newfoundland owed much of its importance to its strategic position in the imperial navy's plans. The wooden houses, the irregular lanes, the impermanent appearance of the town also showed Britain's long-held intention to maintain Newfoundland only as a trading centre and a naval base, rather than a settled colony. By the 1820s this design had failed. In 1827 there were almost 60,000 people on the island. But its development as a community had been severely retarded. Although a circuit court system was erected in 1824, and an executive council in 1825, Newfoundland still lacked representative government and, more important, it lacked a sense of settled authority and order. Its economic system added to its instability. Like the timber trade, Newfoundland's staple, the fish trade, was risk-filled. The only people reasonably sure of making steady profits were the great merchants who advanced money and supplies to the fishermen. All too often the fishermen were unable to meet these debts, and were ruined. Yet another factor contributing to social instability was the largest group of settlers, the Irish. Most of the Irish who came to Newfoundland were poor, illiterate and violent. With little police power to awe them, suffering under an uncertain and exploitative economic system and driven by Catholic–Protestant animosities imported from Britain, the Irish represented a volatile element in the Newfoundland of the 1820s. The brutality which was always near the surface in this province was best exemplified by the fate of the aborigines. Hunted down like animals for centuries, the Beothuk Indians were wiped from history. In 1829 at St. John's, Shanandithit, a Beothuk woman, died—the last of her race.

The most stable social group in British North America was the peasantry of Lower Canada—so stable as to be stagnant, English critics said. Travellers commented on the cheerfulness, honesty and sense of order of the rural French Canadians. Despite a flagging agricultural economy and the beginning of migrations from unproductive land (especially to unsettled portions of New Brunswick), this bucolic picture was still generally true in French Canada in the 1820s. The cities, Quebec with its strenuous, rowdy timber trade, Montreal with its industries, its spreading affluence, and its growing immigrant population, seemed far less tranquil. Quebec's timber coves required large gangs of brawny dockside labourers to load the great square timbers aboard ship. There were the throngs of shipyard workers, the seamen and the raftsmen "on the spree," after bringing their clumsy, massive cargoes down river. Montreal was a lively, if materially minded centre, as was testified to by a Scots traveller, John Duncan, who visited that city just before the twenties began:

> If you enjoy good eating, card playing, dancing, music, and gayety, you will find abundance of all. If literary society is your choice, you will discover I am afraid but little; and if religious, still less. I was particularly struck with the extent to which card-playing and the dice-box abound; they seem indeed to be almost the only resource in an evening party, if it is not professedly a dancing one.

The literature of the city may be estimated by the fact, that there is at present but one book shop in it, whose collection of English authors has even moderate claims to respectability; a few others are to be found with Romish prayer books, and monkish legends, but their shelves can boast of little else except a few articles of stationery. . . . And of the British residents the greater part are eagerly intent upon the acquisition of wealth, and in general anticipate a return to their native country to spend it; and if in their hours of intermission from other pursuits, they can glance at a novel, or a fashionable poem, it is all that in most cases is attempted.

Despite the disturbing presence of Quebec and Montreal, the social conservatism of the *Canadiens* gave a somewhat settled character to the Lower Canadian community at large. Upper Canada, in contrast, was a chaotic melting pot. A place like Loyalist Kingston seemed civilized and structured in the traditional class system of Britain. Yet Kingston was overrun with taverns where the endemic frontier vice of drunkenness was indulged, with its inevitable socially disruptive results. In the absence of established police forces, the weak authority of the magistrates was challenged in many communities. Colonel Thomas Talbot, overlord of a vast tract of land in the western part of the province, was unable to restrain disorderly conduct among his Highland Scots settlers. In the Ottawa valley timberers and labourers on the Rideau Canal endangered the very bonds of society with their rioting. A petition from the inhabitants of Bytown, on the Ottawa, to Lieutenant-Governor Maitland in 1828, summed up the problems of many areas. Complaining about the absence of magistrates and police, they pointed out the need for authority: the canal works, they said, "had drawn together a numerous population of a mixed description; and from their heterogeneous nature, frequent differences arise which require the interference of legal authority. . . ." In the absence of such authority, or at least its absence in effective power, people tended to take a very loose and relative view of the law. That same year at York the populace expressed its displeasure at attempts to enforce laws which had long been ignored. When one Emmanuel Burgess turned informer, giving the magistrates evidence of violations of the liquor licensing laws, he was beaten with a stick on the street outside the courthouse, before a large cheering crowd.

III

Disorder was a sign not only of inadequate authority, but of growth as well. It was one price of rapid development. That it was not more widespread or more serious in its implications was due in part to the leadership of small semi-aristocratic groups who filled the vacuum left by the absence of established institutions. In many localities, merchants and landed gentlemen used their prestige and their talents to maintain the basic services—local government, the magistracy, churches, and charitable institutions—of their communities. Their counterparts at the provincial level were the oligarchies which flourished during this decade in most of the colonies.

Perhaps the most unsuccessful, at least in terms of retaining the support and trust of the population, was the loose grouping of government officers, merchants and French-Canadian seigneurs at Quebec, the dominant côterie often termed the "Chateau Clique" from its supposed clustering around the governor's residence, the Chateau St. Louis, from where all favours were presumed to flow. In any case, this group, entrenched in the appointed Executive and Legislative Councils, was regularly opposed by the popularly elected Assembly. The first two elements were separated from the French-speaking majority of the people by language, customs and outlook; the latter, by moving away from their estates to the capital and by associating themselves with the development plans of the English government, weakened their links with the *Canadien* population. At a time when the government under the active but insensitive leadership of the Earl of Dalhousie, governor general between 1820 and 1828, seemed determined to offend French-Canadian sensibilities with its development programs, it was virtually impossible for the seigneurial elite to keep the favour of both the executive and the people.

Far more successful was the so-called Family Compact of Upper Canada. Its functioning core was the small group of officials who dominated the Executive and Legislative Councils at York. While Sir Peregrine Maitland was lieutenant-governor, from 1818 to 1828, the Compact operated within a genial environment. They shared with him tory values, hostility toward the United States, and a sense of earnest dedication to the job of government. Until Maitland's successor, Sir John Colborne, began to shake them from their hold on the administration, John Strachan and John Beverley Robinson were dominant figures. Strachan, Anglican archdeacon of York, and Robinson, attorney-general and member of the Assembly for York until 1829, attempted to impose on the province their conception of a British society, a class-conscious society. The upper classes would pay for the deference and offices they received by a serious attention to the good of the province. The bargain was kept through most of this decade. The Compact received both deference and office—by the public will, they liked to think—and their tory allies maintained at least an equality with the opposition in the Assembly, except for the session of 1828-30. In return, the oligarchs provided dedicated, competent and honest government. Although of the inner group only William Allan, president of the Bank of Upper Canada, was a businessman, they supported the business community's development schemes. The Welland Canal was the prime example. Once the Compact had become convinced of the value of the project, they not only threw the weight of government behind it, but many personally invested. Without the need to satisfy a retrenchment-minded electorate, the elite could afford to gamble on grandiose projects in the interest of the general good of the province.

Their conversion on the Welland Canal scheme emphasized the anti-Americanism which was a major element in their ideology. Most of the Compact leaders had played significant roles in the defence of the province during the War of 1812, an experience which heightened their hostility toward the United States. This animosity had positive results, when it led them to support development projects to strengthen the province. It also had negative aspects. They developed a "garrison mentality," seeing themselves as the sole repositories of loyalty, suspecting all opponents of traitorous pro-Americanism. They were led, as well, to place undue emphasis upon those things which seemed to distinguish Upper Canada from the United States. Chief among them was the Anglican Church. More than a religious body, the Church was seen by Strachan and his colleagues as a bulwark of the British constitution in Canada, and as a device for inculcating loyalty in the population. Despite continued opposition to such symbols of Anglican pretensions as the clergy reserves—opposition even among more moderate tories—the government persisted in its attempts to strengthen the Church. One of the most unpopular expressions of this determination was in educational policy. At York a common school had been established by public subscription. In 1820 the government took over the common school for the establishment of a Lancastrian school, to be operated on Anglican principles under the watchful eye of the provincial administration. Maitland saw this Upper Canada Central School as the training centre for a corps of ultra-loyal teachers who would fight republicanism in the schools of the province. Because of poor administration and the rigidity of its Anglican teaching, the school was a failure, and the government's arbitrary expropriation of a publicly-supported institution won it considerable hostility. Nor did King's College, the elite university chartered in 1827, win wide support. Even Governor Colborne thought this Anglican college was unrealistic, and blocked its opening. The government satisfied itself by establishing an almost equally elitist secondary school, Upper Canada College, in 1829, a school staffed by Anglican divines from Britain. It too was a source of controversy and bitter criticism from the non-Anglican majority in the province. Tying the reputation of the Compact so closely to that of a pretentious minority church could only weaken the oligarchy in the long run.

The Family Compact combined in its membership Loyalists, like Robinson and George Markland, and immigrants who had come from Britain before 1812—for example John Strachan and the Boulton family. A similar blend was to be found in the oligarchy at Halifax, a typical combination of government officials, members of the learned professions and leading businessmen. A more sophisticated character was added to the Halifax gentry, however, by the military and its aristocratic outlook. According to McGregor, Halifax's upper class had "more refinements, more elegance and fashion, than is to be met with probably in any town in America." In part this was because it was an older aristocracy, holding its position long enough to pass both social outlooks and offices on from generation to

generation. Its characteristic family was the Uniackes, at full aristocratic blooming in the 1820s. An Irish-born lawyer, R. J. Uniacke
was the chief law officer of Nova Scotia for thirty-three years,
evolving from a rebellious Irish youth to a dignified aristocratic old
age. One son, Norman, after studying law in England, became
attorney-general of Lower Canada until he accepted a judgeship
at Montreal in 1825. Another, Crofton, was a judge of the Vice-
Admiralty Court. A third, James Boyle, became tory leader in the
Nova Scotia Assembly. Richard John Uniacke, Jr., in 1820 was
elected to the Assembly for Cape Breton. This undoubtedly con-
soled him somewhat for the unpleasantness he had just lived
through. On July 21, 1819, he had killed a young Halifax merchant,
William Bowie, in a duel. Brought to trial he faced the court surrounded by his distinguished family—Judge Crofton, Attorney-
General Norman, his grieving father—and successfully defended
himself by explaining that Bowie had impugned his honour. Honour
was all; Richard Uniacke was acquitted. His name more than
compensated for his temporary notoriety in the Cape Breton election of 1820 which soon followed, the first in a series of victories at
the polls for the young aristocrat.

More so than the Family Compact, the Nova Scotian elite was
a commercial oligarchy. The leading figure of the business group
was Enos Collins. From a New England merchant family, Collins
built a successful business in shipping, but he made his fortune
during the War of 1812 in privateering, a respectable and patriotic
profession in Nova Scotia. His wealth and his extremely conservative instincts made him a useful ally for the government; in 1822
he was appointed to the Council of Twelve, the ruling body of the
province, where he was the major voice for the business community
and organizer of the Halifax Banking Company, popularly known
as "Collins' Bank." He cemented his membership in the aristocracy
by marrying the daughter of Halifax's leading social figure, Judge
Brenton Halliburton. The urge to enjoy the prestige of the English
country gentry was strong even among urban commercial men like
Collins. His wealth secure, the Honourable Enos built a fine home
outside Halifax, Gorsebrook, and there enjoyed the dignity of a
gentleman farmer.

Around the Council of Twelve gathered a group of political allies, mostly lawyers and merchants. The lawyers dominated the Assembly throughout the 1820s and rarely opposed the Council. This was entirely natural, for most lawyers had been educated at the oligarchy's pet institution, the tory-Anglican King's College, and had articled under the Loyalist established lawyers. There was an additional motivation supplied by the Council's patronage power. Of the fifteen lawyers who served in the Assembly between 1812 and 1830, thirteen received judicial or other appointments from the government.

Nevertheless an opposition movement was stirring in Nova Scotia. The major issues were the same as they were elsewhere in British North America: the right of the Assembly to control public revenues, and discrimination against non-Anglicans. The two issues coalesced in the extended struggle over the privileges of Pictou Academy. Founded by Thomas McCulloch to train Presbyterian ministers and to educate those not served by the Anglican King's College, the Academy became a political storm centre. It was attacked by King's, by the new Dalhousie College at Halifax which feared a rival for government support, by tories who suspected McCulloch's liberal views and by Church of Scotland supporters who opposed McCulloch's radical "Antiburgher" form of Presbyterianism. The controversy became provincial in scope when, in 1823, the Council rejected a bill passed by the Assembly granting Pictou Academy a permanent government endowment. The fight over the endowment, and over government attempts to restrict the school's policy of accepting students and staff of all religions, became an annual affair in the legislature for the rest of the decade. The defence of the Academy, and the resultant resentment against Anglican privileges, sparked the beginnings of a reform movement. With the founding of the *Colonial Patriot* at Pictou in 1827 by Jotham Blanchard, a former pupil of McCulloch, the opposition had an articulate organ of dissent. Joseph Howe would admit that he had been converted to reform by the "Pictou scribblers." In 1830 opposition members won a majority of seats in the Assembly, largely on the education issue. It was a disorganized, non-party opposition, with typical Nova Scotian moderation. But a tradition of dissent had been established, to be exploited in the future by effective leaders.

Dissent was heard in Newfoundland and New Brunswick, as well, but in rather different forms. The fight in Newfoundland was at a more primitive level. The dissenters, led by the Scots surgeon William Carson and the Irish merchant Patrick Morris, were struggling to gain the representative assembly enjoyed by the other colonies for decades. The religious issue was present, in the violent hatred between Protestant and Catholic. Although some progressive Protestants, such as the St. John's merchant Benjamin Bowring, followed Morris, the political spectrum was divided religiously, Catholics being liberals, Protestants conservatives. New Brunswick in its usual eccentric fashion, added some new elements to the political cacophony of British North America. The issue there, naturally enough, was control over the crown lands, and therefore of the vast forest reserves on those lands. A series of administrators sent out from Britain attempted to maintain a government hold on the lands and to raise large revenues from them. Thomas Baillie, who became surveyor general in 1824, was especially fervent in his drive to make the forests pay. This provoked great cries of outrage from timberers and from members of the Assembly. What made the situation unusual was that it was the gentry of Fredericton and Saint John who led the opposition. It was a curious picture, these tory gentlemen attacking imperial officials. In part their actions may be explained as a defence of what they saw as the legitimate interests of the province; in part they sprang from the personal investments of the elite threatened by the forest policy; and in part it was an issue of power, for officials like Baillie threatened to usurp the effective power in the province from the gentry. To protect themselves and their monopoly on government, the oligarchy would fight Baillie for a decade, in the process expressing the popular opposition to any restraints on the timber trade.

Political opposition was not new in Lower Canada. In the 1820s the old struggles—government against Assembly, merchant against agrarian, English against French—were personalized in the characters of Governor General Dalhousie and the Assembly's speaker, Louis-Joseph Papineau. Dalhousie had been a very successful governor in Nova Scotia, where his Scottishness and his strong belief in the royal prerogative had satisfied an imperialist and conservative people. The same approach was disastrous in Lower Canada where Dalhousie's evident anti-Catholicism and his arbitrary views on government would bring him into conflict with the leaders of the Assembly. Papineau was the leader of an Assembly majority dominated by professional men, a majority increasingly hostile to a merchant-controlled oligarchy. Their hostility sprang both from their conviction that the oligarchy was pursuing policies inimical to the interests of agrarian French Canada, and from their personal frustration—frustration that their Frenchness barred them from the upper reaches of office and power. Their major tactic both to influence government policy and to win at least patronage power for themselves was to gain control over the public revenues. This Dalhousie, jealous of the royal prerogative, would never agree to. Indeed Dalhousie went far beyond opposing the Assembly's demands for power over the public purse. He made little attempt to maintain a good relationship with Papineau, admittedly a difficult task given Papineau's hot temper and often arrogant manner. Perhaps his major purpose in dissolving the Assembly in 1827 and calling an election was to oust Papineau as speaker; when the new Assembly immediately re-elected Papineau as its leader, the furious governor prorogued the obstinate Parliament.

Dalhousie's support of the union bill of 1822 demonstrated both his alienation from the people and his lack of understanding of them. This measure introduced into the British House of Commons would have joined Upper and Lower Canada in a union dominated by the English, governed by a parliament whose proceedings would be in English, a parliament elected under a franchise so high it would exclude most French Canadians. The violent opposition of the *Canadiens* and Papineau's mission to Britain finished the idea of union. In the process the British government's good sense won for it the trust of French-Canadian political leaders. A myth developed that the troubles of Lower Canada sprang from arbitrary governors and the executive cabals around them, who misled the good-hearted British authorities about Canadian conditions. This myth would help calm politics when the hated Dalhousie was removed in 1828, and replaced by a more genial figure, Sir James Kempt. It would not help when Britain dashed this faith in the decade ahead.

Upper Canada, too, had its tyrant, in the eyes of opposition members. Sir Peregrine Maitland, tory of tories, did much to aid the development of the province before he left in 1828. But he also involved himself in a series of unfortunate disputes which alienated significant portions of the community. Early in his administration he was associated with the persecution of Robert Gourlay, an incident which produced the first genuine opposition members, the "Gourlayites," elected to the Assembly in 1820. His government's association with the alien question produced a strong contingent of reformers in the succeeding election of 1824. The attempt to enforce the alien laws, which would have disfranchised American immigrants and denied them the right to hold land, threatened a large percentage of the population and was a major stimulus to the formation of a reform party. By 1826 the governor was inextricably associated with the Family Compact. When in June 1826 the young bucks of Compact families decided to punish the presumptuous opposition editor, William Lyon Mackenzie, of York's *Colonial Advocate*, by smashing his press, the reaction against this tory violence included Maitland; as indeed it might, for the governor's confidential clerk, John Lyons, was one of the hoodlums. It was only one of a series of apparent acts of tyranny in these years: the suspension of the pension of a reform politician, Captain John Matthews, for asking a visiting American orchestra in a York theatre to play "Yankee Doodle" during a performance on New Year's Eve, 1825; the firing of the king's printer, Charles Fothergill, for voting against the government in the Assembly; the use of soldiers to remove an offending private fence at Niagara Falls; the removal of the reformers' darling, Judge John Willis, for disrupting proceedings of the Court of King's Bench in 1828. There were large issues producing strong opposition, as well, issues like the Bank of Upper Canada, the clergy reserves, the power of the Assembly as against the Executive and Legislative Councils. And there were the local issues, roads and bridges, local power struggles, which so often determined the results of elections. Yet, at the provincial level, the significant matters were so often relatively petty clashes, the conflict of strong personalities like Maitland and Mackenzie. As John Strachan wrote in 1825, "In a colony such as ours opposition is commonly personal and bitter."

Strachan himself was all too often at the centre of such disputes. His attacks on the Methodists, begun in his sermon on the death of Bishop Mountain of Quebec in 1825, enflamed the religious animosities in Upper Canada and created an unnatural alliance between the reformers and the Methodist Church. Egerton Ryerson, the young Methodist leader and editor of the church paper, the *Christian Guardian*, was a naturally conservative man, who nevertheless led his denomination into the opposition camp to fight Anglican pretensions and to counter Strachan's attacks. Although the reformers were effectively led in this period by the moderate Marshall Spring Bidwell and William Warren Baldwin, the tone of opposition politics was set by Mackenzie.

Editor of the most popular newspaper in the province, noisiest member of the Assembly after 1828, Mackenzie's violent rhetoric and his powerful sense of injustice served to polarize the political scene. As member of the Assembly for York County, Mackenzie broadened out the appeal of the reform group. Respectable and cautious, the reform leaders expressed the viewpoint of a professional middle class, disturbed by misgovernment and anxious to share in power, but essentially content with the basic institutions of society, Mackenzie, the product of Scottish poverty, was not content. His appeal was to the "honest yeomen" he saw as the backbone of Canadian society. For them the governmental system, the educational system, the economic system, must be changed to break the hold of oligarchs and merchant exploiters. Agriculture, he said, was "the most innocent, happy and important of all human pursuits," and the task before Upper Canada was to remove the restraints on it. At the end of the decade he was confident that with the support of Britain the necessary reforms would be accomplished. Britain's warm reception of the reformers, as with the delegation of 1827 which won resolution of the alien question, fostered the belief that the imperial authorities would, if they had adequate information, redress all grievances in the colonies. Like Papineau, the depth of Mackenzie's disappointment with Britain in the years ahead would spring in part from the unrealistic height of his euphoric faith at the end of the 1820s.

Many governors, such as Maitland and Dalhousie, were accused of being tyrants. Perhaps only Charles Douglas Smith, lieutenant-governor of Prince Edward Island from 1813 to 1824, actually fitted the description. By 1820 he had alienated most of the leading men in the colony by his arbitrary procedures, his filling of public offices with relatives and his cavalier treatment of the legislature. When the Assembly elected in 1820 was dismissed by the governor after a few weeks sitting, it was the fourth session to meet that fate under Smith, and the last—for he did not recall the house during the remainder of his term. The sins of the Assembly had been two-fold: they had demanded control over the burgeoning government expenditures; and they resented the governor's protection of his son and son-in-law, who had insulted and even physically attacked members of the legislature. With the Assembly prorogued in 1820, Smith ruled despotically. He appointed one son-in-law registrar of the province and another, J. E. Carmichael, provincial secretary, although it was Carmichael who had invaded and insulted the Assembly in 1818. The courts disregarded their own legal proce-dures, land was distributed to the governor's favourites, and there were well-founded suspicions about the honesty of the law offices.

In 1823 indignant meetings were held in the counties of Prince Edward Island to denounce the governor. For reporting these meetings the editor of the Charlottetown *Register*, J. D. Haszard, was called before the Chancery Court, with Smith presiding as chancellor. "I caution you," Smith thundered at Haszard, "when you publish anything again, keep clear, sir, of a Chancellor! Beware, sir, of a Chancellor." In October 1823, the organizers of the meet-ings were arrested. But John Stewart, a former speaker of the Assembly, escaped to England and there successfully put the province's case. Lieutenant-Colonel John Ready assumed the gov-ernorship in May 1824, and the tyranny of Charles Douglas Smith was at an end. Despite continued disputes between Assembly and Council over control of the revenues, public life in Prince Edward Island took on under Ready the same tranquillity as the landscape.

IV

Throughout the colonies political life was becoming agitated by disagreements over the direction of development, over the distribution of power, over schools, churches, forms of government, all the institutions of a maturing society. Yet while the problems of growing maturity were being struggled with in the settled colonies, there was still a frontier of hardship and adventure in British North America. It was found in the northwest where the fur companies merged into a greater Hudson's Bay Company in 1821 and pressed forward their exploitation of the prairies and the Pacific slope. While Upper and Lower Canada were engaged in arguments over canals and roads, the difficulties were more elemental at the Bay Company's struggling Red River colony. Grasshopper plagues, prairie fires, floods—these were the enemies for the colonists there in the 1820s.

The frontier of adventure, above all, was to be found in the north in this decade. Shifting polar ice after 1815 had opened up freer access to the Arctic waters, and renewed the romantic search for the northwest passage. Two men symbolized the spirit of adventure impelling this quest. One was John Franklin, a naval captain who made two overland treks to the polar sea in the 1820s. The first journey, commencing in 1819 and ending in 1822, saw Franklin and his expedition follow the Coppermine River to the Arctic Ocean, and from there explore the coastline east to Hood River. Forced to turn back by lack of provisions, their return to the Coppermine and the fur forts there was a nightmare of cold and starvation. One after another of the party died on the way, two of the Canadian *voyageurs* being killed and eaten by an Indian guide. Yet at the first opportunity Franklin was back in his Arctic torture-house. In the spring of 1825 he journeyed again to the polar sea, on the second of his epic adventures, adventures which would continue until his final disappearance into the Arctic in 1847.

The other great adventurer was William Edward Parry, like Franklin a naval officer. Parry tested himself against the north four times in the 1820s. Exploring the eastern Arctic by ship, Parry proved himself a man of outstanding ingenuity. His ice-locked vessels were turned into school houses for the crews, and the north's first newspaper, the *North Georgia Gazette and Winter Chronicle*, was published aboard the ship *Hecla* in 1820, all to combat the misery and boredom of the frozen winter. Parry's greatest triumph, in terms of fortitude if not of science, was his trek across the ice from Spitzbergen in 1827. Dragging two specially constructed boats for moving between floes, his party struggled north, subsisting on ten ounces of biscuit and nine ounces of pemmican a day for each man. Driven back by drifting ice at 82° 45′ north, they had come closer to the pole than any men before them. They remind us that this was still a very new world in British America; they remind us that political battles should not disguise the primitive which was yet so close in this infant Canada.

8: The 1830s

G. M. CRAIG

Canadians used to think of themselves as moderate, law-abiding, and cautious people; decent and tolerant enough, but devoted to the safe, middle ways of a safe, middle power. Whether or not they still accept this characterization, they might look again at an earlier day of vehemence, the 1830s: at the extravagant and ferocious political debate; at the bitterness and open contempt with which neighbours and fellow-colonists of another religion or language or national origin were regarded; at the regular recourse to violence and intimidation to settle differences, especially during elections; at the constant readiness to argue virulently about education and cultural development while concentrating almost all effective energy on the pursuit of material gain and political preferment (i.e., jobs); at the equal readiness to blame the outsider, preferably in another country or colony, for all existing

difficulties; and finally, at the two armed insurrections. This closer
look at their British North American forbears might possibly lead
Canadians today to ask themselves whether this heritage of turbulence, acrimony, and intolerance bordering on bigotry bears any
relationship to our own enlightened times.

I

The two Canadas, the most populous of the settled regions of British
North America, were also the most severely wracked by various
kinds of dissension; and they will have to occupy most of our
attention here. First, however, we should attempt a quick overview
of all the British possessions in North America, to include the "lower
provinces" by the Atlantic and the vast regions stretching north to
the Arctic and west to the Pacific where the Hudson's Bay Company
was striving to rule supreme.

Although priding itself on having both the oldest and the closest
ties with Britain of all these colonies, Newfoundland had only
recently ceased to have the legal status of a fishery, and it was not
until 1832 that it acquired representative institutions in the form
of a legislative assembly. At once, however, it began to exhibit most
of the traits of political and social discord and instability—in an
exaggerated form, to be sure—to be found in the mainland colonies.
A wide franchise was given to a population that had suffered
decades of neglect, was largely illiterate, had no political experience,
and was scattered (indeed, almost isolated) in scores upon scores of
coves and outports. The consequent insularity of outlook was greatly
sharpened by the religious antagonisms resulting from approximately equal numbers of Protestants and Roman Catholics. With
the appointed Council solidly in the hands of the Anglicans, who
looked after the interests of the Protestant merchant class, ambitious
Catholics sought, with considerable success, to control the elected
Assembly. Political contests were marked by campaigns of organized
intimidation in which the clergy, led by "an illiterate and vulgar
Roman Catholic Bishop" (in the governor's words) took an active
part. A notorious event was the cutting off of the ears of a newspaper editor who criticized clerical influence in politics, and in

many places Protestants stayed away from the polls to avoid being beaten up by the mob. In the Assembly itself each group relentlessly pursued its own interests, or sought vengeance against its opponents. Before the end of the decade it was widely felt that the experiment of representative government should be suspended, and early in the 1840s it was in fact considerably modified.

Nova Scotia, on the other hand, had had more than seventy years' experience of representative institutions, and at first glance seemed to be a stable and orderly, if rather complacent, provincial community. In 1830 Joseph Howe asserted that "a more contented and happy population is not be found within the wide circle of the British Dominions." But in almost the same breath he sharply attacked the appointed Council which was dominated by Halifax mercantile and financial interests, and which always conducted its business behind closed doors. In the developing contest with the Assembly, the Council was ready to bring the operations of government to a full stop to prevent the slightest interference with the economic activities of its members. Nor did the Assembly seek to operate on a much more exalted level of political and public responsibility. In the absence of disciplined political parties, its members were chosen in contests that were marked—again to quote Howe— by "murders . . . lawless mob dominion . . . gangs of ruffians . . . [and resort to] the most palpable frauds, the lowest and most humiliating tricks, to obtain votes. . . ." Once elected, the deepest concern of each member was to secure as much of the public revenue as possible to distribute to his constituents.

It was not easy to rouse Nova Scotians from an unquestioning acceptance of the old ways. Howe tried it in his newspaper, and then in the Assembly, by urging the voters to turn away from their excessive concern with personalities and to develop a grasp of political principles. T. C. Haliburton tried humour and ridicule. According to Sam Slick, with the Bluenose it was "all talk and no work. . . . I guess if they'd talk more of *rotation*, and less of *elections,* more of them 'ere *dykes* and less of *banks*, and attend to *top* dressing, and less to redressing, it'd be better for 'em." More important still, they should "make a railroad from Windsor to Halifax."

Across the Bay of Fundy, the people of New Brunswick thought of only one topic—timber. After nearly three decades of prosperity their discontents were few, and the only cloud on the horizon was the possibility that the mother country might be so faithless as to reduce the preference. There was general satisfaction with the status quo. In particular the Assembly was happy with a system that gave it substantial control over revenues and which permitted each member to supervise the disbursement of his share of the revenue to his own constituency. Electoral contests revolved around personalities and around the clashes of rival lumbering firms. Sometimes they became pitched battles between rival gangs of hundreds of lumberjacks hurling stones and pieces of coal or even firing scrap iron from cannon until the troops were called out to restore order. New Brunswick, in the words of its historian, was "a democracy, direct and unrefined in character," firmly under the control of the descendants of the Loyalists who looked with a mixture of "compassion and contempt" upon the thousands of immigrants pouring into the province.

Political divisions were not based on liberal and tory principles but reflected the clash of interests of Saint John merchants, strong in the Assembly, and the "official party" based on Fredericton. The strongest asset of the latter was the Commissioner of Crown Lands, Thomas Baillie, who was determined to get a sufficient revenue from the forests to make the executive independent of the Assembly. But in the end the Assembly gained control of the crown lands, and New Brunswick, a frontier democracy in which the lumber barons had full scope for their activities, resumed its cheerful course.

In the Gulf little Prince Edward Island was still engaged in the tight and bitter class war of the tenants and the proprietors. The former sought to use their numbers to intimidate and terrorize the latter, and had some success in the sense that after elections marked by frequent violence the Escheat Party gained control of the Assembly. But the landlords still had strong support in London, and they remained in firm command of their estates at the end of the decade.

Turning for a brief look at the Canadas (before examining them in more detail), we find many of the same tendencies noticed in the Atlantic provinces.

On the political level, there was the same disorder at election time. The polls sometimes were kept open for more than three weeks while partisans, spurred on by unlimited amounts of free liquor, used every trick they knew and every element of force they had to overawe their opponents and prevent them from voting. To a limited extent, the 1837 insurrection in Lower Canada was, in its origins, a culmination of the electoral clashes that had disfigured the Montreal area for several years. In that province, also, crown officers regularly interfered in elections, helping to establish a tradition of corruption that lasted long after these years; in the upper province, similar efforts were most noticeable in the campaign of 1836. In the Canadas there was also the same conflict between the elected and the appointed branches of the legislatures, each representing distinct economic and class interests. In each of these provinces, too, the executive was "irresponsible"; that is, it was immune to pressures emanating from the elected Assembly and relatively free to distribute patronage without regard to the Assembly's views. As in the Atlantic provinces, the members of the Canadian assemblies sought every possible means of securing funds and jobs to disburse to their constituents. Another feature of the system, usually obscured, was that the executive authorities were administratively incompetent and generally inefficient and incapable of coping with provincial problems.

On the imperial level, the 1830s opened with repeated assurances from the British government that it was anxious to give the colonies the largest possible control over their own internal affairs. "Reform" and "change" appeared to be the watchwords, as the movement for parliamentary reform gathered strength in England and the cause of liberal nationalism won victories on the continent. But the promise of reform added little to provincial peace and contentment. Tories saw it as a craven surrender by weak-kneed British ministers, which would leave faithful subjects at the mercy of disloyal demagogues and open the way for the engulfment of the provinces by the rapacious Americans. Reformers and radicals soon doubted the sincerity of the British offers, especially since they were not accompanied by a willingness to agree to any basic changes in provincial constitutions. Not only that, but Downing Street, or at least many influential permanent officials in the Colonial Office, kept right on intervening in the internal affairs of the provinces. Well-meaning colonial secretaries, often in office for only a few months, tried earnestly to keep up with what was happening across the Atlantic, but were rarely successful.

On the economic level, the most unsettling factor was the headlong boom evident in the first half-dozen years of the 1830s in the nearby American states. The Montreal merchants, and their allies at other points on the St. Lawrence navigation system, were goaded to new heights of furious indignation and helpless frustration as they tried desperately and unsuccessfully to compete with their rivals in New York state. The reaction of the upper province was to enter so enthusiastically into the internal improvements craze that it came within an ace of bankrupting itself. On the whole, the economic growth of all the provinces was satisfactory and in some ways even striking in these years. Yet it never seemed enough to those colonists who were dazzled by the "go ahead" Americans. There was a sense of satisfaction for many when the American boom collapsed in the Panic of 1837.

Only a few aspects of the social scene in the Canadas can be touched on here. Of all coherent population groups, the French Canadians were of course the largest. When Alexis de Tocqueville travelled among them in 1831 he found them to be gay, lively, still very French in their manners, but also unenterprising, uneducated, and naively committing "all their hopes . . . [to] their representatives." His delight at finding a large French community in North America somewhat blinded him to the many dangers in its archaic social structure in the bustling world of the 1830s. He did, however, find many indications that French Canadians were "a conquered people." In particular, almost all commercial undertakings were in English hands, and those French Canadians who were educated were beginning "to feel their secondary position acutely." The "peasantry" seemed comfortable enough, but if Tocqueville had seen more of the farming area around Montreal he might have sensed something of the crisis that was developing there. He did note the "jealousy" with which the French-speaking population regarded "the daily arrival of newcomers from Europe. They feel that they will end up by being absorbed." As yet, however, "the English and the French merge so little that the latter exclusively keep the name of *Canadiens*, the others continuing to call themselves English."

The "others" were being prodigiously reinforced, mainly from England but also from Ireland and Scotland. The early and middle years of this decade saw the largest immigration yet to enter British North America, about four-fifths of it destined for Upper Canada. (Much of it that reached the Canadas kept right on going, until it reached the United States, although alternatively, another stream came into the Canadas via New York.) One of the heaviest influxes occurred in 1832, and in that summer also arrived the cholera epidemic, killing about one-twelfth of the immigrants as well as many of the existing residents, forcing the beginning of Canadian public health legislation and regulation, and in general (it returned in 1834) unleashing the greatest social calamity the provinces had ever seen. French Canadians, already suspicious of immigrants as Tocqueville had noted, were infuriated by what many of them took to be a deliberate campaign to destroy them by exporting disease into their midst. Their reaction is perhaps symbolized by the report (Quebec *Gazette*, July 4, 1832) of crowds turning out with weapons on the shores of Lake Champlain and threatening to fire on the steamboats unless they turned back.

Upper Canada, on the other hand, although also appalled by the plague, never wavered in its eagerness to receive all the immigrants who would come. Foremost in his enthusiasm was the lieutenant-governor, Sir John Colborne, who laboured unceasingly to ease the way of the newcomers. It was the last chance to make Upper Canada "a really British Colony." The province had been allowed "to fall into the hands of foreigners" (that is, the American settlers), but now their influence might be counteracted by the flow from the mother country, particularly of "half pay Officers and respectable families." As the writings of Susanna Moodie, her sister Catharine Parr Traill, and many other "respectable" British settlers reveal, the adjustment was not an easy one, for the tone of society in Upper Canada long remained deplorably "Yankee" in many respects.

One final feature of provincial life may help to make political and social developments more explicable. In the 1830s British North Americans entered fully upon the newspaper era and became passionately, at times almost exclusively, addicted to this form of reading. Many of the journals were ably conducted, contained long columns of useful and enlightening information, and played essential roles in communities that were rapidly growing more complex. But nearly all were intensely, even virulently, partisan—to a degree that would seem incredible in these days when plain speaking is at a discount. It was widely believed that the rather coarse level of society and public discussion, the recurrent agitation and violence, were to a great degree directly attributable to the newspapers. The *Christian Guardian* (of York, which in 1834 was incorporated as the city of Toronto), despite its name did not spend all its time turning the other cheek. It blamed the "disordered state of society in this Province [on] a malicious spirit engendered chiefly by means of an abusive, slanderous and inflammatory press." On another occasion the shooting in a Montreal by-election was blamed on newspapers that had encouraged violence by resorting to "direct falsehoods," "mean insinuations" and other irresponsible tactics. But the papers were avidly followed, passed around, and read aloud to the illiterate and semi-literate whose numbers were large in every province, especially Lower Canada. In 1837 Anna Jameson remarked that the commercial news-room in Toronto was "absolutely the only place of assembly or amusement, except the taverns and low drinking-houses"—of which there was an abundant supply. Thus, as another observer put it, the minds of the people were "kept in a perpetual state of feverish excitement. . . . Everyone is reading, inquiring, talking, and disputing about politics [which produced] strange effects" on "uncultivated, haughty and independent minds." Sam Slick thought they would be better off minding their own business instead of everybody else's.

Such, then, were some of the characteristics of these colonies in the 1830s. Their total area of settlement was only a fraction of that of the later Canadian confederation. Stretching thousands of miles to the north and to the west lay the domains of the Hudson's Bay Company with which the colonists and the *Canadiens* had little contact in this decade. But the role of the Company deserves a brief mention before we turn to the troubled history of the Canadas, for its successes and failures would help to determine the outlines of the later confederation.

Like the St. Lawrence merchants to the east, the Company struggled constantly against the aggressive competition of American traders and against the threatening advance of the American settlement frontier. In the border regions west of Lake Superior, stretching to Red River and beyond, the Company held its own in these years. An agreement with the American Fur Company, which lasted to the end of the decade, successfully protected the monopoly north of the 49th parallel.

Farther west, however, the situation was much more critical. To be sure, an accord reached with the Russians maintained the Company's monopoly of the north Pacific coastal trade. But in the lower Columbia valley it was another matter. Before the end of the 1830s the first few scores of American settlers had reached the Willamette, and the Company failed in all its efforts to counter this potential threat. The shadow of the impending retreat north of the 49th parallel was beginning to lengthen.

II

In Lower Canada at the beginning of the decade, there was a promise—false, as it turned out—of a new era of political harmony. The arduous efforts of Sir James Kempt had done much to pacify the discordant parties, and there was hope that his successor, Lord Aylmer, who reached Quebec in October 1830, would continue this good work. Progress was made in implementing the recommendations of the British House of Commons Committee of 1828, particularly those regarding the enlargement of the Legislative Council. Moderates became more influential in the upper chamber, which for about two years cooperated reasonably well with the Assembly, itself now considerably expanded to include both English-speaking members from the townships and additional representation for the rapidly growing French-Canadian population. The British government appeared willing, even anxious, to concede the principle of full control of internal affairs to the local legislature, and took an important concrete step in 1831 by surrendering to the two Canadian legislatures the right to appropriate the customs duties raised under the Quebec Revenue Act of 1774. With the home government's recognition that control of the revenue should reside in the representative assembly the attainment of full colonial self-government seemed to be plainly in sight.

Yet, despite these appearances, affairs in Lower Canada soon reached an impasse far worse than that of the Dalhousie years, with many factors contributing to the deterioration.

The British government must share some of the blame. The appointment of Lord Aylmer, another Wellingtonian general without political intelligence, suggested how superficially the problems of Lower Canada were understood in London. Moreover, the proclaimed readiness to march cheerfully towards colonial self-government was not in fact shared by many of the strategically placed permanent officials in the Colonial Office. The frequent changes of government and personnel in the 1830s, added to the normal delays of the period, in any case made a coherent policy impossible. Besides, there was an insuperable internal contradiction: Lower Canada was to be conceded control of its internal affairs, but only if the rights and interests of the English minority were adequately protected. This reservation, which was frankly avowed only as the crisis developed, made British talk of colonial self-government sound like the worst kind of hypocrisy to a growing number of French Canadians.

The English minority also played their part in bringing about the breakdown. Many of them were flexible and moderate, ready for an evolution of the political system that would give much greater power to the French-Canadian majority in the province. But the loudest and most influential English voices in Lower Canada were as intransigent as ever. They bitterly denounced the British government for truckling to the French Canadians. They contemptuously dismissed the French Canadians as ignorant, illiterate and backward, and demanded that their absurd laws and institutions be tossed onto the rubbish heap to make way for more up-to-date replacements. They held on tenaciously to most of the best political jobs, and increasingly insisted that the resources of the province be put at their disposal to further their business enterprises. They openly called for measures, *any* measures, that would overwhelm the French Canadians.

Among the *Canadiens* a combination of a new awareness, new fears and new problems were having an increasingly disturbing effect. In this dawning era of national movements they had a new consciousness of themselves as a people, as a collectivity, with their own language and institutions and an identity to maintain. But at the very time that they were acquiring this new consciousness their collective life seemed to be threatened as never before. There was the influx of immigrants, who were taking up land that would be needed by the next generations of French Canadians. Legislation passed in England (notably the Tenures Act of 1826) was aimed at weakening the land system they knew and at bringing in new laws they did not understand. Furthermore, there was incorporated (also in England) a land company to which was surrendered vast quantities of land for speculative purposes. All this was happening just when the pressure of rural over-population in the regions around Montreal was being felt, when agricultural prices were falling, and when the wheat-fly epidemic was playing havoc with the major crop. It became increasingly feasible to convince the habitant that the English capitalist was the cause of all his trouble.

To the English the French Canadians seemed to be a monolithic bloc, but this was far from being the case. The clergy, close to the people and sharing their nationalist aspirations, were nevertheless increasingly opposed to the Papineau faction, especially after this group had sponsored the *loi des fabriques* aimed at weakening the control of the clergy over church property by letting parishioners attend and vote at meetings of the local church councils (vestries or *fabriques*). The Assembly leaders were splitting up into moderates and radicals. After the cholera epidemic of 1832 and the Montreal West Ward election of the same year, when British troops fired on the populace and killed three *Canadiens*, the moderates weakened and almost disappeared.

As for the radicals, led first by Bourdages and then by Papineau, they moved from their earlier focus on English constitutional principles and practice to a more abstract natural rights framework of ideas which drew much from both the French and the American revolutionary and republican traditions. This new outlook made them impatient of compromises and of piecemeal adjustments and prepared them for a frontal attack on the constitutional system of 1791. Of immediate importance, from a practical point of view, the new mood of the radicals made them adamantly opposed to the acceptance of office by any of their number. This stand was greatly reinforced by the temperamental inflexibility of Papineau, who understood systematic resistance but not gradual accommodation. From now on, *Canadiens* who did accept office were attacked and destroyed politically. The chasm between the administration and the opposition widened.

Despite their new rhetoric, the radicals associated with Papineau were not in fact very radical, for they were also nationalists. The seigneurial system, the old French laws, the ancient customs—all of the framework of a traditional agricultural society—must be preserved and defended against alien forces from the outside world. Although deeply anti-clerical, Papineau also favoured retaining the pervasive influence of the Church, as a necessary part of the social cement. On the other hand not all of Papineau's associates followed him in this conservatism. Some of them wanted deep-running changes in the structure of French-Canadian society. Thus the radicals were divided among themselves.

These positions set the stage for the political battle of the 1830s, and that battle reached a first climax with the famous 92 Resolutions, adopted (56 to 24) by the Assembly in February 1834. In this sustained assault by verbal violence the Legislative Council was denounced as "the most active principle of evil and discontent in this Province" and as "the servile tool of the authority which creates, composes and decomposes it." It must be made elective in order to conform "to the wishes, manners and social state of the Inhabitants of this Continent." Of particular significance was number 75, stating that out of approximately 600,000 inhabitants of the province, "those of French origin are about 525,000, and those of British or other origin 75,000"; that the civil government establishment of 1832 showed 157 posts held by people "apparently of British or Foreign origin"; and that the list contained the names of only 47 who were "apparently natives of the Country, of French origin." Towards the end the resolutions called for the impeachment of Lord Aylmer and of his "wicked and perverse Advisers." The Assembly followed up the Resolutions by refusing to vote supplies (for the second year in a row), and in the election later in the year Papineau's party nearly swept the boards.

In the new Assembly there was not a single merchant or spokesman of the mercantile interest and in some regions, notably the city of Quebec and environs, English-speaking representation had been wiped out entirely. Neilson's moderate Quebec *Gazette* observed that the one-fifth of the population "possessing at least one half of the property and capital in the country . . . having interests and connexions in the other British provinces on this Continent, which contain a population, in the whole, more numerous than that of French origin in Lower Canada have a right to know what they have to expect: whether they are to depend on the protection of their Sovereign, or solely on their own efforts."

Other English voices, notably in Montreal, were sharper and more threatening. An address *To Men of British or Irish Descent* (December 1834) from a committee headed by John Molson asserted that "the want of education among the French majority, and their consequent inability to form a correct judgment of the acts of their political leaders [has] engendered most of our grievances." It was ridiculous for "the leaders of the French party [to affect the] character of liberals and reformers, whilst they have sedulously fostered a system of feudal exactions and feudal servitude," and done everything possible "to inflict injury upon commerce." There was a hint, which would become more open in later statements, that if the English of Lower Canada were deserted by the mother country they would turn to their American neighbours (where "we recognize the lineaments of kindred blood and national character") rather than submit to "French oppression."

The response of the British government to this worsening situation was to appoint a Commission of Enquiry, headed by Lord Gosford, who also succeeded (in the summer of 1835) Lord Aylmer as governor. A mild-mannered civilian, Gosford was charged with a mission of "conciliation and the reconcilement of all past differences," and "admoni[shed] to secure the confidence of the House of Assembly, and to cultivate the good will of the Canadian People of all ranks and classes." The amiable Lord Gosford set out at once to act in the spirit of these instructions, and soon he was the object of bitter attacks from the "English party."

From the summer of 1835 this party was in fact bestirring itself as never before. "Constitutional Associations" in Montreal, Quebec, and elsewhere held frequent meetings and issued strongly worded addresses. Adam Thom's *Anti-Gallic Letters* illustrated the escalation of vituperation. Delegates were sent to England to try to bring the mother country to its senses and to get rid of Lord Gosford. A hint of more direct measures was contained in the formation of the British Rifle Club in Montreal. Disbanded by Gosford, it was reorganized as the Montreal British Legion early in 1836, but was dissolved soon afterward. The atmosphere remained "feverish with excitement, and those whose loyalty would under a proper Government have carried them thro' fire and water for their King and Country (as the *old* fashioned phrase was), now talk with a sort of savage satisfaction of a Union with the U. States—anything, say they, rather than the despotism of an ignorant cruel french faction" (an official, writing in May 1836).

But Gosford's honeymoon with the Assembly lasted only a few months. A full disclosure of his instructions revealed that the commission was not empowered to recommend basic changes in the constitution, such as an elective legislative council, and the *parti patriote* quickly insisted that the whole commission was founded on hypocrisy and bad faith. A session of the legislature in September 1836 lasted only twelve days, and another year had gone by without supplies being voted.

With its policy of conciliation collapsing, the British government now tried a different tack. Following the report of the Gosford Commission, which opposed the main demands of the Papineau party, Lord John Russell presented Ten Resolutions to Parliament at the beginning of March 1837, the eighth of which authorized the governor to take funds from the provincial treasury to defray the expenses of government without prior appropriation by the legislature. The imperial Parliament was being asked to use its supreme authority to break the impasse. Parliament quickly agreed.

From now on the situation rapidly deteriorated. The *Vindicator*, a leading newspaper of the *patriote* cause, announced (April 14, 1837) that

> the die is cast; the British ministry have resolved to set the seal of degradation and slavery on this Province, and to render it actually, what it was only in repute—the 'IRELAND' of NORTH AMER-ICA. . . . One duty alone now remains for the people of Lower Canada. Let them study the HISTORY of the AMERICAN REVOLUTION. . . . The monies which fill the coffers at Quebec and are about to be illegally disposed of by the British Parliament, are collected by duties on Brandy, Rum, Wines, Tobacco, Tea, and such like articles. The people must abstain from the consumption of these articles. Instead of drinking Brandy or Rum, let them drink home-made Whiskey, if they require such like stimulus, and encourage the smuggling of Tea, Tobacco, and other articles from the United States.

Before following the course of events leading to insurrection, we must consider developments in Upper Canada in these same years.

III

Like the other colonies, Upper Canada opened the 1830s on a fairly optimistic note. The recently appointed lieutenant-governor, Sir John Colborne, was generally better liked than Maitland had been, and seemed to be less in the toils of the oligarchy, the "Family Compact." Reformers were disappointed at losing control of the Assembly in the 1830 elections but they took heart at the coming to power of the Whigs in Great Britain. The *Colonial Advocate* called it "GLORIOUS NEWS!" to see "The Duke of Wellington and his old Tyrannical Tories put down in England! Now, we shall have good government assured to Upper Canada . . . and the base mercenary hirelings, who . . . have so long kept the Province in strife and confusion, will follow their arbitrary master into oblivion. The people will have their day." The Upper Canadian conservatives were pleased at their election victory. "Here at home," as one of them wrote, "things are assuming a more peaceable aspect

—the change in our Election has been a good one, & I trust Hon Members will set to work heart and hand for the good of the country, & shew the people who are their real well wishers." With the prospect of greater political harmony there could be renewed concentration on economic development as the province moved into an era of internal improvements, heavy immigration, and more diversified and complex institutions and activities.

To a very considerable extent these expectations were in fact realized. It is true that the din of partisan debate increased rather than slackened, and radicals and tories reached new heights of extravagant language. But Upper Canada escaped the complete impasse between executive and assembly that Lower Canada suffered from in these years, and moderates—men of the middle— were not driven out of politics nearly to the same extent. In the end, Upper Canada too had a rebellion but, as we shall see, one far less symptomatic of deep-seated disorder than the insurrection in the lower province.

To be sure, Upper Canada continued to have its grievances. A petition of 1831 mentioned the "exclusive privileges . . . extended by the Colonial Government to certain religious sects or denominations," the crown and clergy reserves, defects in the land-granting department, lack of control by the Assembly over all the revenue, the "monopoly" of the Bank of Upper Canada, judges and clergymen holding seats in the Executive and Legislative Councils, and many more. It was the quarrel in the Assembly over action on this petition that led Mackenzie to denounce the conservative majority as "sycophantic" and subservient to the executive, words (with many more like them) that started the train of events leading to his repeated expulsions. But in fact the conservative Assembly was not a subservient tool of the Family Compact. On many matters it took a distinctly independent position. Nor were its members always agreed; by playing one group off against another the reform minority under Bidwell was often able to get its own way. Government in Upper Canada was inefficient and essentially leaderless, but it was never dominated by the passion and intransigence developing in Lower Canada.

On one subject the conservatives were as firm as the reformers, in some ways even firmer: opposition to Colonial Office interference in the internal affairs of the province. It was, after all, Mackenzie who went to London in 1832 to badger Lord Goderich with his interminable memoranda, one consequence of which was the dismissal of the tory attorney-general and solicitor-general. And it was the tories who reacted by denouncing this "high handed and arbitrary" act of a "foolish Colonial Minister" and who threatened that this "insulting and degrading course of policy" would drive the loyal people "to 'cast about in their mind's eye' for some new state of political existence, which shall effectually put the Colony beyond the reach of injury and insult from any and every ignoramus whom the political lottery of the day may chance to elevate to the chair of the Colonial Office." Moreover, a few months later tories and more moderate conservatives joined with reformers in a nearly uanimous Assembly vote to denounce Colonial Office disallowance of two bank bills as an action that reduced Upper Canada "to a state of mere dependence upon the will and pleasure of a Ministry that are irresponsible to us, and beyond the reach and operation of the public opinion of the Province." Conservatives and reformers were generally agreed in asking for a larger measure of colonial self-government. Conservatives saw no reason for any change in the structure of government, while reformers were demanding an elective legislative council, or executive council responsible to the Assembly, or both.

Within this general framework the party battle continued furiously. A combination of superior political organization and growing resentment on such topics as church and state, land policy, poor educational facilities, and unrest among the farmers enabled the reformers to regain control of the Assembly in 1834. They returned to many of their favourite subjects—the clergy reserves, intestate estates, jury selection, vote by ballot, and several others—only to have many of their bills rejected by the Legislative Council. For his part Mackenzie, now back in the Assembly and chairman of a grievance committee, set out with frenzied energy to expose the evils under which he felt the province was groaning. The result was the famous Seventh Report on Grievances (1835), containing the voluminous evidence of many witnesses and a wide-ranging attack on the existing system of colonial government. Mackenzie succeeded in offending many members of his own party (particularly because of his attacks on the Methodists), but his report did hasten the end of Colborne's term. For some time colonial secretaries had unsuccessfully been trying to get more information from Colborne about the state of the province, and in 1835 Lord Glenelg was thunderstruck to receive this bulky book of grievances, apparently endorsed by the Assembly, after years of Colborne's laconic assurances that everything was calm and everyone contented in Upper Canada. If there were real grievances in Upper Canada, they must be immediately attended to, according to the same policy of conciliation that Lord Gosford was to apply in Lower Canada. Accordingly, to implement this policy, Colborne was replaced by Sir Francis Bond Head, who reached Toronto early in 1836.

Possessed of an adventurous disposition, a lively if rather shallow mind, and a very fluent pen, Sir Francis was exhilarated by the challenge of governing Upper Canada. After ten days in the province he concluded that "a good feeling pervaded a majority of the people . . . who [were] naturally desirous to be tranquil, and equally disposed to be loyal," but that it was being kept in a state of excitement by "party feeling . . . and struggle for office" and by "strong republican principles" that had "leaked into the country from the United States." The reform majority in the Assembly did not represent "the general feeling and interests of the inhabitants." This "implacable . . . republican party" would be satisfied by "no concession," and his course must be not "to conciliate any party."

To be sure, he did begin by enlarging the Executive Council to include two well-known reformers, Robert Baldwin and John Rolph, but he also made it clear that he would consult the Council only when he saw fit. Soon all of its members, old as well as new, resigned, and were replaced by men who were prepared to accept Head's conception of what their duties should be. The Assembly, which had already set up a select committee to investigate the resignations, now voted want of confidence in the new Executive Council, and its contest with the governor intensified when it became known that fifty-seven rectories had been designated as endowments for Anglican clergymen. As always in Upper Canada, political and religious controversies were inseparably linked. The committee's report castigated Head's "deceitful" conduct and characterized the secret endowment of "57 government parsons" as further proof that the province needed "a responsible Government." The Assembly went on to stop the supplies. Head retaliated by refusing to approve any money bills, and by dissolving the legislature. Early in May 1836, Upper Canada was plunged into a fateful election campaign lasting some two months.

This campaign revealed the striking difference in the politics of the two Canadas. In the lower province opposition leaders, enjoying the unwavering and continuing support of the majority of the French-Canadian voters, were able to maintain complete control of the Assembly as long as the 1791 constitution was in effect. But in Upper Canada, although many constituencies were also politically unchanging year after year, the political climate generally was much more volatile, and when conditions were right, supporters of the executive government and opponents of constitutional change could win control of the Assembly.

Conditions were opportune in 1836, and the reformers were routed. Many voters, influenced by the economic boom in the nearby American states, felt that the province was falling behind and wanted, as one petition put it, to direct attention "to the improvement of the land we live in, rather than to the consideration of abstract questions of Government" which might bring on "the dismemberment of this Colony from the Parent State, and the establishment therein of democratic institutions, uncongenial to the habits and sentiments of its British population." Such feelings were reinforced by suspicions that the reformers had close connections with the French-Canadian radicals; there was, for instance, Papineau's public letter to Mr. Speaker Bidwell asserting that "the state of society all over continental America requires that the forms of its Government should approximate nearer to that selected . . . by the wise statesmen of the neighbouring Union." Periodically Upper Canadians have felt a deep need to give themselves over to an orgy of anti-continentalism. In 1911 the slogan was "No truck nor trade with the Yankees"; in 1836 it was Sir Francis's rousing cry, "In the Name of every Regiment of Militia in Upper Canada I publicly promulgate—*Let them come if they dare!*" This appeal to British loyalty might itself have been enough to win the election, but the "constitutionalists," as the conservatives now called themselves, also relied heavily on the time-honoured techniques of Canadian elections. Riot, intimidation, bribery, corruption, biased returning officers and the careful selection of polling places all contributed to the result. Of particular importance, Orangemen and Catholics temporarily stopped clubbing each other in order to unite against reformers. Sir Francis had "contend[ed] on the soil of America with Democracy," and had won.

After this emotional binge the province fell back into some months of relative quiet. Many moderate reformers, notably Bidwell and Robert Baldwin, withdrew from politics entirely. The new Assembly, in which moderate "constitutionalists" as well as die-hard tories were prominent, pressed ahead with a good deal of useful legislation and was no longer in perpetual conflict with the Legislative Council. Particular attention was paid to the apparently popular demand for "improvement." Bills relating to canals, harbours, roads and railroads, and banks poured out of the legislative hopper so rapidly that the provincial debt began to spiral upward. When financial panic hit the western world at the end of 1836 Upper Canada was in a dangerously exposed position.

While the people of the province may have been disturbed and confounded by the economic crises, it never occurred to the overwhelming majority of them that an armed uprising would be any answer to their problems. But some of the radical reformers came out of the election and then into the panic in an increasingly angry frame of mind. They felt that fair elections were no longer possible, and therefore that government was carried on in defiance of the true public opinion. There was, they thought, no longer any point in appealing to a mother country which always came down, in the long run, in support of the Family Compact. They saw the wealth of the farmers being gambled away in mad speculation and banking frenzy. It seemed that the old settlers and their families, who had built up the province, were being thrust aside while most of the favours and openings and jobs went to newcomers, mainly from Britain.

Mackenzie, who started a new newspaper, *The Constitution* (*everybody* was for the constitution) on the interesting date of July 4, 1836, increasingly gave voice to these feelings. Another reformer, W. B. Wells, published a book in London early in 1837 warning that "the people" would rise if things went on unchanged. "*Arms and ammunition have long since been secured.* The days of 1776 are again to be renewed in 1837." But events in Upper Canada would depend heavily on what happened in the lower province.

IV

The years 1837-40 saw strenuous political debate in every British North American province set against a background of bad times, passionate controversy in the Canadas leading to armed clashes, harsh repression and prolonged border fighting, and finally, the first glimpses of the constructive political adjustments to come.

Throughout the period Lower Canada, the most populous and the most distracted province, was the focus of attention. The *patriotes* had been directly challenged by Lord John Russell's Ten Resolutions and in response their Permanent Central Committee organized a large public meeting early in May 1837, at Saint-Ours on the Richelieu River. The delegates adopted resolutions denouncing the "lying promises" of the "oppressive" British government, stating that Lower Canadians were now bound to it only by force and that their "true friends and natural allies were on the other side of the 45th parallel." The non-consumption of imported goods was endorsed, as was smuggling, and an association, reminiscent of the American Association of 1774, was projected to add coercion to endorsement. Similar resolutions were passed at many public meetings in the following months in the counties of the Montreal, Richelieu and, to a lesser extent, in other regions. Formally proclaimed as the national leader and propelled forward by men more radical than himself, Papineau was driven on to new flights of anti-British and pro-American rhetoric. On the one hand, he called for an extra-legal convention of delegates elected by the county meetings (a proposal bound to conjure up memories of the

French Revolution in English minds); on the other, he tried to convince his followers that there was no need to resort to force. But was the constant escalation of verbal violence consistent with a reliance on peaceful means?

The English party, joined by some French Canadians, mainly office-holders, answered in kind. The Montreal *Gazette* scornfully dismissed Russell's Ten Resolutions as "entirely inadequate [to end] the thraldom of a FRENCHIFIED revolutionary faction." It denied that there was any "chance of coming to an amicable arrangement" with this faction, and warned that "BRITISH Colonists" would easily prevail in any resort to force. "GREAT LOYAL" or "Constitutional" meetings were convoked, mainly in Montreal and Quebec, to denounce "Papineau and his faction," to warn Americans that they had nothing to gain by sympathizing with the *patriote* cause, and to "declare our determination to maintain the unity of the empire—to oppose all treasonable designs—to adhere firmly to our connection with the Parent State."

As summer moved to autumn the tension mounted. In *patriote* strongholds north and south of Montreal French Canadians were boycotting the English minority. Through a program of harassment (shaving the manes and tails of horses at night and conducting threatening charivaris) they were patently trying to drive the English away. Lord Gosford, still under constant attack for "conciliating" French Canadians, issued a proclamation against the Papineau meetings and later followed it with the dismissal from office of magistrates and militia officers who had attended. In reply, the *patriotes* made plans to conduct their own elections of such officials. Taken in conjunction with the call for a convention, this step suggested the construction of a parallel framework that would ignore the existing government. These developments were punctuated by an abortive session of the legislature in August, which lasted little more than a week. About this time the British government returned to a policy of conciliation, abandoning the plan to take money for government expenses from the provincial treasury without legislative grant and increasing the number of French-Canadian appointments. The change of policy was, however, probably too little and certainly too late.

In September and October there was increasing recourse to direct action. In much of the countryside north and south of Montreal the *patriotes* were in effective control. In Montreal itself, where the sides were evenly matched, the *Fils de la Liberté* and the Doric Club provoked each other with noisy parades. Towards the end of October Bishop Lartigue issued a *mandement* declaring that it was a Catholic's duty to obey the established government, but this document only infuriated the *patriotes*. They had no clear plan, as far as is known, for an uprising, although there apparently was a good deal of rather vague talk of actions to be taken when the river was frozen. On the whole, they were mainly seeking to bring about a disintegration of the existing authority. Still loyal to his policy of conciliation, Gosford was reluctant to react with military force.

A street fight on November 6 between the *Fils de la Liberté* and the Doric Club, resulting in broken heads and property damage, finally forced Gosford to accede to the demand that law and order be restored. The troops were called out, meetings were prohibited, and warrants were issued for the arrest of the *patriote* leaders. Their flight to the Richelieu stronghold of their cause led to armed clashes at Saint-Denis and Saint-Charles in that area, and to the subsequent use of regular and volunteer troops to overwhelm the *patriotes* at Saint-Eustache and elsewhere. As the English party had always claimed, in a trial by battle the *patriote* cause was at a hopeless disadvantage.

Meanwhile, in Upper Canada, Mackenzie had been following these events with the closest attention. In May his paper echoed the call for non-importation: "Buy, wear, and use as little as you possibly can of British manufactured goods or British West India merchandize or liquors." In July he was asking: "Can the Canadians Conquer?" and he gave the ringing answer: "Yes! with the exception of the fortress of Quebec, the Canadians, whenever they see fit to do it, can make the power of their Downing Street Tyrants vanish instantaneously." He alluded to officers coming from France, garrisons likely to desert, Americans ready to help. A few weeks later he and his associates issued a declaration paraphrasing the document of 1776, congratulating Papineau and urging "the Reformers of Upper Canada . . . to make common cause with their fellow citizens of Lower Canada." It called for a convention of delegates which would have authority "to appoint commissioners to meet others to be named on behalf of Lower Canada and any of the other colonies, armed with suitable powers as a Congress, to seek an effectual remedy for the grievances of the colonies." Mackenzie then spent most of August organizing public meetings north and east of Toronto and in some other parts of the province, asking the farmers to bring with them "good stout hickory sticks." A repeated theme was that if the French-Canadian *patriotes* were overwhelmed, the Upper Canada reformers would be next. In September Mackenzie tried to show that there was no need to worry about British power: "We are far from the Sea—for five months our shores are ice bound—the great republic is on one side of us; The Lower Canadians on another; Michigan and the wilderness, and the lakes are to the west and north of us. The whole physical power of the government, the mud garrison, redcoats and all, is not equal to that of the young men of one of our largest townships."

When Sir Francis sent the regular troops to Lower Canada at the end of October, Mackenzie was doubly certain that it was time to act. On November 15 he published a constitution for the State of Upper Canada essentially based on that of the United States. On the 29th he was arguing that when the demand for reform had been met by oppression, revolution became "a bible duty"; besides, there were "not now twelve soldiers in U. Canada" and the "reformers [were] as ten to one." By such language Mackenzie deluded himself and his followers and prepared the way for the abortive and botched attempt to take Toronto early in December.

Mackenzie's rebellion had some analogies with the Lower Canadian insurrection, though the contrasts were stronger. Each movement was directed more against the local oligarchy than against British authority, although widespread exasperation with the British was evident in 1837. A considerable number of respectable, established and middle-aged farmers, artisans and professional people in both Canadas were sufficiently disaffected to feel absolved from allegiance to the existing government; indeed, a considerable proportion of them believed that the state governments across the line were a desirable model to follow. In each province economic hardship, caused by the business depression, bad harvests and other factors, added to the atmosphere of instability and the willingness to contemplate violence.

But Mackenzie's uprising was at once more a deliberate act of rebellion and less a serious movement than its Lower Canadian counterpart. Mackenzie had a definite plan, however clumsy and unrealistic, to march on the capital, disperse those in office, and establish an elective democracy on the American pattern. The plan was unrealistic because it had only the slightest support; at the first word of the uprising, loyal men from every part of the province poured out to defend the government. In Lower Canada there was the same inefficient—indeed irresponsible—leadership, but it is less certain that there was a deliberate plan to move against the government. (In any event, that government was at Quebec and the *patriote* strength was in the Montreal area.) There was, however, deep and profound rural discontent among a significant proportion of the French Canadians which expressed itself in an unyielding determination to resist the English interloper's attacks (as they seemed to be) on their laws, their customs, their language, their religion and their land. The French Canadians were not adept at the use of force, but nevertheless it took considerable numbers of regular and volunteer troops, drawn in part from the Maritimes and Upper Canada, to put them down.

V

The sequel must be stated very briefly. In Lower Canada in 1838 the constitution was suspended and the French Canadians were again ruled as a conquered people by Sir John Colborne (in temporary authority as military commander-in-chief), while many in the English party called loudly for their utter destruction. In Upper Canada the tories were riding high; the reformers were on the defensive; and there was a sharp increase of anti-American feeling arising from cruel border outrages by raiders from the United States—sometimes moved by enthusiasm for the Mackenzie "patriot" cause, and sometimes by delusive hopes of power and plunder. Nova

Scotia and New Brunswick felt great upsurges of British loyalty at the news of rebellion in the disorderly Canadas. Anger at the Americans was also stimulated there by the long-persisting Maine–New Brunswick boundary dispute. The atmosphere did not seem to be conducive to progressive change or to the broadening of self-government in British North America.

Outside Lower Canada, however, the normal political battle was quickly resumed. It was soon clearer than ever that elected assemblies could gain almost any degree of control over the local government that they were prepared to press hard for. Indeed, the New Brunswick Assembly achieved its main demands in the very year of the rebellions. In Nova Scotia, where Howe's followers were often cautious and wavering, it took somewhat longer to press the case for enlarging the authority of the Assembly and for an executive government responsible to the Assembly. In Upper Canada middle-of-the-road reformers regrouped under new leaders such as Robert Baldwin and Francis Hincks and in a year or so it was apparent that the days of the Family Compact and the rule of the oligarchy were numbered.

The crucial problem was what to do about Lower Canada. It was to Lord Durham, a prominent "advanced" Liberal, that a troubled British government turned for an answer. And indeed Durham thought he had the answer even before he reached Quebec in the spring of 1838, on his five-month mission in Canada: a union of all the British North American colonies. Closer observation served only to confirm this view. As he put it later, in his celebrated *Report* of 1839, French Canadians were "an old and stationary society, in a new and progressive world"; it had been a mistake to try "to preserve a French Canadian nationality in the midst of Anglo-American colonies and states." In order to elevate them from "hopeless inferiority" they must be given "our English character" by being engulfed in a British North American union. It would then be to their advantage to assimilate to the English-speaking majority. Durham was equally ready to condemn the failings of the old oligarchic colonial governments, however, and to recommend that government should be responsible to the legislature henceforth, on the British parliamentary model.

Before long, Durham found that the Atlantic provinces wanted nothing to do with his larger union. He then had to fall back on a proposal for dual union of the Canadas, still with the objective of submerging the French Canadians, but still with the grant of responsible government—which would be safe enough, he thought, as long as the *Canadien* element was duly subordinated in a loyally British community. This proposal could be imposed on Lower Canada, where the constitution was still suspended, under rule by a Special Council, and the rather reluctant, but nearly bankrupt, Upper Canadians could be enticed by the promise of an imperial loan. Such was the plan recommended and soon implemented. The 1840s would reveal whether union meant the end of French-Canadian nationality in British North America.

9: The 1840s

JACQUES MONET, S.J.

October 19, 1839, was a windy, cool, and dark day; but thousands of Quebecois lined the streets of their ancient city to watch the colourful parade as Sir John Colborne, erect on his black charger and in the full gold and scarlet of a major-general, led the officers of his staff out of the Chateau Saint-Louis towards the harbour. There, in the frigate *Pique*, awaited the Rt. Hon. Charles Poulett Thomson, later Lord Sydenham, the highly competent, forty-year-old English businessman who had been commissioned to come to the Canadas and by "frank and unreserved personal intercourse," reconcile them to Lord Durham's plan for their union. In mid-afternoon, after the whole garrison had assembled, the new governor general, short, slender, supremely self-confident, stepped briskly off the gangplank, took the salute, and drove to the Chateau to issue a proclamation announcing his assumption of power. The decade of the rebellions in British North America had effectively ended. That of the union of the Canadas and responsible government had begun.

The Durham *Report* had reached Quebec and Halifax eight months before, and colonists and *Canadiens* had lost no time in expressing their frank and unreserved opinions about its chief recommendations for union and responsible government. They were not uninfluenced, of course, by the reaction of imperial statesmen in the mother country. While these had rather spontaneously agreed to union and assimilation in the Canadas, they had remained sceptical, to say the least, about responsible government. To the latter, the prime minister, Lord Melbourne, declared himself "entirely opposed," the leading spokesman of the opposition dismissed the idea as of "a perfectly subordinate nature," and the colonial secretary opined that responsible government "meant separate independent powers existing in Great Britain and in every separate colony. . . . It would be better to say at once 'Let the two countries separate'." Clearly, Canadian union was one thing, colonial responsible government another. And in the colonies as well, there were not a few ready to draw the same distinction. Some opposed both, others agreed with both, others yet welcomed or resisted either one.

Tory leaders in British North America felt instinctively that both of Durham's proposals would be fatal to their rule. In Nova Scotia Judge Haliburton, who had earned an international reputation with his literary creation Sam Slick, had not even awaited publication of the *Report* to ridicule it. After burying himself in eight hand-carts of assorted documents, he had emerged with his acid *The Bubbles of Canada*, in which, among many other remarks, he commented: "When a nobleman advocates democratic institutions, we give him full credit for the benevolence of his intentions, but we doubt his sanity." In Upper Canada, the chief justice, John Beverley Robinson, reacted in very much the same manner. He also shut himself up for days before publishing a retort which, naturally, censured the union and responsible government, both of which, he foresaw, would involve the upper province in all the troubles of Lower Canada. Later, his sentiments would be echoed by the Committee reports of each house of the tory-dominated legislature in

Toronto: while the union might be acceptable for economic reasons, responsible government would "lead to the overthrow of the great Colonial Empire of England."

In Lower Canada, powerful voices had also arisen against Durham's plans. John Neilson, the veteran constitutional reformer and editor, since 1797, of the colony's leading newspaper, the bilingual *Quebec Gazette*, declared himself strongly. He attacked the union project. By its provisions for the rearrangement of the *Canadiens'* ancestral legal system, by its strictures upon French-Canadian culture, by its recommended reorganization of Lower Canadian education, it violated the special national rights repeatedly confirmed to the French by Great Britain, rights enshrined by prescription and defended in two wars at the price of *Canadien* and British blood; by joining two cultural groups into one legislative system, it threatened the whole social order in which property and freedom were secured. This strong opinion was seconded by the powerful French-Canadian clerical elite. The courtly, white-haired Archbishop of Quebec, Joseph Signay declared "notre opposition à un semblable plan," while Bishop Jacques Lartigue, his suffragan in Montreal, called it "très dangereux pour les Catholiques." They both left no doubt they would resist the policy designed, as Bishop Lartigue put it, "pour nous *anglifier*, c'est-à-dire nous décatholiser par une union législative et un système d'écoles neutres."

Some, however, approved. In Nova Scotia Durham's *Report* threw light and hope on Joseph Howe's long struggle for political reform. True, the editor of the *Novascotian* disagreed with any hint of a union with the Canadas: "A Confederation, instead of leaving the Province with its present evils in connection with the Colonial Office, would establish an Office in the backwoods of Canada, more difficult of access than that in London." But with responsible government he was in total accord. Indeed, he wished that "a copy of this *Report* was in the hands of every head of family in Nova Scotia." In Lower Canada, most of the anglophones—Quebec officials and Montreal business leaders—rejoiced expectantly over continued English-speaking rule under the proposed union. The mistake made in 1791 would be righted, interprovincial barriers would be removed from the rich trade which they could now fully control up the great

Laurentian waterway, and, since they need no longer fear a hostile French majority in the Assembly, they could finish the St. Lawrence canal system and conquer the natural barriers to their hinterland. Their journals generally gave the *Report* a warm welcome. So, of course, did those of the reformers in Upper Canada. "No document has ever been promulgated in British North America that has given such general satisfaction as this report," wrote Francis Hincks in his Toronto *Examiner* before setting off to organize hundreds of "Durham meetings" and "Durham Constitutional Clubs" with "Durham flags" and "Durham songs," to the benefit of the reform cause. Indeed, in Hamilton, a gathering which mustered some two thousand people—half the population of that town—passed enthusiastic resolutions approving of "responsible government as recommended by Lord Durham." Within six months many such large meetings were held; by the end of the year 1839, the "Durhamites" seemed to constitute a large proportion of the population of Upper Canada. By then Durham's recommendations also seemed to have secured the support of an important number of French Canadians.

In Quebec the highly respected journalist Etienne Parent, editor since 1831 of the nationalist *Le Canadien*, had translated the *Report* as soon as it arrived, and published it by instalments. Then, in a remarkable series of articles published between May and November 1839, he carefully unfolded his thought upon it. Since Great Britain had now determined on the union, his compatriots had no choice but to resign themselves. They must, however, insist on the union's twin: responsible government. "En nous résignant au plan de Lord Durham," he wrote on May 13, "nous entendons qu'on le suive dans toutes ses parties favorables." With and by these two, union and responsible government, he considered the margin of gain was worth the loss. The *Canadiens* would achieve at last their goal of thirty years, victory over the local oligarchy of officials and merchants. By the union they would be joined to the reformers of Upper Canada whose strength they needed and who also needed them. Together, as he foretold on August 2, they would force from English politicians "un gouvernement satisfaisant, responsable, condition indispensable de bonheur et de prospérité." In fact they would even gain the help of reformers throughout the whole of British North America.

Parent urged what appeared to French-Canadian *nationalistes* to be the supreme sacrifice. Yet, at the same time, he seemed to be aware that such cultural self-denial might not be necessary. For throughout his penetrating analysis of the *Report*, he underlined that *la survivance* of the *Canadiens* as a distinct national group went hand in hand with the British constitution. It was by using the constitution that had been granted to them that the *Canadiens* had, so far, preserved and developed their own distinctive cultural patterns, the survival of which still depended upon its flexibility and organic vitality. Without it, would they not long ago have fallen under the overwhelming numbers and influence of their immediate neighbours? Would they not have inevitably lost their identity? So, to save themselves, they had twice defended Britain's empire at the price of their blood, and—a subtle thought—had they not kept the other colonists British by setting up a rival culture to that of the merchants and American Loyalists? "Du moment qu'elle n'aura plus à craindre ou à jalouser une nationalité française dans le Bas-Canada," he argued, the English-speaking British American population would sound the tocsin of revolt exactly as it had in 1775.

The British constitution, therefore, and French Canada's distinct nationality were co-relatives: the stronger the nationality the greater the permanence of the Empire, and vice versa. And once the *Canadiens* had achieved responsible government, they could utilize it to nullify assimilation, and open up a broadening future for their language, their institutions, and their nationality. Or, as Francis Hincks wrote to Parent's close associate, the young politician Louis-Hippolyte LaFontaine: "On the Union question you should not mind Lord Durham's motives but the effect of the scheme. . . . I have already told you that I have always supported the Union *without reference to details* because by it alone I felt convinced we would have a majority *that would make our tyrants succumb.*"

All this might well be, but as the new decade opened, the times for French Canada seemed dark and dangerous indeed. Disillusion and disappointment had set in. In November 1839, Governor Poulett Thomson had summoned Colborne's old Special Council to

Montreal and submitted the union project in a closed session, calling for a vote before any of those likely to oppose it could discuss amendments. The terms, besides, were clearly unfair to Lower Canada. Its population of 650,000 was to have in the united legislature the same representation as the upper province's 450,000, and the Upper Canadian debt of £1,200,000 (huge compared to Lower Canada's £95,000) was to be charged to both. And obviously the terms contained nothing about responsible government. The governor next moved on to Toronto, where Durhamite ardour for union seemed to cool in proportion to the decline in guarantees of responsible government. He won acceptance for the union in the Upper Canadian legislature, but at the price of more discrimination against Lower Canada. Now, the *Canadiens* learned, the capital of the province would have to be moved to Upper Canada (to, of all places, what they came to call, "cet enfer de Kingston"); and English would become the only official language of the united Parliament. Clearly this was not the union Hincks had dreamed of, nor that Parent had been ready to accept. In any case the Union Act went through the British Parliament later in 1840. Yet when, on February 10, 1841, the union was officially proclaimed, almost every French Canadian greeted it with horror. "Nous entrons cette nuit dans une route obscure," sighed John Neilson, "à l'entrée de laquelle sont le mensonge et la corruption."

II

Despite *Canadien* misgivings, the decade would be for all the colonists as well as for themselves one of progress and resolvings. There would be growth and change of pace. There would be signs and symbols of prosperity. As Nova Scotia's seaborne commerce mounted further, Halifax—incorporated as a city in 1841—virtually became the capital of the North Atlantic. The British North American Mail Steam Packet Company, founded by the native Haligonian Samuel Cunard, was sending "steamships on schedule" across the ocean, and gained a practical monoply of transatlantic steam navigation. When the city was connected to Boston by telegraph in 1849, it was there that American newspapermen came to pick up the latest news from Europe which, arriving in the morning, could be published in New York evening journals. In New Brunswick, despite a short-lived decline in the second third of the century, the timber trade continued on its exciting upward curve. As for Prince Edward Island, where the four thousand inhabitants of Charlottetown proudly watched the rise of their fine new provincial building (in somewhat dated Georgian style), the province had now achieved a notable degree of farm-based self-sufficiency: oats forging ahead as its principal earner of credit. And Newfoundland, too, enjoyed increased prosperity, as sealing developed markedly. Vats for the manufacture of seal oil grew ever larger at Fogo, Twillingate, Greenspond, and Trinity. Some years as many as 650,000 seals were shot or clubbed to death (to be exact, 685,530 in the peak year, 1844). Gold bullion also was acquired as Spanish vessels, encouraged by the preferential duties of their government, came to buy fish at island ports.

Although during the widespread depression late in the decade there were business failures—Joseph Howe claimed that in New Brunswick there was "scarcely a solvent house from Saint John to Grand Falls," though skilled workmen abandoned the shores of Fundy for Australia and New Zealand, while Nova Scotia suffered from the shrinking of overseas trade after 1847, the Maritimes, generally, would end the 1840s in a sounder financial state than they had begun it. Howe, exuberant and energetic as usual, might well exhort his fellow colonists: "Boys, brag of your country. When I'm abroad I brag of everything that Nova Scotia is, has, or can produce; and when they beat me at everything else, I turn around on them and say: 'How high does your tide rise?'"

In the new united Province of Canada, the tide continued to flow with British immigrants. They arrived, some 25,000 to 40,000 a year, to boost the total population up to near the two million mark—a net increase during the decade of some 692,000. Most travelled to the chief settlement frontier in the upper section, now denominated Canada West, doubling its population in ten years to some 952,000 (compared with some 890,000 in Canada East). There they established themselves on the large fertile land area stretching inland from Lake Huron, or southward towards Lake

Erie, or again north of Toronto or along the Ottawa. Some went to the urban communities: London in the heart of the western peninsula with its population of some 2,000 in 1841; Hamilton, 3,400, at the head of Lake Ontario. Others went to Kingston, the stone-built garrison town of fewer than six hundred houses which had suddenly become the capital of an enormous province, where hundreds of labourers were busy remodelling the municipal hospital into a Parliament. More still travelled to Toronto, a city most definitely on the move: it would mushroom from 14,000 in 1841 to over 30,000 in 1851. There, according to one traveller in 1842,

> all is in a whirl and fizz, and one must be in the fashion; everything and everybody seem to go by steam; and if you meet an acquaintance in the street he is sure to have arrived from some other place three or four hundred miles off, and to be starting upon a similar expedition in some other direction. After a short experience of this mode of life one quite forgets that there is such a thing as repose or absence of noise, and begins to think that the blowing of steam is a necessary accompaniement and consequence of the ordinary operation of the elements.

The fact was that in Toronto as throughout the West, the 1840s were breeding a considerable class of businessmen closely involved with the extensive growth of the western agrarian community, supplying its wants and marketing its crops. By the end of the decade, these would shape a new upper and middle class of merchants and entrepreneurs—men such as the Scots importer Isaac Buchanan, the Irish wholesale merchant William McMaster, or the American stove manufacturers Charles and Edward Gurney. They would ally with professional men and "gentry" in the towns or countryside to prompt and guide the results of the population explosion. They would prosper, of course, from the increased sales of wheat and the steady expansion of the Ottawa lumber empire. They would build numerous churches (in percentage the western population in 1841 was roughly 22 per cent Anglican, 20 per cent Presbyterian, 17 per cent Methodist, and some 14 per cent Roman Catholic). And they would support the constant proliferation of newspapers across Canada West, and even the foreshadowing of a periodical press, evidenced by the *Victoria Magazine*, "a cheap periodical for the Canadian people," founded at Belleville in 1846. This, indeed, was edited by Susanna Moodie and her husband; but though she also wrote for the similar (and longer-lived) Montreal *Literary Garland*, her classic account of pioneer life in Upper Canada, *Roughing it in the Bush*, was published in England, as were a number of other literary works on Canadian immigrant and pioneering experience, which then found a ready British market.

At the same time a more populous, settled Canada West was developing an effective, publicly maintained school system. In 1844 the powerful and controversial Methodist leader, Egerton Ryerson, was appointed Chief Superintendent of Education for Upper Canada. Under Governor Sydenham, the Union Parliament had passed the first of the decade's important series of school acts in 1841, essentially enabling the two sections of the union to develop their own patterns of state-supported education. That for the Upper Canadian half became basically one of non-discriminational schools, though with provisions for separate schools for the religious minority. That for the Lower Canadian section provided for religious-based, or confessional schools—Catholic for the majority, Protestant for the minority. But in Upper Canada it was the work of Ryerson, above all, that established a system of elementary public education across the West, dependent on central grants and standards but with a good deal of local authority (and some taxes) in the keeping of locally elected school boards. In short, the basis of the Ontario school system was laid during the 1840s. But more than that, the decade also witnessed notable beginnings in Ontario higher education. The Methodists' Victoria College emerged at Cobourg; Ryerson was its first president before he became educational superintendent, the post he was to hold for over thirty years. Queen's was founded as a Presbyterian college at Kingston in 1841, while the long-delayed Anglican King's College finally began teaching in Toronto in 1842.

As for the eastern, largely French-Canadian section of the united province, despite Neilson's dark forebodings—and perhaps even more so Durham's disparaging assessment of French Canada—the union soon generated a new ferment and vitality among the *Canadiens*. They grew out of the "grand découragement" that had hung over the beginnings of the decade. Gradually they caught the infectious nineteenth-century spirit of progress. They became more aware of their national identity and, as the 1840s moved on, they became restless to express it. In cultural affairs, in newspapers, literature, and thought; in their Church; in reviving industry; they looked at things with new pleasure. At the beginning of 1843 there were in French Canada five large bi-weeklies, *Le Canadien* and *Le Journal de Québec* in the old capital; *L'Aurore, Les Mélanges Religieux*, and *La Minerve* in Montreal. By 1850 these had multiplied to over a dozen, and the older ones now appeared three times a week to compete with the new radical *L'Avenir* and with a host of other, keen little papers. There were also the anthologies such as Michel Bibaud's *Encyclopédie Canadienne*, in which the French could read chapters from François Xavier Garneau's new national *Histoire du Canada*, and a steady stream of productions from native authors: wild, romantic novels, like Joseph Doutre's *Les Fiancés de 1812*, theatrical plays like *Le Rebelle*, endless epic poems—uneven, ugly tangles of captive heroines, brigands, handsome officers, passionate lovers, but for all that, the first drafts of what would one day be the *Canadiens'* own national literature.

They also flocked to lectures, filling parish halls and hotel lobbies to hear new, exciting ideas percolating over from the salons of Europe on the most modern topics of the day: education, hygiene, exports, independence of character, and "la position de la femme." Especially they listened to Etienne Parent. In five great lectures delivered in Montreal between 1846 and 1849, the former editor of *Le Canadien* now turned civil servant, outlined a new social and economic philosophy which, had they heeded it, might well have given the *Canadiens* the key to the new economic order then being founded. He proposed sweeping reforms in all social, educational, and religious institutions; more importantly, in the habits of thought of the habitants. He was not followed, of course, as fully as he would have wished. "Il a exprimé," noted *La Minerve* on December 18, 1884, "beaucoup d'idées qui paraissaient toutes neuves à une grande partie de son auditoire." Still, in a way, he testified to the new mood.

So, in another way, did the new Bishop of Montreal, Monseigneur Ignace Bourget. Shortly after succeeding Bishop Lartigue in 1840, this energetic and authoritarian young churchman began to renew the face of Catholicism in French Canada. Within his first year, he had organized a great mission throughout his diocese, preached by Bishop de Forbin-Janson, one of France's foremost orators. Between September 1840 and December 1841 the latter travelled across French Canada, visiting some sixty villages and preaching rousing sermons to crowds numbering sometimes as many as ten thousand. Meanwhile the Bishop of Montreal had left for Europe to arrange for the immigration from France of the Oblate Order (December 1841) and the Jesuits (May 1842), of the Ladies of the Sacred Heart (December 1842), and of the Sisters of the Good Shepherd (June 1844). Before the end of the decade, he had also founded two Canadian religious congregations of his own, and established the Saint Vincent-de-Paul Society. Of course, this enthusiasm, this multiplication of religious houses and charitable foundations spread beyond Canada East to new fields in Toronto, the northwest and the Oregon country on the Pacific: "Cette vaste chaîne de sièges épiscopaux," commented the *Mélanges Religieux* in 1843 on the occasion of the consecration of a French-Canadian bishop in Oregon, "qui doit s'étendre un jour, nous l'espérons de la mer jusqu'à la mer: *a mari usque ad mare*." Essentially, however, it was a Lower Canadian phenomenon. So was the excess of enthusiasm over temperance.

In Canada West a temperance movement developed in response to the frontier brawling and family suffering caused by the "liquor evil." Toronto's Temperance Society had over a thousand members in 1841. In New Brunswick an unfortunate government would experiment with prohibition in the 1850s. But in French Canada East the movement was part of the Catholic revival and turned upon the personality of "le petit père Chiniquy," a sensitive, frail, passionate young abbé who was obsessed with the problem of alcohol. He began his crusade in March 1840 by administering the pledge to thirteen hundred of his parishioners at Beauport, near Quebec. Thence he progressed, brimful with temperance, across the Quebec diocese. In the Montreal district he sometimes enrolled as many as seventeen thousand people in one month. In fact, he moved Montrealers to such a pitch of sobriety that they planned to erect a marble statue of him on Place d'Armes: in his left hand he would carry a tablet with a bilingual history of the temperance cause and his own name in gold letters, and from his right hand there would fall through the fingers a fountain of water—the beverage he recommended so highly. In 1849, he gave some fifteen hundred sermons in one hundred and twenty parishes to over 200,000 people. In all of this, of course, the Apostle of Temperance was doing more than fostering sobriety: he was witnessing that the Catholic Church in French Canada had become one of the more powerful advocates of change.

Indeed, Bishop Bourget was concerned with more than spiritual things. He followed Parent's lectures with great interest, and detected among the *Canadiens* a growing regard for business matters. True, the French Canadians as a whole remained less overtly concerned with these than their new compatriots in the western section or in Montreal; but their leaders were. Bourget gave his patronage to a new *Banque d'Epargne*; the Sulpicians in Montreal became proprietors of large blocks of shares in the proposed Saint Lawrence and Atlantic Railway; other leaders started a new steamship company— La Compagnie du Richelieu—and invested in the *Banque du Peuple*. When Joseph Masson, owner of extensive seigneuries and a most influential importer, died in 1847, he was reputed to be the wealthiest merchant in the two Canadas.

As for the other classes, they could no longer consider economic activity to be subordinate: their newspapers were filled with stories of new railway projects and steamship services. Besides, the union had evidently brought them a return of prosperity. The first Canadian agricultural protective tariff in 1843; the acts of 1844 and 1845 that raised grants to farmers to £150 for each county in Lower Canada; the employment provided by the beginning of the new Beauharnois Canal, and by the gradual increase of shipping in Quebec city from about 12,000 tons in 1841-42 to 40,000 tons in 1846; the fleet of paddle-wheelers sailing the St. Lawrence between Montreal and Quebec, and the construction of the greatest of them all, the *John Munn*, the most luxurious and fastest ship in Canada, called "le roi du Saint Laurent," launched at Quebec on May 22, 1847— all of this brought encouragement.

It may be that in bare numbers of population, the *Canadiens* had become a minority in the united province, but due especially to their high birth and declining death rates, they were growing proportionately in the eastern section. Montreal, where the proportion of the population of roughly 40,000 in 1841 was some 60 per cent anglophone, increased to 45 per cent (of 57,000) French-Canadian in 1851; Quebec would rise to 58 per cent French; the Eastern Townships from some 27 per cent French in 1841 to almost 41 per cent in 1851, as British immigration there tailed off. As for the chief cities, Quebec, of course, was the busy centre of the "immigrant trade," Canada's chief lumber port and shipbuilding centre, British North America's military headquarters, and French Canada's religious capital. But thanks to the union, Montreal was becoming the economic heart of the commercial metropolis of the province and in 1845 became the political capital as well. There the aggressive mercantile and financial community established along Notre-Dame and Saint James streets directed the economy, if not the lives, of the Irish and *Canadien* labourers, of the new immigrants from Scotland, and of the buoyant habitant farmers from the countryside come to the daily market.

As the climate of opinion in cultural, religious and economic affairs grew more enthusiastic, the *Canadiens* found anew their joyous and hospitable sense of fellowship. They began to join new social and patriotic clubs. Napoléon Aubin, a Swiss emigré and *littérateur*, founded the Société Saint Jean Baptiste in Quebec in June 1842, and seems to have set the example. In 1843, Ludger Duvernay, editor of Montreal's *La Minerve*, decided to resurrect the Saint Jean Baptiste Society there. Within the year several others were set up. And on December 17, 1844, some two hundred young Montrealers met in the chambers of another recent foundation, the *Société d'Histoire naturelle*, to start the more famous *Institut Canadien* that would have a noted influence as a centre for advanced liberal political and social thinking.

From commerce to literature, in church and in the salon, the *Canadiens* were out of discouragement, out of the misery of the thirties. They placed no limit now on their enterprise.

III

Before the end of the decade the *Canadiens* had become veritable political masters of the union. This was no easy task—after all, the project had been designed to crush their national aspirations. But it was Louis-Hippolyte LaFontaine's achievement, above all. He was not the scholar Parent was; he had none of Papineau's passion, none of John Neilson's urbanity. He had no charm, no sense of humour. But as circumstances would make him French Canada's main spokesman, he revealed that he could think clearly and practically about his nationality and about its connection with the British constitution. Like Etienne Parent, he understood how responsible government could bring the *Canadiens* to overcome the past. It was not retreat into a French Lower Canada they needed as much as to deal with the British on their own terms, to argue on grounds which no British subject or statesman could deny. Soon he came to identify his country's cause with his own ambitions, and then he found that his personality could be turned into an invaluable political asset. His strange mixture of ambition and stubborn idealism coincided well with the constant pressure needed to force the concession of responsible government. Before the end of the decade he would head a responsible cabinet, and be the first among his own people to actually express and direct the national aspirations of French Canada.

When union was proclaimed in 1841, most French Canadians agreed with John Neilson, the powerful Denis-Benjamin Viger, (Papineau's cousin and coadjutor), and the various other politicians of the Papineau family who favoured a separatist solution. Militant idealists, these found the key to *la survivance* in the isolation of French Canada upon a territory where the *Canadiens,* living as a compact national group, would be undisputed masters, secure against alien Anglo-Saxon contamination. The union having been adopted in spite of them, they decided to cooperate as little and as superficially in politics as possible. They decided to join on a mere temporary basis whichever one of the Upper Canadian parties offered them the most interesting concessions. Later, in 1845, in another form of abstention, they invented the theory of "double majority," a device according to which a law of the union would not be valid until it was sanctioned by a distinct majority of the two groups, English and French. Still later, after Neilson's death in 1847 and the return from his Paris exile of the great, uncompromising hero, Louis-Joseph Papineau, these ardent nationalists improved upon isolation by promoting the idea of a French-Canadian national republic, which, joining the American republic as a 34th state, could become a little Louisiana of the north.

LaFontaine thought otherwise. Ten days after the Act of Union was announced, he accordingly published his celebrated *Adresse aux Electeurs de Terrebonne*. In this, he admitted that the union was unjust—"elle est un acte d'injustice et de despotisme." But it did not follow, he argued, that the French should abdicate their rights as British subjects, and adopt a course which must inevitably lead to national suicide. No, they must play their rightful part, fight the next election, then unite with sympathizers from Upper Canada to form a political majority that could force through responsible government. With this, "le principal moteur de la constitution anglaise," they could win back all that they had lost. But without it, there could be no political liberty, no cultural future. The call was clear: accept the union, join with the reformers of Canada West, force the Colonial Office to grant responsible government. Fortunately he found western reform associates, like sharp-witted Francis Hincks, eager to urge the cause of "Reform alliance," and the austere, clear-sighted Robert Baldwin, who commanded wide respect for his unswerving devotion to the principle of responsible rule.

Nevertheless, LaFontaine spent nearly ten years accomplishing his purpose. It was not until the elections of 1844 that he succeeded in rallying a majority of his fellow *Canadien* politicians. And it was not until 1846 that he managed to win the support and influence of the clergy, which until then feared his projects of school reform. He had to suffer the effects of the political reversals of his friends, the reformers of Upper Canada, who were temporarily beaten by western tory-conservative forces between 1844 and 1847, led by able William Draper and the demagogic but forceful Sir Allan MacNab. LaFontaine even had to face the beginnings of a revolt among his own followers in 1846-47. Not until the end .of the decade could he be certain of victory. Still, after a decade of fistfights on electoral platforms, scandals, riots and racial fury; after a luminous, dynamic, and flexible partnership with Robert Baldwin; and strengthened at last by the almost unanimous support of his compatriots, LaFontaine achieved his goal.

He needed Robert Baldwin as leader of the Upper Canadian reformers, who could prove to *Canadien* electors that Upper Canadians were aware of their sensitivities. This Baldwin did, for example, in refusing to enter the Executive Council in 1841 because he considered the Oath of Supremacy he was asked to take would be insulting to the Pope, and thus to French-Canadian feelings and traditions. Another time, in a warm gesture towards the *Canadien* leader, Baldwin persuaded his own constituents in the Fourth Riding of York in Canada West to elect LaFontaine in his place. At that time Etienne Parent underlined the significance of the gesture in his *Canadien*: "Que je vous dise un mot des braves gens que j'ai rencontrés à Newmarket. Si tous les habitants du Haut-Canada leur ressemblent, je peux prédire les plus brillants résultats de l'Union des Canadas." LaFontaine also needed the help of that gentle gentleman, the governor general, Sir Charles Bagot (Sydenham's successor) a man of the world, fluent in French, who moved through Lower Canada in 1842 conversing with *jeux d'esprit* and wit. It was his task to prove that the union did not necessarily mean assimilation, indeed that some good might come out of it. And this he did by conceding to the *Canadiens'* most urgent wishes in education, in the judiciary, in the area of municipal reform, indeed in a long list of popular appointments, not least of which were LaFontaine's and Baldwin's to the attorney-generalships of the province. Then, too, LaFontaine needed the help of Francis Hincks, the best election-winner in the two Canadas, who moved to Montreal in early 1844, and more than anyone else created the powerful reform alliance which allowed LaFontaine and Baldwin eventually to dominate the Assembly—and the Canadas.

Once he had become political master in his own house, LaFontaine set to work to transform the administration and implement reforms in the municipal and judicial systems, and much else besides. He also made certain, excellent politician that he was, that by a judicious allotment of favours all the *Canadiens* became permanently involved in self-rule. For two generations, the *Canadien* professional class had been struggling to secure an outlet for its ambitions: so now, with a kind of bacterial thoroughness it began to invade every vital organ of government, and divide up among its members hundreds of posts as judges, Queen's Counsels, justices of the peace, medical examiners, school inspectors, militia captains, postal clerks, mail conductors, census commissioners. And as the flatteries and salaries of office percolated to other classes of society —from merchants who wanted seats on the Legislative Council down to the impoverished habitants on the crowded seigneuries— the French Canadians came to realize how parliamentary democracy could be more than an admirable ideal. It was also a profitable fact. And henceforth, because of LaFontaine's crucial role in achieving responsible government, there could be guaranteed for all of them the possibility of room at the top.

In addition, LaFontaine turned his energies to development and expansion. In the Eastern Townships and the Saguenay region, he pushed forward a new policy of colonization, of improvement of agricultural methods, and of reform in depth of the seigneurial system. In education, he encountered the new primary schools being founded by the new Superintendent of Education for Lower Canada, Jean-Baptiste Meilleur, and the multiplication of new *collèges classiques* climaxed, after the end of the decade, by the grant of a royal charter to Laval University in Quebec. Indeed, by 1848, he had become identified with the mission to defend French culture and language. Hence when he finally came to power, he wished to inaugurate his regime by formally reinstating the official use of his mother tongue.

At the beginning of 1848, the reformers swept the elections in both Canadas. Lord Elgin, the statesmanlike governor general who had come to Canada the year before, called upon the leaders of the Assembly majority to form a government, as indeed it was now British policy to do. He turned to LaFontaine to head the ministry, since he had the larger following, with Baldwin as his leading colleague. LaFontaine now had his moment for the reinstatement of the French language, the supreme moment of the colony's political and ceremonial life: the opening of Parliament in his own city of Montreal. Accordingly, on January 18, 1849, amid traditional panoply, and through rows of troops that had taken their places like monuments along the route, bright scarlet against the snow-banks, Governor General Elgin slid smartly in a large sleigh down Notre-Dame Street to the Parliament at the Marché Sainte-Anne. There, white-plumed and splendid in his dark-blue and silver tunic he proceeded to the red chamber, crowded for the occasion by dark, formal-coated councillors and their wives in bright dresses. Seated under the huge red and gold canopy, he read his Speech from the Throne. He paused and, his courtly diction filling the chamber, he himself repeated it once over in elegant French. Thus, in one fine, royal, unprecedented gesture, he wiped out forever the last national iniquity of the union. And as he stepped out a few minutes later into the fresh and open air, the fanfare must have seemed to ring out with greater sound. In all events, as the vice-regal procession receded, LaFontaine's old opponent Denis-Benjamin Viger exclaimed in tears: "Que je me sens soulagé d'entendre dans ma langue les paroles du trône!" Indeed, asked *La Minerve,* "Quand notre nationalité a-t-elle été plus respectée, plus honorée?"

IV

In Upper Canada, too, the LaFontaine–Baldwin combination that had taken office in March 1838, as the first completely reform party cabinet, brought notable changes to laws and institutions. For one thing the vexed "university question" of the decade—as to the nature of the publicly endowed Upper Canadian provincial univer-sity, King's College—was given a lasting settlement. In the mid-forties various bills had been put forward to make that institution a completely secular state university, to share its endowment among several religiously based colleges, or to work out some form of asso-ciation for them all. None had succeeded, as advanced reformers sought full secularization, confirmed tories defended an Anglican King's College, and moderate conservatives sought some com-promise, often backed by the various religious college interests. But in 1849, the reform government secularized King's College, though denominational institutions could have a loose affiliation with the new non-sectarian University of Toronto that replaced it. From this, ultimately, would stem a federation of private denominational colleges with the public university, a significant model for Canadian higher education.

Equally significant was the Municipal Corporations Act of 1849, that set up a pattern of municipal self-government throughout Canada West. This aptly christened "Baldwin Act" really extended its initiator's belief in responsible rule into the vital area of the local community. It created a complete system of elected, locally responsible authorities, both rural and urban, that would remain at the core of Ontario's political and administrative life for well over a century, and have influence as well on the development of other municipal institutions in the far broader Canada of a later day. Also important, at least for its own day, was the Guarantee Act of 1849, put through by Francis Hincks as the finance minister of the new regime. The guarantee it offered for the bonds of projected railways that everyone was talking about by the close of the forties did much to encourage their rapid construction in the next decade.

Whatever the consequences of the coming of responsible government in Canada, it no less made its impact in the Atlantic provinces. Indeed, Nova Scotia was actually first to achieve it in British North America, for in January 1848, two months before Canada, a responsible party cabinet of reformers took office in Halifax, headed by James Boyle Uniacke and Joseph Howe. Howe himself had shaped a powerful campaign for the cause, skilfully directing Durham's ideas against the Halifax oligarchy and, in particular, writing a widely read set of public letters to Lord John Russell, then colonial secretary, refuting the latter's objections to colonial self-government with telling wit and realism. After bringing down one government by duly parliamentary methods, Howe perhaps was ill-advised to join a supposedly "non-party" coalition Executive Council in 1840 under a new governor, Lord Falkland. But when he found he could make no further headway with his tory colleagues there, he went into opposition in 1843, and worked vigorously at building a strong party front in the Assembly. Success came under still another governor, Sir John Harvey, who now—like Elgin in Canada—was authorized by changed imperial policy to accept a government from whatever party could control the elected house. And the reformers carried the elections of 1847, so that when the Assembly met in 1848, they took office. Nova Scotia had achieved democratic self-government "without the shedding of a drop of blood . . . the breaking of a pane of glass," as Howe liked to proclaim.

New Brunswick did less to attain self-government for itself. Indeed, politics in that province were relatively uneventful during most of the decade. The external irritant of the disputed Maine–New Brunswick boundary was finally settled by the Ashburton Treaty of 1842, although New Brunswickers might complain that the settlement took away valued tracts of timberland as well as blocking off their shortest land routes to Quebec. In internal affairs, the Assembly by the late thirties had already gained such full control of crown revenues and lands (and thus timber resources) that reform leaders like Lemuel Wilmot saw little need to press further. There was a shifting succession of coalition administrations under Sir William Colebrooke, governor from 1841 to 1848, but personal contests for office and patronage did not really alter the general political tranquillity—"the Reign of Smoothery," the Saint John *Loyalist* termed it. In 1848 an earnest new governor, Sir Edmund Head (who would later succeed Elgin in Canada) did seek to apply the principles of responsible government that had now been recognized by the imperial authorities; yet New Brunswick was only gradually adapting to that system at the end of the decade. More meaningful perhaps, was the underlying fact that by 1850 the business power of Saint John had wrestled ascendancy away from the old conservative gentry of Fredericton, and so would dominate in politics thereafter.

In Prince Edward Island through much of the forties, Governor Sir Henry Huntley carried on a bitter feud with the Speaker of the Assembly, Joseph Pope, whom he regarded as one of the dangerous "party of the Escheators" who sought "unlimited control." Thus he opposed Pope's resolution in the house in 1846 for responsible government, and poured scorn on "this abstruse subject." But then the change in imperial policy revised his ideas. Still, there were further angry struggles in the little island political cockpit before a responsible ministry took office in 1851. As for the larger, still angrier cockpit of Newfoundland, political clashes there were so acute that the movement to popular self-government even went into reverse for part of the decade. Wild election violence at Carbonear in 1840 brought the suspension of representative government, and when it was resumed in 1843 it was within a single mixed chamber of appointed and elected members. Under more conciliatory leaders, chastened Newfoundland politicians made the system work. By 1848, in fact, as they saw responsible government being applied to neighbouring colonies, they began to seek it for themselves, notably through a "Catholic Liberal" party that emerged under Philip Francis Little. The divided, scantily organized island was scarcely ready for it yet, however. And when responsible rule did come, in the next decade, it was chiefly because British policy was now generally granting it to all white colonies of settlement.

There was no question of granting responsible government to the rest of British North America. Apart from trading posts and missions, in the immense wilderness area west of the bounds of Canada there was still only the little colony at Red River in the keeping of the Hudson's Bay Company; and it was too remote and immature for such a grant, though it was developing a regular administrative and court system. In 1849, it is true, a new colony was founded on Vancouver Island, after the Oregon Treaty of 1846, extending the boundary along the 49th parallel from the Rockies to the Pacific, had brought British interests to withdraw from south of that line. But the island colony was still under Bay Company auspices, and it would not rise to representative institutions for several years. In all the lands between, from New Caledonia (that is now mainland British Columbia) to the posts along the Peace, Saskatchewan and Athabaska, the Bay Company fur trader held sway; and generally gave just treatment to the Indians of the region, who were, after all, the essential suppliers and customers of the great fur monopoly.

V

The Canadian union had turned out to be a positive achievement of the forties; responsible government assuredly was another. But the decade also had its disasters, its dangers and depression. Indeed, before its end it would see new violence and destruction. One such disaster was fire, given crowded, flimsy houses in the towns and inadequate water supplies. In Quebec in 1845 two spectacular conflagrations almost totally destroyed the city. In the fire of May 28 about one hundred Quebecois perished and nearly 16,000 were rendered homeless, while on June 28, 12,000 homes were burned, leaving another 18,000 without shelter. Colonists throughout British North America came to the relief of the ancient capital, and over £100,000 came from private donations in Britain, Queen Victoria herself contributing liberally from the privy purse. The Quebec disaster had another unexpected, but not uncharacteristic, effect: some ten dozen dispossessed and unemployed prostitutes had to move to Montreal.

A year later, on June 9, 1846, St. John's was almost wiped out, at a cost of over 12,000 homeless and a million pounds in estimated damages. Colonists and *Canadiens* were brought together in catastrophe, and liberal donations were subscribed to ease the grim tragedies.

Nor was this all. In 1847 a host of destitute and starving immigrants began arriving in British North America, fleeing from famine and dispossession in Ireland. With these "famine Irish" came dreaded disease, to be a constant threat to the end of the decade. "L'année 1847," wrote Ludger Duvernay in *La Minerve*, "sera nommée dans notre histoire l'année de l'émigration. Près de cent mille malheureux ont quitté l'Irlande pour venir chercher du pain sur le rivage du Saint Laurent; pour comble de malheur la fièvre les a décimés." "La fièvre" was the dreaded typhus. Within the year, some 16,000 Irish immigrants would die of it, and miserable thousands of *Canadiens* and colonists be infected. Government, the churches, and private charity struggled desperately but could not cope. Doctors and clergy died, newspapers listing new obituaries in each new issue. "I visited the [immigrant] sheds one Sunday afternoon," an old Montrealer reminisced some fifty years later. "They formed a large square with a court in the centre, where the coffins were piled; some empty awaiting the dead, and some full awaiting burial. I tried the weight of one coffin standing above another which appeared to be empty, but on lifting the lid found a skeleton within. On one occasion I saw the mayor, [John Mills] and Lord Elgin visiting the ships on horseback, and afterwards riding towards the sheds." Mayor Mills of Montreal, Bishop Michael Power of Toronto, Monseigneur Hyacinthe Hudon, the Vicar-General of Montreal, and eighteen nuns from Quebec all succumbed to the fever, along with so many other inhabitants and immigrants alike in port cities and inland towns across the country.

After these squalid miseries, 1848 seemed healthy by comparison. Yet, by the beginning of June, the abbé Félix Cazeau, who led the relief for the sick in Quebec, already had more orphans to place than he normally had in a whole year. Then in 1849 cholera replaced typhus; and between July and September, some 1,200 died in Quebec and 974 in Montreal. 1850 would bring some relief. But throughout the colonies there lingered a feeling of disturbance and insecurity.

It might well. For throughout the last half of the decade, forces from outside the province, from the republic to the south and from the mother country, seriously threatened the colony's economic stability. In 1845 and 1846 the American Congress passed the Drawback Laws remitting duties on goods destined for Canada which were imported through the United States, and on Canadian exports sent overseas the same way. Upper Canadians would now be able to use the Erie Canal route to the sea. And in fact Montreal merchants grew increasingly desperate, as more and more western wheat went by the Erie and imports passing through Montreal for the inland country declined sharply. The whole St. Lawrence commercial system was now fully exposed to American competition. Meanwhile, in Britain, a vigorous railway boom was coming to an end, with consequent disastrous results for Canadian timber merchants. Moreover, in 1846 the powerful agitation of the British Anti-Corn Law League culminated in the repeal of the duties on grain, the climax of the advancing British movement to free trade. Britain's adoption of free trade might have removed earlier objections there to the recognition of responsible government, since free trade doctrines saw little need for closely controlled and subordinated colonies. But at the same time it loosened the bonds and removed preferential duties between 1846 and 1849 that had given Canada much of its economic prosperity. The results, wrote Lord Elgin, were to ruin "at once mill-owners, forwarders, and merchants. The consequence is that private property is unsaleable in Canada, and not a shilling can be raised on the credit of the Province."

The fact was that British North America, and especially the Canadian merchants in the staple trades, were feeling the impact of world trade depression, which spread from 1847 onward from Halifax to Sarnia, as well as through Europe and America. But the most obvious factor was the change in imperial trade policy, and the removal of the old protections given colonial commerce. To solve all this, somehow, the new prime minister, LaFontaine, turned to his new inspector-general, Francis Hincks, who set himself to the unenviable task with his customary efficiency. He began commercial negotiations which would eventually lead to a reciprocal trade treaty with the United States. And after persuading his fellow reformers Lemuel Wilmot of New Brunswick and William Young of Nova Scotia to initiate a trade conference in Halifax, he travelled down to the Maritime capital to exchange views—and talk railways. By the end of the 1840s the world depression was lifting. It grew apparent that the prosperity of the first two-thirds of the decade would return. But not quite yet.

There was still the question of rebellion losses—a complicated piece of legislation debated on and off throughout the decade and designed to compensate those whose property had been destroyed during the Rebellions of 1837-38. Upper Canadians had received £40,000 in 1845; and in February 1849 LaFontaine introduced a bill to cover damages suffered in Lower Canada. For the new prime minister and his council the measure was designed as a broad unstinting gesture that would finally put to rest the bitterness of 1837. But for many in Montreal's commercial class, already suffering the pangs of deep financial depression, and for many of the tory politicians who had just lost political control of Lower Canada for the first time since 1791, the issue became a symbol. They reacted with all the primitive, panic-stricken, almost standard fury of the recently dispossessed. On the evening after Lord Elgin had given his royal assent to the Rebellion Losses Bill (April 25, 1849), a tory mob gathered in Montreal, some fifteen hundred strong, and broke into the Parliament, rioting, tearing, smashing. Some threw rocks at the great clock, others hacked at the throne; one, mounting the steps of the speaker's chair pronounced: "I dissolve this French House"; another, seizing the splendid silver-gilt mace ornamented with Canadian beavers and the imperial crown, hurled it out a window to the excited crowd below. Someone set a fire. Soon the flames, feeding on the escaping gas and whipped by the wind blowing through the broken windows, were burning out of control, licking the walls about the roof. At midnight the rioters were still there running about the building, singing, cavorting, yelling, celebrating the ruin (they thought!) of French domination. They had turned away the firemen, cut the hose, and the huge bonfire raged uncontrolled high into the black night.

In the spring and summer of 1849, Montreal's tory commercial community could concentrate on nothing but French and reform domination. And after a contagion of violence—a senseless attack on the person of the governor general, the destruction of LaFontaine's home and Hincks's furniture, several weeks of breathless disorders which, if not in lives lost at least in property damage and national bitterness, formed a revealing counterpart to the rebellions that closed the previous decade—Montreal businessmen turned to what they considered more practical means of regaining control of the colony. By abolishing the Corn Laws, they reasoned, the British had ceased to protect their own; by acknowledging responsible government they had abandoned them to what they termed "the tender mercies of a voluble French faction." Why not, therefore, join the United States, and even at the cost of being American, regain control of the colony for Anglo-Saxon Protestants? On October 11, 1849, they issued the Annexation Manifesto.

To Louis-Joseph Papineau and the radical separatists dubbed *rouges* who had been campaigning for repeal of the union and for annexation, this "démarche imprévue," as Papineau put it, "semble être un secours providentiel qui nous advienne." They signed the Manifesto and with their new-found allies set off on what turned out to be a short-lived press and speech campaign in favour of "la colossale République du nouveau-monde." Short-lived because

Canadiens remained unattracted by this small *nationaliste* republican head somehow attached to a larger anglophone tory body. Short-lived also because conservatives outside the metropolis and in Canada West seemed equally unimpressed, and reformers ardently hostile. At a grand meeting of the British North American League in Kingston in July, they had overwhelmingly declared their British allegiance. By the end of the year, annexationism in its tory and *nationaliste* varieties had been reduced to an ineffectual nuisance in Canada.

Indeed as the decade ended, prosperity was returning all across British North America. Responsible government and the British constitution were secure; LaFontaine, Baldwin and their united reform party solidly entrenched in Canada. Judge Haliburton and John Beverley Robinson had been proved wrong: the union and responsible government did not mean the end of the British connection. The end of Family Compact, oligarchic rule perhaps, but not of the connection. The Montreal merchants, the Roman Catholic bishops, and John Neilson had been proved wrong: the union had not crushed French Canada's nationality and religion. On the contrary, it had fortified them. It was Joseph Howe who had been right: responsible government had strengthened the British constitution. It was Francis Hincks, Robert Baldwin, Etienne Parent and Louis-Hippolyte LaFontaine who had been right: the union and responsible government had reinforced reform, nationality, and allegiance. And for the *Canadiens,* the union, responsible government and reform had saved "notre langue, nos institutions, et nos droits"; they had consecrated the Union Jacks flying over imperial citadels at Quebec, Kingston and Halifax.

10: The 1850s

J. M. S. CARELESS

It was a time of widespread prosperity for the peoples of British North America, and of mounting discord within the big province of Canada itself. It was a decade of such material growth that real possibilities emerged of bringing the separate colonies into one united framework—and a period of such French-English friction within the existing Canadian union that the need to remodel it became manifest indeed. These, then, were the 1850s: years of passage from the gaining of self-government by the communities of British North America to the achievement of their federal union in the following decade.

It might seem that the fifties were only an interlude between the more noteworthy eras of Responsible Government and Confederation; but these, after all, are simply useful labels that historians apply. Colonists and *Canadiens* in the forties might not have felt that their ordinary daily lives were bound up with gaining responsible rule, nor even, through much of the sixties, that their whole future hung on the outcome of Confederation. In the 1850s, however, the bulk of the people were surely well aware of the boom that lasted until late in 1857, seven remarkably fat years such as they had seldom known. And they were no less aware of the introduction of the railway in their midst, of the rapid growth of towns, the soaring of business fortunes, and the swelling of debts and taxes that generally accompanied this revolution in the technology of land transport.

At the same time they could see that the ending, by 1849, of the old British colonial system of imperial protective tariffs had not brought the economic ruin predicted by opponents of free trade. The colonies proved able to work out successful new trading patterns, particularly through gaining better access to American markets; and gave thought as well to improving commercial contacts amongst themselves. Some of their people also began to consider the prospects of expansion into the vast northwest beyond the Great Lakes, which had so long been the fur trade preserve of the Hudson's Bay Company; and still farther away, they marked the beginnings of new British colonies on the distant Pacific coast. In short, this decade of the fifties was not just a prosperous interlude, but a time when older, more localized colonial concerns were being displaced by newer, broader outlooks of even continental scope. The basis for a confederation movement, and for a future nation-state stretching across the northern half of North America, was being laid.

As for the province of Canada, its inhabitants could scarcely ignore the rise of conflict in this decade between English-speaking, Protestant Upper Canadian interests and French-speaking, Catholic Lower Canadians. They clashed strongly on questions of education, taxation, representation, and the relations of church and state. Still, the very sectional and sectarian problems of the union of the two Canadas led to proposals for altering it: for constitutional changes that might even bring in the other British provinces as well. Hence the growing disunion between Canadas East and West itself fostered the trend to fresh ideas. There was eager hope, as well as angry ferment, among Canadians of the fifties.

The Atlantic provinces faced no such deep internal discords, but they had stresses of their own. In Newfoundland, only granted responsible government in 1855, religious rivalry continued to create sharp divisions in politics. A Catholic Liberal regime took office, but Protestant sentiment rallied to Conservative opposition forces. The situation was the more complicated because the Catholic Irish were largely concentrated in or near St. John's, the capital, which was also the headquarters of the Conservative "fishocracy," the big merchants of Water Street to whom most of the island's fishing population was regularly in debt. The revival of the French Shore issue in 1856-57, after Britain had granted France enlarged exclusive rights on the western coasts, did bring a temporarily unanimous mood of protest, until the agreement was dropped; but Newfoundland's internal social and religious strains remained. In the smaller island province, compact Prince Edward Island, there was similar religious friction, which engrossed the people with partisan local politics as if the little legislature at Charlottetown controlled the fate of half the world. One enduring issue, however, still stood out above all others, the continued hold of absentee proprietors over the lands, and therefore much of the life, of this largely agricultural community. Still, the Islanders felt comfortable and jauntily independent on their million-acre farm of rich red soil bounded by the blue waters of the Gulf.

New Brunswick presented a somewhat different case. Having been so long dominated by the timber interests that exploited its thickly forested river valleys, the province's political life, under responsible government as before, was more a matter of practical dealing to gain timber revenues or build local works like roads and bridges than an ardent clash of party factions. An all, one-party (reform) cabinet only took office in 1854, under Charles Fisher. The reformers or Liberals generally ruled throughout the decade—their ablest leader by its end was a shrewd Saint John businessman, Samuel Leonard Tilley—but party lines were blurred, and crossed as opportunity arose. Moreover, public opinion in New Brunswick was often highly localized, separated as its settled areas were by rough uplands between them. Thus the sprawling lumbering districts of the Gulf of St. Lawrence or north shore had little contact with the old Loyalist farmlands of the lower Saint John valley, or with south shore farmers and fishermen along the Bay of Fundy. And the nicely ordered, patrician world of Fredericton, seat of officialdom, Anglicanism and learning, had little in common with the hard-driving lumber and shipbuilding magnates of seaport Saint John, nor with the unionized ship labourers of its extensive dockyards.

Nevertheless, the province in the 1850s did experience one common, overriding issue, the "temperance crusade," which has been called "the first mass movement in the history of New Brunswick." For a time at least, a heterogeneous society focused on that cause. In 1855 a law was carried prohibiting the sale or consumption of alcohol, sponsored by Tilley, who had been unanimously chosen Most Worthy Patriarch of the Sons of Temperance of North America. The law was overturned the next year, however, to the accompaniment of a ministerial crisis and excited elections that drove Tilley and the Liberals from office. Though they returned to power in 1857, they left prohibition in the discard, for New Brunswick's brief moment of enthusiasm had definitely passed.

Nova Scotia was in many ways the most mature and unified society in British America of the 1850s, the level-headed, firmly rooted, self-respecting Bluenose being widely recognized as an established social type. Yet even here the Gaelic-speaking Catholic Highlanders of rugged Cape Breton Island varied considerably from the Baptist farmers of the fertile Annapolis valley, the simple schooner fishermen of Lunenburg from the wealthy mercantile elite of Halifax —or, in cultivated circles, the Presbyterian academics of Pictou from the Anglican Loyalist gentry of Windsor. It was true that Joseph Howe and the reformers had achieved responsible rule in 1848 in notably ordered fashion, and remained in power well into the fifties. But he and his party associates would hardly have considered that boisterous elections and slashing journalism showed that Nova Scotians were a mild, easily managed breed: especially after resurgent Conservatives threw them out of office in 1855 and kept them out till 1860, thanks largely to that stalwart emerging Conservative champion, Dr. Charles Tupper. Nor were Nova Scotians prepared to accept their own substantial achievements as sufficient. There was restiveness appearing over the confined limits of their provincial community, a concern about its future possibilities of development, a tendency to fear it might be bypassed—as expressed in a bit of dubious "poetry" in a Halifax paper of 1852:

Why are we thus so far behind
All other portions of mankind,
Are Nova Scotians mad or blind –
Not really wise?
Or else some pluck would stir their mind
To enterprise.

In fact, it was chiefly in comparison with deeper sectional cleavage in the Canadas that the Maritime provinces might congratulate themselves on internal unity and orderly development. And if they grew less stormily, they also did not grow as fast or far as their big St. Lawrence valley neighbour during the prosperous mid-century years. Hence that region kept the lead in population and economic advance. In 1851 there were, in round numbers, 1,840,000 people in the province of Canada, 275,000 in Nova Scotia, 193,000 in New Brunswick, 122,000 in Newfoundland and about 67,000 in Prince Edward Island. By 1861 the respective figures were 2,500,000, 330, 000, 252,000, 138,000 and 80,000. Montreal grew from some 57,000 to 90,000 inhabitants over this period, Toronto from 30,000 to almost 45,000, while Halifax and Saint John increased more moderately from 20,000 to 25,000 and 22,000 to 27,000. Similar comparisons in miles of railways built, steam mills and factories established, or in the value of provincial trade, would convey much the same picture. With its greater extent and wider resources Canada experienced the boom most fully, though considerable wealth was also amassed in Nova Scotia.

The good years really began with 1850, when the world depression of the later forties lifted and international trade revived, stimulated particularly by the gold discoveries in California. Canadian grain, flour and wood found renewed markets in industrial Britain. So did New Brunswick square timber and wooden ships built for sale abroad, while Nova Scotia thrived on supplying the British West Indies market, and on the Bluenose shipping that plied the oceans of the globe. Newfoundland's sealing and cod fisheries were buoyant; Prince Edward Island farms provisioned Newfoundland fishermen and New Brunswick lumbermen alike. The recently completed chain of St. Lawrence canals grew busier each year; the wheatfields of Canada West produced rich yields; and the Canadian lumber frontier pushed further and further up the Ottawa River. Then the Crimean War in Europe from 1854 to 1856 added further stimulus, since it cut Britain off from alternative sources of raw materials in Russia and the Baltic.

Meanwhile, the Reciprocity Treaty of 1854 with the United States had given still another spur to the provinces' economic activities. Since the British adoption of free trade in 1846 Canadians had hoped for a commercial agreement with the republic that would open American markets and thus offset the loss of tariff preferences and protection in Great Britain. For several years, however, the United States had shown little desire for lower trade barriers with its northern neighbours, being largely controlled by high protective tariff forces of its own. But in 1854 a conjunction of low tariff proponents in that country with New England fishing interests seeking access to the valuable fisheries to the north, enabled a British diplomatic mission to conclude a treaty in Washington on behalf of the colonies. To run for ten years from 1855, and then be renewable by mutual consent, it provided for reciprocal free trade in natural products between the provinces and the United States and for joint access to their North Atlantic inshore fisheries.

While the precise effects of this Reciprocity Treaty are open to argument, there is little doubt that it greatly enhanced the north-south flow of trade between the British provinces and the United States. Canadian and New Brunswick lumber went out in volume to supply rapidly expanding American factories and cities. Upper Canadian wheat and Lower Canadian coarse grains and livestock also found American markets, though much of the wheat shipped might go on through United States' ports to Britain. Prince Edward Island was pleased to find its trade enlarged. Nova Scotians, however, at first disliked the treaty, because they feared American competition in their fisheries—or at least had hoped to bargain with them to gain a better agreement for themselves. But they soon felt the advantage of having the huge American market open for their catch. So did Newfoundland, where ties with Boston increasingly grew up in its outports. In general, then, reciprocity widely ministered to the good times in British America. Yet whether or not prosperity would have continued without the treaty, it is also true that another potent factor was supplying money, jobs and confidence to the mounting boom: railway-building on a large scale was under way.

II

The 1850s really brought the railway age to the people of the provinces. When the decade opened there were only some sixty-six miles of track in all British North America. Before it ended, there were eighteen hundred miles in Canada alone. The world economic recovery from 1850 onward had much to do with this, of course. British and American capital became available for investing in railways in a broad area like Canada, where needs were evident and returns looked very promising, especially as Canadian trade continued to climb. In this prosperity, moreover, Canadian capital was accumulating, and at the same time railways had caught the popular imagination. Much of the capital influx would come from Britain, but the Canadian contribution—above all, through public expenditure—was highly important as well. The Maritime provinces seemingly offered smaller possibilities, attracted less outside capital and had only limited private resources. None the less, lines were built, in Nova Scotia and New Brunswick at least; and the people shared in the widespread railway fervour that inspired Thomas Keefer in Montreal to write *The Philosophy of Railways* (1849), or the *Acadian Recorder* in Halifax to declare in 1851, "No country can be great without Rail Roads."

Whatever the significance of the lines once they were in operation, there is no doubt that their building much increased economic activity, inflated land values and wages, and soon raised prices and costs. Very often, too, the projecting of a line was almost as important as its building. Well-publicized promotion led to overhopeful speculation, out of which, usually, only promoters and politicians gained at the general expense of both railway companies and public. Financiers and contractors like Samuel Zimmerman of

Hamilton, Casimir Gzowski of Toronto, David Macpherson or Luther Holton of Montreal, piled up fortunes and founded a new plutocracy. But when the rail boom finally broke in 1857, it bequeathed a monumental load of private and public debt and unfinished or over-extended lines for the provincial people to contend with.

Nevertheless, the consequences of the railways that were built and completed by 1860 can scarcely be overestimated. Much of the results would only become evident over the years; but even during the fifties the transforming potentialities of railways grew evident. They fostered the rise of towns at strategic points on rail routes. They stimulated a demand for rails and rolling stock which in some cases led to the beginnings of heavy machine industries. They changed social horizons, as access to provincial centres and to city newspapers improved. Inland areas no longer needed be cut off by the freeze-up of water routes, isolated by the mud and thaws that closed primitive roads for weeks in spring and fall. And for the first time long-range internal land transport systems could be conceived to overcome geographic barriers, link up provinces, and surmount the continental distances of British North America.

Of the lines constructed, the first of major importance was the St. Lawrence and Atlantic, joining Montreal with the ice-free port of Portland, Maine, to enable the Canadian metropolis to compete with American seaboard rivals for western trade despite the winter freezing of its St. Lawrence outlet. Begun in the depression years of the later forties, most of the line was built in the fifties and finished by 1853. Its successful completion owed much to the determination of Alexander Tilloch Galt, president of the company after 1849, a far-sighted entrepreneur who would soon make a mark in public life as well. So would a rising Montreal *Canadien* politician and lawyer, George Etienne Cartier, solicitor for the St. Lawrence and Atlantic.

The Montreal-Portland scheme, however, had been rivalled by an alternative plan to unite the river of Canada and the Atlantic through British territory: the Quebec to Halifax, or Intercolonial Railway. This project had been explored in the late forties as a means of strengthening colonial defence and of fostering interprovincial trade in view of the loss of British tariff protection. A route had been recommended—Major Robinson's route—down the north shore or eastern side of New Brunswick. But the scheme had failed to advance, because of daunting costs and arguments over the route. Saint John interests were particularly opposed to a line so remote from their western side of the province, even though it was held to be more defensively secure in its distance from the American border.

In 1851 the Intercolonial scheme revived when, largely through the missionary work of Joseph Howe, the British government expressed a willingness to guarantee the financing of a railway from Halifax to Quebec, to be built jointly by Nova Scotia, New Brunswick and Canada. Provincial delegations met in hopeful conference. Howe, eloquently championing the project, saw it as the precursor of a railway to the Pacific, through which "many of this room [in Halifax in 1851] would live to hear the whistle of the steam-engine in the passes of the Rocky Mountains." Francis Hincks, the skilful finance minister who now became premier of Canada, put a bill through the Canadian house for a "main trunk railway," to link with the Intercolonial at Quebec and run on across Canada to its southwestern limits. Then in 1852 the Intercolonial negotiations broke down in London, because of disagreements over the route and the terms of the British guarantee. The project was not to be forgotten, however. Colonial delegations to London took it up again in 1857 and 1858, as did subsequent interprovincial meetings in the early 1860s. The idea, or the vision, was notably influential in the Maritimes, looking for rail access to the continental interior, and to bring new trade down to their harbours. Hence in due course it became a crucial factor in the confederation movement of the sixties, when it appeared that only a union of the provinces could carry it through.

Meanwhile, in New Brunswick, ground had been broken with great ceremony at Saint John in 1853 for the European and North American. This grandly titled route was to be extended westward to Maine to link with the American railroads and the Portland line to Canada, and eastward to reach the Nova Scotian border. Actually only the track east from Saint John to Shediac on the Atlantic shore was completed, a 108-mile, government-owned railway that opened in 1860. "Western extension," long an issue in New Brunswick politics, was not to be achieved until after Confederation, nor the eastern extension to Nova Scotia until the Intercolonial finally went through. In the latter province, Howe had reluctantly put aside the Intercolonial and turned to building a provincial system. In 1854 he became chief commissioner of a Nova Scotia Railway Board, which under his vigorous supervision began branches from Halifax to Windsor and Truro. By 1858 Nova Scotia had some ninety-five miles of track crossing from Atlantic to Bay of Fundy waters, and with a good starting point at Truro for an Intercolonial route.

As for Canada, Premier Hincks had come back from the Inter-colonial discussions of 1852 in London with a plan instead to pro-ceed with the railway across his own province by private rather than public enterprise. In fact, he had reached an agreement with one of the world's leading railway-building firms, Peto, Brassey, Jackson, and Betts, to construct the Canadian main line. Accordingly, he carried legislation chartering the Grand Trunk Railway of Canada, a company with a capital of £9.5 million, to be built and financed by the Brassey interests in conjunction with great London bankers like Thomas Baring and George Glyn, and, of course, a host of British shareholders.

At the same time the Grand Trunk was not, and could not be, a wholly private concern. The province's credit and extensive financial assistance were inevitably involved in so large a project. Politics and the railway were tied inextricably together, as cabinets could not afford to let the line go down, while the railway used its powerful influence to support its political friends—with consequent loud outcries against Grand Trunk "waste" and "corruption." The powerful Toronto *Globe* led in deploring Grand Trunk influence in politics, the jobbery and lowering of public morality it produced. Thus it wrote of the passage of a new Grand Trunk aid bill in 1857: "The big Grand Trunk pig has had its fill from the trough, and now the smaller unclean animals may come in. Look out for rapid legislation and a general saturnalia among jobbers. Oh, for a Cromwell or a general election to cleanse the Augean stable of this Parliament!"

The line indeed proved lavishly expensive: not only because costs had been underestimated through ignorance of Canadian conditions of weather and terrain, but also because of the need to buy out Canadian railway entrepreneurs with competing designs of their own. And so a huge, shaky concern emerged, to run from Lévis (across from Quebec city) in the east to Sarnia in the west, and leasing the Montreal to Portland line as well. It was small wonder that the Grand Trunk was enmeshed in financial troubles from the outset. None the less, it was an enormously important and imposing achievement. The track to Lévis was open in 1854, from Montreal to Toronto, the core of the system, in 1856, and on to Sarnia in 1859. It gave Canada one great unified overland route, eleven hundred miles in length, from the sea coast to Lake Huron. Here was a whole new version of the St. Lawrence commercial empire centred on Montreal—of iron rails this time, not rivers and canals—reaching to the heart of North America. Despite its costs in political scandals and bankrupt investors, one could scarcely imagine what the country would have been like without the Grand Trunk.

Still other lines were built in Canada in the fifties; much shorter, but significant. The Great Western ran across Canada West from the Niagara River to the Detroit frontier by 1855, and was quickly extended from Hamilton to Toronto. The latter city's own first line, the Northern, began building in 1851. By 1855 its broad-stacked, wood-burning locomotives were pounding to Collingwood on Georgian Bay, on a hundred-mile passage from the lower to the upper Great Lakes that tied a rich hinterland and great timber resources to Toronto. Other lines reached north as well to tap lumber areas for American markets, until the province had a basic net of rail transport, largely focused on either Montreal or Toronto. Both cities expanded markedly through their power to dominate larger hinterlands; but so did smaller centres such as Hamilton, London or Bytown—in 1855 incorporated as the city of Ottawa.

For a'l the importance of the opening of the railway age of steam and iron, however, this was still an era of wood, wind and water. The bulkier goods still went by waterway in the open season: huge square-timber rafts down the Ottawa, St. Lawrence or Saguenay to British America's leading lumber port, Quebec; grain cargoes by

the Welland, St. Lawrence and Erie canals out to markets overseas. Around the Maritimes, the seaborne coasting trade carried far
more goods than railways. And while officious steamboats were much
in evidence for passenger traffic on lake, river or ocean, freight
mainly moved by a multitude of humbler sailing craft. Indeed, the
Maritimes were just reaching the last and golden age of sail, that
made them the fourth-largest shipping owner in the world.

Furthermore, the great wooden windship was reaching the perfec-
tion of its design at Quebec, Saint John and a host of Maritime
harbours. The towering *Marco Polo*, launched at Saint John in
1851, won world speed records. At Halifax, which flourished more
by shipowning than shipbuilding, Samuel Cunard's pioneering transatlantic steamship line was thriving though he had since removed its
main headquarters to England. From the sealers of Newfoundland to
the Great Lakes schooners there was plentiful evidence that the
1850s yet lived by water—however fast the continental age of rail
was taking shape.

III

In the early stages of the railway boom in Canada, common enthusiasm for construction projects brought together people of both
languages and of widely divergent political opinions, so that it
seemed that an era of notable good will might be in the making.
Yet new divisive forces were emerging at the selfsame time. And
nowhere was this more apparent than in the rise of radical elements
in both sections of the province.

The *rouge* movement of Canada East had already taken shape, of
course, in the later forties, inspired by the apparent triumphs of
democratic revolutions in Europe in 1848, the return to politics of
the o'd French-Canadian *nationaliste* radical champion, Louis-Joseph Papineau, and the lively annexation movement of 1849 that
had centred in Montreal. Young *rouge* idealists had dreamed of
establishing a liberated *Canadien* state in the American union. While
by 1850 annexationism was fast losing popular appeal, the *rouge*
faction continued to advocate fully democratic institutions and
sweeping reforms in church and state. They made inroads in the

left wing of the Lower Canadian reform movement, and might have made more if their attacks on clerical influence in state affairs had not roused traditionally powerful Roman Catholic forces in French Canada against them.

In Canada West, a radical movement had only taken definite form late in 1849, when a somewhat similar combination of youthful idealists and resurgent old radicals sought to reinvigorate the Upper Canadian reform party—in order to "roll the country down to a commonsense democracy," as the young Toronto lawyer, William McDougall, earnestly proclaimed. Soon dubbed "Clear Grits" by Upper Canadian Liberals who upheld the existing reform ministry under Robert Baldwin and Louis LaFontaine, the western radicals also began to make significant headway. While not so much associated with republicanism or annexation as the *rouges*, the Clear Grits also wanted to move on beyond the British system of responsible cabinet government to a written constitution on American elective lines, with manhood suffrage, vote by ballot, and other measures then considered as decidedly advanced democracy. These proposals were put forward at enthusiastic popular conventions in the countryside, and embodied in the Grit's new journal, McDougall's *North American*, particularly addressed to the "Farmers of Canada." By 1851 radicalism created such a stir in politics that both Baldwin and LaFontaine retired in frustration, leaving the government to their chief lieutenants, Francis Hincks and A. N. Morin.

Still other disturbing new forces were appearing, however: notably the voluntary movement. Voluntaryism, the doctrine that churches should be voluntarily maintained by their adherents without any state connection or financial support, had long been expressed in Upper Canada by those opposed to the clergy reserves granted to the Church of England. When in the 1840s income from the reserve lands had been distributed to other churches also, with the lion's share still going to the Anglicans, voluntaryists had continued to oppose the very principle of state aid, urging instead the total separation of church and state. The Clear Grits themselves took up the demand for final abolition of the reserves. They accused the government of delaying, and thought that this was due to the influence of French-Canadian supporters who, as Roman Catholics, accepted links between religious and secular affairs. The Catholic Church, declared the *North American*, "is to all intents and purposes the established church of this country."

Voluntaryism was also fervently espoused in some of the Upper Canadian Protestant denominations, notably among the Scottish Free Church Presbyterians. One prominent Free Kirk Scot and Liberal was George Brown, the massive, red-haired editor of the Toronto *Globe*, which he had made the strongest reform paper in Canada, since launching it in 1844. Brown had vigorously opposed the Clear Grit movement from the start, chiefly because he believed in the superiority of the British parliamentary system over the American political model. Nevertheless, he did become worried himself over the government's inaction on the reserves. He took the *Globe* on a strongly voluntaryist course and was soon elected to Parliament to pursue it there as an independent reformer.

Even more important for the long run, Brown and other Upper Canadian voluntaryists became strenuous opponents of Roman Catholic "aggression" in public affairs, chiefly in regard to school legislation. In Canada West, the School Act of 1850 had considerably enlarged Roman Catholic rights to state-aided separate schools. The *Globe* and its Protestant following saw this as an "entering wedge" threatening the majority's non-sectarian public school system in Canada West. The Catholics, on the other hand, claimed rights equal to those enjoyed by Protestants in Canada East, where the majority schools were religious and Catholic. The fact was that the Upper Canadian Roman Catholic population, enlarged by the heavy Irish immigration of the late forties, was mounting a drive for its own state-supported school system. Backed by Lower Canadian Catholic votes in Parliament, they were able to obtain a measure of improvement in 1852-53; though this to many Upper Canadian Protestants only appeared as French and Catholic dominance of the educational policies of the West. "We shall consider no institution safe from priestly encroachment, if this bill is carried," the *Globe* had darkly warned.

In any case, just as there was ardent voluntaryism growing in Canada West, so there was a strong resurgence of Catholic zeal in Canada East, seeking new enactments also to incorporate church bodies for teaching, charitable and hospital purposes. These ecclesiastical corporations seemed the very contradiction of voluntaryist desires to separate church and state. "We can never have peace in Canada," thundered Brown, "until the principle is acknowledged that every church is to stand on its own foundation without aid from the government or legislature." There were angry rows in Parliament between the two strongly held viewpoints; and outside there were violent episodes, such as the Gavazzi riots of 1853 in Quebec and Montreal, where shots rang out between embattled Protestant and Catholic factions.

Still further, to add to this sharpening sectarian and sectional division, it became evident from the census reported in 1852 that Canada West had passed Canada East in population, the figures now standing at 952,000 to 890,000. That fact gave whole new meaning to a principle already raised in Parliament, representation according to population. If this replaced the existing equal representation of the two Canadas in the united legislature, then Canada West would have a majority of members there. Representation by population thus would be a means of combatting the "dominance" of the close-knit French-Canadian block that was inevitably influential in any union government.

George Brown moved it in Parliament in 1853. Though defeated, "rep. by pop." increasingly gathered support from Upper Canadians. It seemed eminently just to them, underrepresented and controlled by the East as they held themselves to be—particularly when, as they claimed, they also paid the larger share of provincial taxes because the West's trade was larger and more active. But French Canadians quite naturally rejected rep. by pop. out of hand, fearing to see themselves under a hostile English domination once again.

The prominent Quebec journal, *Le Canadien*, thus expressed it:

> In the nineteenth century, in an English colony, a British subject dares to proc'aim as a principle of government that a mill'on French Canadians deserve proscription on account of their origin and their faith. Before such savagery of sentiment what else can the Lower Canadian representatives do than stand squarely before this terrorism and say to it, "You shall not pass."

Hence sectional strains only grew more acute, and the existing political party structure began to break up. In 1854 Hincks resigned and a new political alliance took power. It was composed of the Lower Canadian moderate Liberal followers of Morin, those Upper Canadian ministerial supporters who had stayed with Hincks, and Tory-Conservative forces led by Sir Allan MacNab. The resulting MacNab-Morin government was thus a Liberal-Conservative coalition, dedicated to keeping the existing union going, proceeding with the Grand Trunk, and at least settling two rooted problems of the two Canadas, the clergy reserves in the West and the old seigneurial system in the East. Acts of 1854 finally abolished the reserves endowment, transferring its funds to municipal purposes, and ended the old land-holding system of the St. Lawrence that dated back to the days of New France. The Liberal-Conservative coalition established itself firmly in power.

It was, after all, an effective combination of the main French-Canadian group (increasingly concerned to conserve *Canadien* identity from radical and sectarian attack) with conservative but dynamic business-minded elements who stressed material development for the province. Very soon, moreover, the alliance came under the control of younger, abler leaders, the amiable and highly astute John A. Macdonald and the combative but very perceptive George Cartier. By 1857 the coalition government had become the Macdonald-Cartier ministry, heralding one of the great political partnerships of Canadian history and the founding of a future national Conservative party that broadly combined both Canadians and *Canadiens*.

Meanwhile the remnants of the old reform forces that had remained outside the coalition—the *rouges,* the Clear Grits and the voluntaryist followers of Brown—were coming together themselves as a rival, Liberal, political formation. They were, indeed, a much looser formation, lacking the helpfully unifying factor of having offices to allocate. But eastern *rouges* and western reformers could agree at any rate in attacking the Conservative regime's alleged misuses of power, especially in regard to its sustaining Grand Trunk extravagance and immorality. Furthermore, the Grits and Brown, at least, came closer together in an increasingly potent western Liberal alliance. After another school act in 1855 was manifestly put through by Lower Canadian votes, Brown brought the Grits behind him in a clamorous concerted campaign for rep. by pop. The latter laid aside their earlier demands for elective constitutional reforms in order to concentrate with him on the sectional wrongs of Upper Canada. In 1857, an Upper Canada Reform Convention in Toronto sealed the bargain by adopting a common platform for "no sectarian schools," rep. by pop.—and the acquisition by Canada of the great northwest beyond the Lakes.

At the end of that year, Brown and his reorganized Grit Liberals swept the elections in Upper Canada, worsting Macdonald's Conservative following. In Lower Canada Cartier's supporters, now termed *bleus,* defeated the *rouges* under A. A. Dorion in Lower Canada and kept the balance fairly even (though there were some doubtful returns in one Lower Canadian constituency, where George Washington, Julius Caesar and Judas Iscariot were each recorded as having cast their votes). It was evident in any case that another future national party was also taking shape: the Liberal party, which across Canada today still widely bears the name of "Grit," as in George Brown's time.

IV

In October 1857, financial panic spreading from London and New York soon brought an end to the great boom in Canada. Railway speculation collapsed, overextended merchants had to face their creditors, and for the next year or so trade prospects were gloomy. Yet 1857 brought something else as well: a whole new interest in the northwest of British America. It was not just coincidence that the Upper Canadian Liberals made the acquisition of the northwest a major part of their platform that year, that a select committee of the imperial Parliament held an inquiry into the future of the Hudson's Bay Company's territories, and that two expeditions, a Canadian and a British, were sent west across the great plains to report on their potentialities for settlement. This was, in fact, a time of much increased awareness of western issues in British North America, especially in the western half of the province of Canada itself.

By the 1850s, the once extensive farm frontiers of Upper Canada had largely been settled. There was still a good deal of filling-in to do; but in general, the Canadian agricultural frontier had come up against the rugged Precambrian Shield. In the mid-fifties it grew clear that would-be farm settlers had to look beyond the existing limits of Canada for new fertile areas to occupy. Some moved on to the American mid-West below the Lakes; but others turned their gaze beyond, to the empty prairies ruled over by the Hudson's Bay Company. George Brown's *Globe* ardently took up the cause. In 1856 it opened a powerful campaign, extolling the value of the great northwest, "the vast and fertile territory which is our birthright." At the same time business interests in the fast-growing city of Toronto were looking for new worlds to conquer in northwestern trade. Their Northern Railway pointed in that direction; they organized a steamboat line from Georgian Bay to Lake Superior; and towards the end of 1856 the Toronto Board of Trade petitioned the legislature to investigate the Hudson's Bay Company's title to its vast holdings. Accordingly, the Upper Canadian Liberal party's demand for the northwest represented a powerful combination of western sectional forces. It brought together a mass of rural voters, strongly Clear Grit in outlook, with an urban business leadership closely associated with George Brown.

The Liberal-Conservative government under Macdonald and Cartier also was concerned to express Canada's interest in the northwest; an interest based on claims from the days when Nor'westers from Canada staked out a fur trade domain all the way to the Arctic and Pacific and, even earlier, from the time of New France when that ancestor of Canada first proclaimed title to the lands beyond the Lakes. Thus the Canadian government sent Chief Justice Draper, a former premier, to London in 1857 to indicate Canada's interests at the imperial inquiry into the Hudson's Bay Company's position. He was not to do much more, however. The Macdonald regime did not think the time had come yet to try to take over the West; and Cartier and the French Canadians felt, with some reason, that the present Grit Liberal proposal to do so meant mainly to expand Canada West enormously, thereby making rep. by pop. still harder to resist.

The imperial government felt its own concern about the future of the northwest, as it saw American settlement steadily spreading across the plains and up towards the 49th parallel, recalling that in the 1840s the Hudson's Bay fur traders had had to abandon Oregon to an influx of American settlers along the Pacific slope. There was also the question of the British Parliament renewing the Company's licence to a trade monopoly in the great areas beyond Rupert's Land—the lands draining into Hudson Bay which it owned outright by its charter of 1670. The need for periodic renewal of the Company's rights to trade and govern in an immense northwestern territory hence enabled Parliament in 1857 to set up a committee of inquiry into the future of the West. After taking detailed evidence, that committee recommended that fertile districts along the Red and Saskatchewan Rivers might be transferred to Canada when it was ready to develop them, and that Company rule and monopoly on the Pacific coast should be wound up. In Canada, some received the findings with pleasure, as indicating that a new era was dawning for the northwest; but others were aggrieved that the whole Bay Company realm was not freely and immediately to be turned over to the province.

In any case it was the handwriting on the wall for the old fur trade empire. The 1850s really spelled its end, preparing the way for its transfer to a new Canadian federal state in the next decade. Since the union of the fur trade companies in 1821, the Hudson's Bay regime had ruled over half a continent peacefully and prosperously, thanks particularly to the masterful supervision of its energetic "little emperor," Governor Sir George Simpson. But now the Company was not only under pressure from outside; there were crucial changes occurring within its domain as well.

At the Red River, the one real colony of agricultural settlement in the Hudson's Bay territory of the plains, the Company had been forced by the fifties to allow free traders to operate, to deal with powerful commercial houses south in Minnesota rather than rely on its older, harder route out northward by way of Hudson Bay. The trade southward with St. Paul in Minnesota was enlarging American ties and penetration, at first by overland trail and long trains of ox-drawn Red River carts, and from 1859 by steamboat down the river itself. A vanguard of Canadians also began arriving late in the fifties, soon to talk of annexing Red River to Canada. The old stable relationships of French- and English-speaking farmers in the little community, and of Hudson's Bay traders and Métis buffalo-hunters were increasingly affected as wholly new horizons opened for the Red River colony.

On the Pacific coast, the Company had been granted Vancouver Island in 1849 in order to found a settlement there. After the lesson of Oregon, the British government wanted a colony to strengthen possession of the great far western territory it still held, reaching northward to Russian-owned Alaska. Settlers were brought from Britain, and an attractive little farming community gradually developed about Fort Victoria, the Company's new far western base. But this distant island colony grew very slowly—until gold was discovered on the neighbouring mainland where the turbulent Fraser swept down from the high Pacific ranges. A host of eager miners rushed north from San Francisco in 1858 and tranquil Victoria, their jumping-off point for the Fraser, became a boom town overnight.

So many American gold-seekers poured into the Fraser valley that James Douglas, the Hudson's Bay chief factor and the governor of Vancouver Island, feared that lawless violence or another Oregon *fait accompli* might occur. Proclaiming his authority over the mainland coast, he worked swiftly to establish orderly control there. In 1858, the British government went further and set up the new colony of British Columbia on the mainland, with Douglas also as governor. Royal Engineers laid out its capital by the mouth of the Fraser, a river bank clearing in the great coastal forest christened New Westminster—and more lightly termed "the imperial stump field." The presence of the Royal Navy on the coast underpinned the raw young colony. But Douglas's firm foresighted actions had done much to ensure that the Pacific portion of British America would be preserved for a transcontinental union, when the rule of the Bay Company in the West was gone.

Back east, in Canada at any rate, these striking western developments of 1857-58 roused a significant response. In the Canadian Parliament in 1858 Alexander Galt, then an independent member, brought in a set of resolutions that virtually forecast the subsequent program of Confederation. Galt called for a general, and federal, union of the British American colonies, one which would also include the western lands and settlements. This met the rising Upper Canadian demand for bringing in the West; but more than that, by indicating that it could be done through federation, it also answered French-Canadian fears that adding the northwest would only enlarge Upper Canada. Galt's plan indeed proposed a general British North American union, which Conservatives had often talked of, and a federal system too, which a Liberal, A. A. Dorion, had already suggested in Parliament in 1856 for the two Canadas alone, as a way of solving the sectional strains between them.

Galt's scheme was thus a comprehensive, constructive compromise. But as yet it was premature; for many still sought to keep the existing Canadian union, many others demanded rep. by pop., and still others advocated the double majority principle, whereby a government would have to hold a majority for its measures from both sections of the province. Nevertheless, the idea of federal union soon took a significant step forward. In the summer of 1858, the uncertain party balance in Canada briefly brought a Brown-Dorion Liberal ministry into office, quickly replaced by a reconstructed Cartier-Macdonald regime. Galt agreed to enter as minister of finance, on condition that the cabinet take up the policy he had proposed as the answer to the country's sectional and constitutional problems. Accordingly, a mission went to England that fall, and approaches were made to the Atlantic colonies to consider a general scheme of federal union. Neither the British authorities nor the other colonies showed any interest, however. As yet they saw no need for such a fundamental change.

Still, Galt had now placed the Canadian Conservative government plainly on record as supporting a general confederation. The next year, 1859, its Liberal opponents also took a major step forward beyond rep by pop to support the federal concept. In November, at a large Reform Convention in Toronto, George Brown and William McDougall swung exasperated Grits away from demanding a simple dissolution of the existing Canadian union, bringing them to accept instead a policy of federation for the two Canadas: each to have their own government for sectional matters under a joint authority for those of common concern. And this federated system, Brown made plain, in time should be extended to include the other British American communities to east or west, "as one great confederation." And so, by 1860, both the parties and some of the chief leaders in the province of Canada had taken up the theme of confederation. Out of disunion assuredly had come the idea of a greater union. Of course, a good deal still had to transpire before that idea could be realized. But even if the fifties had not done so much to lay the groundwork for the confederation years, they would still have been a remarkably lively and productive decade.

The boom, reciprocity, the railway, all suggested activity enough. Beyond that, Paul Kane was painting his celebrated studies of western Indians, Cornelius Krieghoff his equally famed scenes of rural *Canadien* life; Octave Crémazie was founding a noted school of French-Canadian romantic poetry and Pierre Chauveau delineating the classic *Canadien* agrarian novel. At the same time William Logan's pioneering work with the Canadian Geological Survey shaped the science of Canadian geology, while universities like Laval, Toronto and New Brunswick took enduring form. The first became a university as well as a theological seminary in 1852; the second received its basic provincial structure through acts of 1849 and 1853; and the third emerged from the secularization of Anglican King's College at Fredericton in 1859. Nor was this all in widening cultural activity. Rising printing houses, theatres and handsome public buildings—like Toronto's St. Lawrence Hall or Halifax's new Court House—also marked it in their own ways. So did the emergence of the mass circulation daily newspaper, printed on steam-driven rotary presses, whether Montreal's *Gazette* and *La Minerve* or Toronto's *Globe* and *Leader*.

The quality of life was clearly changing from earlier colonial times. Not only were factory whistles sounding in Galt and Hamilton, Sherbrooke and Saint John, but the railway station and planked or gravelled buggy roads began to diffuse the goods and amenities of industrial society into rural areas: the pioneer look was fast disappearing in well-settled portions of the provinces. One less fortunate aspect was that standardized construction methods and materials—mass-produced brick, lumber and machine-made ornament—were replacing older localized building techniques, so that the 1850s also largely marked the passing of attractive indigenous architectural traditions in much of British North America.

In the larger centres the concentrating, growing population also produced sharper class divisions, and the stirring of an organized labour movement. Printers and other skilled trades increasingly formed unions; there were numerous strikes and lockouts also. At the same time the founding of new banks and insurance or loan companies from Halifax and Saint John through to Toronto and Hamilton, the building of provincial or civic hospitals, of asylums and "houses of refuge," all testified to an increasingly affluent and complicated society. It is remarkable how many such institutions appeared in this decade. Many of their buildings still survive today, along with the county court houses, the numerous churches and substantial brick or stone mansions erected in those flush times, having thus far escaped the so-called developer. Indeed, in many respects the 1850s really saw—for better and worse—the beginnings of modern Canada. In a multitude of ways they forecast the ending of one age and the opening of another for the inhabitants of British North America.

11: The 1860s

P. B. WAITE

Neither in North America nor in Europe were the 1860s peaceful. Between 1861 and 1865 the United States fought a long and bitter civil war over the Southern attempt to split the country into two, ending with the assassination of President Lincoln. Mexico was occupied by the French in 1862, who installed Maximilian as Emperor of Mexico, an occupation which ended with the victory of Juarez and the execution of Maximilian by a firing squad in 1867. In Europe there was war in Italy over Piedmont's attempts to unite the Italian principalities; there was war in Germany, between Prussia and Denmark in 1864, between Prussia and Austria in 1866, mainly over attempts to unite Germany; there was to be war between France and Germany in 1870, one result of the North German Confederation of July 1, 1867.

Political unifications in Europe, the North's success in re-uniting the United States, the union of eastern British North America on July 1, 1867, with additions of the West to come in 1870 and 1871, were, all of them, concomitants of railways. It was indeed possible to conceive of a united Italy, a united Germany, a united British North America without railways: with them such unions became feasible in a practical, physical sense. With railways it was possible to stitch together, so to speak, principalities and provinces. The very existence of railways in the 1860s as a present reality, enabled men to amplify their conceptions of their own world.

That railways were desirable, indeed that they were essential, was an assumption natural and easy for British North Americans to make. A small population, vast stretches of forest, had always kept the colonies distant from each other; this had also made ordinary roads difficult to build well, and often extremely uncomfortable to ride upon. The railway could bring colonies together; it could solve at once the problem of a smooth permanent way, available in winter, spring, summer and fall, and which could be travelled at steady speeds that no horse, or two horses, could match. In effecting this revolution railways had thus thrown men's conceptions of distance far outward, from twelve miles a day to four hundred; and for some, it had made worlds that had once seemed comfortable and viable, now seem narrow and visionless.

The restlessness of some politicians of the 1860s, especially those who had moved about British North America and the United States by steamships, or steam locomotives, is understandable in this new context of colonial worlds becoming markedly smaller; it must be also understood, however, that there continued to exist the strong conservatism, especially of rural populations, many of whom had not yet undergone this unsettling experience.

The changes that railways were to bring with them were as yet unheralded, but signs were already apparent: the growth of the influence and power of cities, and of the institutions that cities bred; equally, the beginning of the decay of small rural settlements, and the trades associated with them—blacksmiths and coopers, wheelwrights and carriage-makers. The world would not, for a long time yet, be able to do without blacksmiths; but the ironmongery associated with their trade, to say nothing of the products of other trades, would not for long be able to compete with the products that the railways were now going to be able to distribute from factories in the cities. The power of city newspapers was to grow all through the 1860s as the increase in the circulation of the newspapers of Halifax, Saint John, Quebec, Montreal, Toronto and London was to show; less obvious was the beginning of the decay of the facilities and institutions of country life, the artisan crafts, the inns and posthouses, the quiet, unruffled, concentric circles of communication around the village.

There is an interesting illustration of this as early as 1857, reported by a New Brunswick editor in the Saint John *Morning News* of June 10, who had travelled to Halifax. At that time, the Nova Scotia Railway, a government-built enterprise, had been completed all of ten miles northward out of Halifax, along the shores of Bedford Basin to Bedford at the head of the basin. The new railway had already made Bedford into a thriving village. There the horses and wagons with their hay, lumber, and produce, came in from the countryside, got onto the "cars," as they were called, often horses, wagons, drivers and all, for the ten miles into the city. The Saint John editor noted that the inns and posthouses for the ten miles along the old wagon road into Halifax, which had for so long supplied fodder to the horses, and food and spirits to their drivers, and to the travelling public, were now "deserted and some of them are going to ruin." That little railway had been going for just two years. Society pays a price, often thoughtlessly, and often unremembered, for its changes.

In the Province of Canada, railways were already playing a substantial role both in society and in politics, as they were to continue to do all through the nineteenth century, and after. The last section of the most famous enterprise, the Grand Trunk Railway— 1,100 miles as it came to be, from Portland, Maine to Montreal, through Toronto, Guelph and Sarnia to Chicago—was completed in July 1860. The monumental wrought-iron bridge across the St. Lawrence at Montreal, begun in 1854, was opened for traffic on December 15, 1859.

The Victoria Bridge was the final straw in the tortuous history of

Grand Trunk financing. By 1860 the Grand Trunk had a total indebtedness of $72 million. For an 1,100-mile railway this was not outrageous, provided traffic was high and operating profits proportionate. But neither was. Receipts from operations were only 12 per cent over operating costs, and that 12 per cent, the net income of the company, amounted in 1859 to only $250,000. That kind of money could not begin to pay even the interest on the debt, let alone amortize it, or still more important perhaps, to pay a dividend to the long-suffering shareholders of the company. One exasperated shareholder, H. C. Chapman, came out to Canada from Lancashire in the summer of 1860 to see for himself. One explanation was that

> the Grand Trunk has been used for political purposes and that the provincial Grand Trunk money has been spent in bribery and corruption. Be this as it may, I am quite satisfied that the Grand Trunk has not begun to be managed as a commercial carrying company . . .

An example at Sarnia will illustrate the point. The Grand Trunk wanted to buy a piece of property there, 330 acres, that was under the control of the British War Office, it being ordnance property. The British Treasury authorized its sale for $825. But somehow it got into the hands of a Canadian contracting company, Gzowski, Macpherson & Co., who ultimately sold it to the Grand Trunk for $120,000.

But the Grand Trunk could not be allowed to go under. Neither the Canadian government, already heavily committed, nor the British bankers, could afford to allow it. Partly as a result of Chapman's disclosures, Edward Watkin was made managing director in July 1861 and conducted a vigorous house-cleaning of Canadian operations, with his eye especially upon traffic. Watkin engendered enough confidence on both sides of the Atlantic that a tidying-up bill, with additional funds, was passed without much difficulty by a Reform government in the Province of Canada in July 1862. Watkin became president a few months later, where he remained until 1869. But not even Watkin could solve the formidable agenda of Grand Trunk problems, especially in the face of the shareholders who had endured much, and who by the mid-1860s wanted dividends rather than seeing more money expended on improvements on the line. No full account is possible here of the manifold vicissitudes of the Grand Trunk in the 1860s; but it was going to remain a railway, and ultimately, by the 1870s, it was going to earn dividends.

Much different is the story of the Great Western. Here the enterprise was not only Canadian in inception, but the members of its board were either Canadians or Americans; and though much of the capital was subscribed from England, not a little came from Canada, and about one-fifth came from New York state. The Great Western has been rather neglected in most general accounts of the period; many success stories are, when there are more lurid ones around. The Great Western made money almost from the start, in the limited, but lucrative, constituency of southwest Ontario. It made its fortunes not only from local traffic, but from through American traffic from Detroit to Buffalo, which avoided the long trip around the south side of Lake Erie. The Great Western suffered losses in handling depreciated northern dollars in the civil war years; the Canadian government's insistence on a 5'6" gauge instead of the 4'8½" gauge that the company wanted was an additional handicap: nevertheless, the Great Western prospered in spite of all, and by 1870 its common stock was paying a healthy 6 per cent.

II

In 1862, near the Great Western station of Wyoming, about thirteen miles east of Sarnia, oil was discovered. It had been noted as early as the 1840s by the great Canadian geologist, Sir William Logan; shipments were made to Hamilton as early as 1858; and from that well near Wyoming, C. W., came three thousand barrels of oil a day. It was used at first for lubrication; but through an invention that a Nova Scotian, Abraham Gesner, had discovered, much more important uses were found. Gesner had derived from coal an oil that we sometimes call coal oil, and which he named kerosene. It made a clear, bright, nearly odourless light. Dr. Gesner had tried to form a company in Halifax, but was forced to go to New York, where he sold his patents, thus providing the start for the kerosene refining industry on Long Island. The process was soon applied, and more effectively, to crude oil. From there the refining process was to return to Canada in the 1870s.

Kerosene was to work a great change in the domestic life of Canada from the mid-1860s on, replacing whale oil and candles for domestic use, and soon being a serious competitor with gas illumination. This reciprocity between Canadian inventors and American capital in the development of kerosene was to be illustrated even more graphically with the telephone in the 1870s. As Alexander Graham Bell said, "the telephone was conceived in Brantford, and born in Boston." It could also be said that kerosene was conceived in Nova Scotia and born in New York.

By the 1860s reciprocity of enterprise extended in other important directions. The Reciprocity Treaty of 1854 between British North America and the United States had given the British colonies new markets for their natural products of fish, lumber, wheat and flour. Commercial relations between the Province of Canada and the neighbouring states had been close, and the official figures of trade understate the reality. There was a thriving trade across the Lakes that was rarely recorded on official returns. The Reciprocity Treaty also, while its concession of the Maritime inshore fisheries was resented there, had given the Atlantic provinces a useful *quid pro quo* in free entry of fish and fish products into the United States. Had reciprocity continued, it is possible that Confederation might never have gathered enough impetus to overcome strong regional inertia. But as it was, the Americans began moves to abrogate the Treaty just about the time the Confederation movement was getting actively under way, and about the time when prospects for a Northern victory in the ghastly civil war began to brighten.

The Reciprocity Treaty was to run for ten years from 1854, after which abrogation could take place at any time with a year's notice. In 1859 the Finance Minister, A. T. Galt, put duties of 20 per cent to 25 per cent on hardware, machinery, clothing and textiles. The Canadian government needed the income, and Canadian manufacturers wanted protection. British manufacturers protested, but the British were not in a position to do much, short of vetoing the tariff bill, which the Colonial Office, despite some pressure, refused to do. The Americans disliked the Canadian tariff also; it was, so they said, against the spirit of the Treaty, even though it may have conformed to the letter of its terms. This agitation served as a focus for Congress, and talk about ending Reciprocity began seriously about the time when it was possible to abrogate it. A motion for abrogation of Reciprocity was only narrowly defeated in Congress in May 1864; a similar motion passed the following December, ending the Treaty on March 17, 1866. This in turn forced British North Americans, in 1864, 1865 and after, to think about trade with each other.

Confederation has often been treated as a political event. It was a political event; but support for Confederation came not only from political arguments, and from military ones, but from a great diversity of economic arguments, some justified in the event, some not. In this context, as well as in any political rationale, the Intercolonial Railway was conceived as the central axis of British North American trade and communication.

An Intercolonial railway could be hardly anything but an heroic enterprise; it could not be a lucrative one. If an 1,100-mile railway like the Grand Trunk, through the heart of a province of 2.5 million people, could not make money, there was no reason to expect that a 700-mile railway running from Quebec to Halifax, through provinces whose population amounted to one-fifth of that, would be wildly profitable. So the Intercolonial railway languished; Nova Scotia and New Brunswick went ahead, and under government auspices, built their own bits and pieces, but nothing else happened.

Then in 1861 came the *Trent* crisis. The American civil war had broken out in April 1861. In November of that year two Confederate agents were travelling in the British mail steamer *Trent* from Havana to London. On the high seas in the Bahamas Channel the *Trent* was stopped at gunpoint by a Union warship, and the two agents forcibly taken off. The British had done this sort of thing to Americans during the Napoleonic wars, and Americans had protested bitterly: now, half a century later it was Britain's turn to protest. The British prime minister, Lord Palmerston, was not famous for his pacific gestures; he stormed into cabinet, flung the despatch upon the table, and said, "I don't know whether you'll stand for this, but I'll be damned if I will." Off went a truculent despatch to the American government, toned down only at the last minute by a sensible Prince Consort; off went 14,000 British troops to British North America, just as soon as they could be got together and the ships collected; and the *Trent* crisis was on in earnest. Only one troopship was able to land troops at the mouth of the St. Lawrence before ice closed in, in December 1861; the rest had to go to Saint John and get overland to Quebec and Montreal mainly by sleigh, through January snows.

The *Trent* crisis showed that however useful the Grand Trunk line from Portland, Maine to Montreal might have been in peacetime, it was useless for purposes like these. The crisis passed; the Americans had enough to do with their own war, and they allowed the Confederate agents to proceed to England. Nevertheless, British-American relations were badly strained, and in this atmosphere of tension the fortunes of the long-neglected Intercolonial were given a great lift. The railway, it was now clear, was a military necessity, whatever might be said of its money-making prospects.

There had been an intercolonial conference at Quebec in 1861 on the Intercolonial railway; but much more progress was made a year later when, in September 1862, also at Quebec, the governments of Canada, New Brunswick and Nova Scotia agreed to share the costs of the railway on the proportion $5:31\frac{1}{2}:3\frac{1}{2}$. This was far more useful for the Province of Canada than spending \$1 million on militia, a bill for which had been defeated in the Assembly just four months before, and which had brought down the Cartier-Macdonald Liberal-Conservative government.

There was then a delegation to England for negotiating the essential British guarantee for a bond issue; Gladstone, who was Chancellor of the Exchequer, and no mean watch-dog, insisted on a sinking fund as prerequisite. The Canadian delegates did not like a sinking fund. The Nova Scotians and New Brunswickers also had reservations, although they were willing to negotiate the matter; but the Canadians went home, leaving a disagreeable impression behind them. Still, no one yet believed that the Province of Canada would really break up the agreement completely on what was, so it seemed, a minor point.

But the Sandfield Macdonald Reform government in Canada had never been exactly enthusiasts for the Intercolonial; many were the accusations they had levelled at the Grand Trunk, and by 1863, with the *Trent* crisis fading away, all their latent uneasiness about the whole Intercolonial project came to the surface. Adverse pressure from both western and eastern elements in the Reform party made it no easier. A. A. Dorion had resigned in 1862, ostensibly because of the Intercolonial railway commitments already made, and in any case the Reform government was not strong in the Canadian Assembly. Dorion's rejoining the government in the summer of 1863 was a portent of things to come; in September 1863 the Sandfield Macdonald government, having hedged as long as it could, suddenly made it clear that they were going to abandon the project. They would now only agree to a joint survey. Neither Nova Scotia nor New Brunswick had any intention of contributing to a survey with no prospect of a railway; and on this point, the whole project jarred to a grinding stop, in a cloud of dust and sparks. Perfidious Canada! was the cry that echoed in Saint John and Halifax.

The Maritime union movement of 1863-64 grew partly from this disillusionment with Canada. Maritime union had been thought of for years; once Nova Scotia had been all one; Prince Edward Island was cut off in 1769, and New Brunswick and Cape Breton followed in 1784. Cape Breton was re-united with Nova Scotia in 1820; was a wholly re-united "Acadia" possible? If possible, was it desirable? Lieutenant-governors in the Maritime colonies certainly thought so, and some Maritime politicians did too. Maritime governors thought of Maritime union as a means by which Maritime politicians might be raised from the ruck of their parochial and mean concerns; and it did represent, for a few politicians, an attempt to break free of the little colonies that now seemed confining. And since, in the Maritime provinces, Maritime union was often felt to be an alternative to British North American union, it was not surprising that in the reaction against Canada in the autumn of 1863, perceptible impetus was given to the union of Nova Scotia, New Brunswick and Prince Edward Island. Perceptible, but not enough. For though resolutions approving a conference to discuss it passed all three Maritime legislatures in the spring sessions of 1864, the debates were brief, and unproductive of great public interest. In Prince Edward Island what public reaction there was, was distinctly averse to any union that would surrender to any body, outside of Charlottetown, control over the domestic concerns of the Island. Perhaps if the capital of a united "Acadia" were to be in Charlottetown, Prince Edward Island might be disposed to be more favourable! That was something that Halifax and Fredericton were likely to receive with something less than enthusiasm.

Another event weakened the Maritime union project. The Canadian government decided early in 1864 to set the Intercolonial survey going, all by themselves with Canadian money. It was a useful gesture. Sandford Fleming was appointed the previous autumn; now, in February 1864, he was sent on his way, and by late April he was already in Halifax, having come over the Gaspé mountains from Rimouski, and so via Fredericton to Nova Scotia.

Then came the Canadian coalition of June 1864. The precariousness of Sandfield Macdonald's government of 1862 was matched by the Taché-Macdonald government that succeeded it in March 1864. That new Conservative government lasted only three months. There were two polarities in the province of Canada: the Reform party, strong in Canada West, and with a weak, though interesting, *rouge* wing in Canada East; the other, the Conservative party, strong as the *bleu* party in Canada East, but weak in Canada West. And while there were moderates in between (some of them had helped to form Sandfield Macdonald's government), nevertheless the pull of Canada East and of Canada West, from opposite sides of politics, weakened moderates so that no effective centre party was possible. And there were exacerbations that had made political life increasingly difficult; Canada West believed that when there was a Conservative government the West paid the taxes, and the East spent the money; Canada East believed that if there was a Reform government, the East would be ruled by unfriendly and bitter opponents of their race and religion. In practice, it was nothing like so simple as this; but prejudices are convenient, and their happy owners never consider complications.

The broad truth was that the Province of Canada had outgrown her 1841 constitution. Canada West was convinced that it was being victimized by French-Canadian insistence on the continuation of equal representation of the two sections of Canada in the Canadian Assembly. This system—each section had 65 members—had once worked in Canada West's favour; but the public have short memories and after the 1861 census, when it was obvious that Canada West's population had well out-distanced Canada East's (1.6 to 1.1 million), the cry for rep. by pop. was bound to grow stronger. So the driving force for change came from Canada West.

Answers had been talked of before, in the late 1850s: breaking the union into its two original provinces, for example. But Canada West needed the port of Montreal and the whole transportation complex of the St. Lawrence valley that radiated westward from Montreal. Another solution was federation of the Province of Canada, leaving each section to deal with its own local problems, but having a common central government for common purposes between them. That might have been accomplished; it was what the Reform party in Canada West wanted. But a bigger, more glittering solution was also conceivable, which had the great advantage of securing ice-free ports in British territory, the acquiring of the northwest for Canada West's burgeoning population, and with Newfoundland as the eastern gateway and British Columbia the western. That glittering idea was Confederation, a union of all the British North American colonies, *a mari usque ad mare*.

III

It was a gargantuan, grandiose, some might even have said, harebrained, scheme. There were 3,500 miles between Newfoundland and British Columbia, and but 3.5 million people. What form of government could hold together such a vast agglomeration of territory with so few people in it? Even if such a government could be conceived what kind of moral or political force could it exercise?

Here it can be said that whatever lessons the United States may have had to teach British North America, whether the American constitution was to be followed or avoided, whether a democratic federal republic was good or bad, whatever examples the United States could present to British North America, there was one message that was writ large and plain: it could be done. It was possible to joint Atlantic and Pacific within one form of government. It could be done, for the Americans had done it. It was true that their population was ten times that of British North America—California alone had over a million people; but there the message was, nevertheless. Why not? By 1864 the American transcontinental railway between Atlantic and Pacific had been chartered; the Union Pacific–Central Pacific system was to be completed in 1869. That British North Americans could do the same was at once breathtaking and absurd. And the realization of it was to take not just three years, when in 1867 the first nucleus was established; not just seven years, even though Manitoba and British Columbia had joined by 1871: rather it was to take the energies, money, resourcefulness and courage of Canadians down to, and after, July 1886, when the first transcontinental train, west out of Montreal, would steam into Port Moody, B.C.

Thus when George Brown, the leader of the Reform party of Canada West, proposed to John A. Macdonald and Cartier, leaders of the Conservative party, a coalition to deal once and for all with the problems of the Province of Canada, he was in effect not only making a great personal sacrifice, he was proposing something truly enormous, that was going to take great draughts of persistence and energy to drive through. Confederation was a neat solution for the problems of the province; but it was to create additional ones on a scale that neither Brown, Cartier, nor Macdonald were in a position to fully appreciate.

The Canadian coalition of June 1864 wound up the spring. Nothing is more striking than the immense resourcefulness and determination of the Canadians to push Confederation through at all hazards, once they had decided to put their weight to it. To do this, however, they needed the unstinting support of prescient, capable, and courageous Maritimers, and a strong push from the British in London. As it turned out, they got both. How it was done is the story of the three years between June 1864 and July 1867.

No full account of this fascinating story is possible in this essay. It is a history of intercolonial discovery, of how New Brunswickers and Nova Scotians came to know Canadians, and how they were prepared (some of them at least), to risk their local political careers in the hope of securing something much bigger. Their actions were not without self-interest: Tupper and Tilley, of Nova Scotia and New Brunswick respectively, could expect to receive, and did receive, rewards, by taking their places on a bigger and more imposing stage, and with offices and salaries to go with them. Not everyone, by any means, in Nova Scotia, New Brunswick, or French Canada —to say nothing of Prince Edward Island and Newfoundland— was prepared to accept such a monumental change. Some were conscientiously, some even bitterly, opposed to Confederation. It is too easy to assume that those who supported Confederation were right, and those who opposed it were wrong. Historians need to keep their heads level and remember facts. But even these, for or against Confederation, are fascinating.

This process of discovery began at the conference that opened in September 1864, at Charlottetown—a dusty little place that September—set in a green land nurtured in sea and sunshine. The Canadians had learned about the possibility of a Maritime union conference in June, and had then asked if they could come to it. Whether it would have been held at all had there been no Canadian request is anyone's guess; but the Canadians thus set wheels in motion in the three Maritime governments, and by late July the conference was settled. Charlottetown was arranged because the Prince Edward Islanders were already balking at the idea of Maritime union, and it was thought that it would help to start things off on their own home ground. Virtually the whole Canadian cabinet came down from Quebec by steamer, and the *Queen Victoria* steamed into Charlottetown harbour at noon on Thusday, September 1. "What sort of people are they?" That was the question someone asked one of the Canadian ministers, D'Arcy McGee, in October about the Maritimers. It might well have been the question that Canadians asked themselves about Maritimers, as they went ashore from the *Queen Victoria*. In the course of the next two months, there would be many opportunities to find out.

Important conferences, especially those in British North America in mid-century, were usually provided amply with the good things of this world. The menus worked through by our capacious ancestors would stagger mere mortals of our day, and the wine consumed was proportionate. Victorians were not prudes. Wine can be a great solvent, that is at some stage before it dissolves sensibility, livers and morals. Every conference has its informal side; and while there is no informal substitute for the hard task of resolutions and constitutional tactics, and good staff work beforehand, nevertheless much can be accomplished by way of private progress, by talk, even jocularity, over food and wine. It is perhaps not too much to say that this informal side of the Charlottetown Conference, the *rapport* that it produced, explains why things went so extremely well for the Canadians. They had to do the convincing; they had the sketches of possible constitutional arrangements already to hand, but they had to persuade the Charlottetown Conference to accept their ideas. And persuade is what the Canadians did, so effectively, indeed, that the public, who had not partaken of these powerful draughts, were rather taken aback. After all, said one Saint John paper when the conference was over, the Canadians invited themselves to Charlottetown, and now, where is Maritime union? Nowhere. The Canadians, said a Fredericton paper, "had it all their own way . . . what with their arguments and what with their blandishments (they gave a champagne lunch on board the *Victoria* where Mr. McGee's wit sparkled brightly as the wine), they carried the Lower Province delegates a little off their feet." But even this paper, the *Head Quarters*, had to concede that the Charlottetown Conference would be regarded by many as historic, the beginning of a great change in the fortunes of the British North American colonies.

So it was to be. The Quebec Conference of October 1864 converted the sketch of Charlottetown into a full portrait; and the London Conference, over the winter of 1866-67, touched it up and laid on the varnish. The British North America Act framed it. This act was passed by the British Parliament in February and March 1867, and signed by the Queen on March 29, the day before the Americans bought Alaska from Russia.

IV

The Alaskan purchase was not really an American riposte to Confederation, although it seemed like that to British North Americans. Negotiations had been going on between Russians and Americans for some years past. The truth was that most Americans did not think much about Canada, then or later. Some American politicians did, however, and British North Americans, in that one-eyed way with which they would always regard the United States, assumed that some spoke for all. Still, the noises were disturbing. In July 1866 a bill sponsored by the chairman of the U.S. Senate Foreign Affairs Committee, General N. P. Banks, provided for the admission of the British North American provinces into the United States. It went to committee without division, though it never emerged from it. In March 1867, the Joint Standing Committee of the Maine Senate on Federal Relations reported that the British government were forcing upon British North America a new form of government, with that same "iron hand" that they had used in 1841 with the union of Upper and Lower Canada. The Maritime provinces would be treated in 1867 precisely as Lower Canada had been treated in 1841. Accordingly, the Maine Senate requested the American government "to interpose its legitimate influence in friendly and earnest remonstrance with the British government" against Confederation. A similar motion came from Minnesota a year later, in March 1868, denouncing the Canadian proposal to transfer the Hudson's Bay Company to Canada without a vote of the Red River inhabitants. That very summer Congressman Ben Butler of Massachusetts, with an official congressional party in train, paid a visit to a refractory province of Nova Scotia and a still unconfederated Prince Edward Island.

The United States seemed to expect that British North America would become part of the great American congeries of states, a useful *quid pro quo* on Britain's part for the damages incurred by the *Alabama* affair. The great New York papers, the *Tribune*, the *Herald*, the *Times,* while they differed in degree, from truculence through indifference to expectancy, all found the prospect of the acquisition of British North America attractive. The purchase of Alaska, however quixotic it may have appeared at the time, was characteristic of the attitude of many in the American government (in particular W. S. Seward, the secretary of state) toward the northern, and still unannexed half of the continent.

The purchase of Alaska was also a move that unsettled the British Columbians. The colonies of British Columbia and Vancouver Island had been united in November 1866 in a shot-gun union insisted upon by Great Britain. Here indeed was the "iron hand." The capital was placed, much to the disgust of the mainlanders, in Victoria, on Vancouver Island.

Vancouver Island had been a colony since 1849, a proprietary colony of the Hudson's Bay Company; it had acquired an assembly in 1856 and had become a crown colony in 1859. British Columbia, on the mainland, had been established in 1858 to control the flood of miners who had come in with the Fraser River gold rush that spring. The gold in the lower Fraser had about run out when, in the early summer of 1860, had come the strike in the Cariboo, on the Quesnel River, some three hundred miles north of the Lower Fraser valley as the crow flies, but some five hundred miles by trail. It cost $825 (about $4,000 at present prices) to bring a ton of goods from Victoria to the upper Fraser in 1860. Then in 1861, at Williams Creek, still further inland from the Quesnel River, came the big strike of 1861, when four partners in three months cleared $40,000 (about $200,000). This set the rush going in earnest. The British Columbia government then began the Great North Road, or Cariboo Road as it was more often called, along the Fraser gorges to the north. By the end of 1863 it was good enough that a four-horse stage was able to go all the way from Yale—the head of navigation on the lower Fraser—to Soda Creek, twenty miles below Alexandria.

But the gold rush began to die out after 1863. New Westminster, the capital, became a city of stumps and of disappointed hopes. British Columbia was down on its luck; all that remained were debts and unpaid mortgages. 1865 was a terrible year, ramifying the beggary already prevalent, and producing the conditions that required union of the two Pacific colonies in 1866. By 1867 a feeling of desperation swept the colony; a resolution for federation with the new Dominion of Canada was passed in March 1867, three months before the new Dominion was officially constituted. There was also talk of annexation to the United States. In British Columbia, annexation was always a real possibility, and indeed its rationale more obvious, than a paper connection with distant Ontario and Quebec, a whole world away. The American purchase of Alaska in 1867 reinforced these sentiments. That Confederation survived as a workable idea on the west coast is remarkable, especially considering the enormous pressures of the realities that could work against it. But in the end Confederation did triumph, and annexation did not. By the end of the 1860s the union of British Columbia and the Dominion of Canada was at hand, to become effective in July 1871.

Manitoba joined Confederation the year before, in July 1870. That, too, was a remarkable change in the ten years from 1860. It had only been in 1860 that Captain John Palliser had completed three years of western exploration, that laid out some of the main features of prairie geography and ecology. Palliser had begun from Red River in July 1857, having left England that spring. Not only did he explore much of the western prairies, but with Dr. James Hector, he explored and mapped the Rocky Mountain passes: the Kananaskis, south from Banff; the Vermilion, south from between Banff and Lake Louise; the Kicking Horse Pass, and the Howse Pass near Mistaya Lake, as well as part of the valley of the Columbia.

Red River and the West was still under Hudson's Bay Company rule; but by 1860 that rule was becoming anachronistic. Minnesota —the border was just seventy miles south from Fort Garry—had been made a state in 1858; by 1860 it had a population of 172,000, which would more than double within the decade. And westward, along the 49th parallel, were established in the 1860s a series of officially constituted American territorial governments, Dakota, Montana and Idaho. Against this American expansion were the eight thousand whites and half-breeds of Red River. The prairie west was a vacuum, of population, and hence of power. The people of Red River had a voice—the *Nor'Wester*, begun late in 1859— and its Canadian owners were both impatient with the Hudson's Bay Company, and not above reflecting the genuine sentiments of the colony about annexation. As with British Columbia, the Red

River colony's communications were almost wholly with the United States; many of its necessities came from south of the border; without the United States the economies of British Columbia and Red River would cease to exist. As the *Nor'Wester* said in 1862, "Can it be expected that we should not become Americanized, when . . . American influences of every kind are operating upon us?" The *Nor'Wester* reflected the uncertainties of Red River's future, with a dying, paternal rule of the Hudson's Bay Company, and aggressive and promising proposals from below the border. As the paper put it, "now . . . is a fit time to settle once for all the question of the Hudson's Bay Company. We do not agree with those who clamor for an abrupt, unceremonious and unconditional termination of the Company's *status* in this country. . . . A peaceful and equitable settlement of the Company's claim is . . . an urgent *desideratum*."

The settlement of the Company's claim did not necessarily mean Confederation with eastern Canada. Most people in Red River, white and half-breed alike, preferred to be a crown colony rather than establish political connection with Canada. Despite the fact that the bishop of St. Boniface, A. A. Taché, was the nephew of the premier of the Province of Canada, E. P. Taché, the Roman Catholic Church was opposed to outright annexation to Canada. Oscar Malmros, the American vice-consul, who was appointed to Fort Garry in 1868, believed, rightly, that the whole French population, and most of the others, were opposed to union with Canada.

Louis Riel had come to Red River in the fall of 1864, back from his education in Montreal, and was already, by 1867, assuming the leadership of the Métis. The Métis themselves, who were buffalo hunters, or *voyageurs* with the York boat brigades of the Hudson's Bay Company, were uneasy about the changes that were already in the wind. "Uncertain of their future, sure of their power," as Professor W. L. Morton puts it, they were prepared to listen to Riel. It was already known by 1868 that the new Dominion of Canada was negotiating in London, and with the entire approval of the British government, to buy out the Hudson's Bay Company. Negotiations were completed that year, and by the autumn of 1869 the date of the transfer had been set for December 1, 1869. The people of Red River objected to being blindly transferred from

Hudson's Bay Company rule to Canadian rule, bag and baggage, without being consulted in any way. The Métis, with the support of the English-speaking half-breeds, and the sympathy of some of the white settlers, resolved to seize power from the Company before the Canadians did. They occupied Upper Fort Garry on November 2, 1869. Thus began the train of events that led to the creation of the Province of Manitoba in July 1870. It had never been the intention of the Government of Canada to create a province of Manitoba; that was forced upon the Dominion by the local feeling of the people of Red River, white and half-breed alike.

A similar reaction at this very same time, November 1869, resulted in the refusal of Newfoundland to join Confederation. It was no mean achievement that Confederation become an issue in Newfoundland at all. A decade before 1860 it would have been laughed out of court. But in 1857 came the French Shore crisis. Newfoundland sent leaders of both government and opposition to Nova Scotia, New Brunswick, and to Canada, and had received warm support from the mainland governments in the contest with the Colonial office over the French Shore. As a result of Newfoundland protestations, Great Britain had abandoned the proposed convention with France. Newfoundlanders would remember that support. "We cannot soon forget," said the *Newfoundlander* on April 16, 1857, "our obligations to our Sister Colonies . . . who have identified themselves with our struggle." Thus Newfoundland entered the early sixties with some consciousness of mainland connections, one that was strengthened by the new telegraphic communication with Nova Scotia.

The sixties were hard years for Newfoundland, the result of a grim combination of bad fishing, both inshore and on the Grand Banks. The potato crop was hit by blight in 1863 and 1864. By the time of the Confederation movement on the mainland, Newfoundland was in parlous circumstances. Something over 25 per cent of the revenues of the colony were going for direct relief to impoverished, in some cases, starving fishermen and their families.

The premier of Newfoundland happened to be in Halifax two weeks before the Charlottetown Conference and broached the question of Newfoundland's participation in it to Charles Tupper.

The *Newfoundlander* and the *Patriot* raised the same question in St. John's. And if Newfoundland did not manage to get to Charlotte-town, it did send delegates to the Quebec Conference (observers technically, but functioning as delegates). In November 1864, they brought home to Newfoundland the Quebec Resolutions, which came before the Newfoundland legislature in February and March, 1865. Newfoundland's instinct in 1865 (as in 1887, 1895 and 1948), was to be cautious, and the defeat of Tilley and Confederation in the New Brunswick elections of March 1865, suggested that there was no reason for haste. Despite, or perhaps because of, its own election in November 1865, Newfoundland continued to be cautious; and the urgings of the British government through Governor Musgrave, however well meant, did not really help; rather they tended to make Newfoundlanders more stubborn. So Confederation was postponed in 1866, and again in 1867, despite enormous pressure from the Colonial Office and the governor. In 1868 and 1869, however, it was revived more vigorously; there was a delegation to Ottawa, and in October and November, 1869, the Newfoundland government took Confederation to the people of Newfoundland. It got roundly defeated for its pains. By this time there was evidence that the bitter antipathy of the Nova Scotians had affected all Confederation projects, both in Newfoundland and in Prince Edward Island.

Prince Edward Island had simply refused to part with any vestige of its local power. The bait was not tempting enough. The Inter-colonial railway meant little to them. They wanted the buying out of the absentee landlords of Prince Edward Island (mostly resident in England), for the benefit of the tenant farmers of the Island. They wanted a guarantee of communication with the mainland. None of these things had been promised in the Quebec Resolutions, despite some talk about putting them in. So Prince Edward Island waited and watched. And the anger of the Nova Scotians did little to persuade Islanders to change their minds.

Confederation had been put through in Nova Scotia and New Brunswick in 1866 with the approval of the assemblies and legislative councils in both colonies. But the means used to secure that approval were a mixture of ruthlessness, chicanery and courage, to-gether with the luck of the Fenian scare of April to June 1866, and an unequivocally strong push by the British government. Had there been an election in Nova Scotia in 1865 or 1866, Confederation would have been defeated. But happily for Charles Tupper, the premier of Nova Scotia, and for the cause of Confederation, no election was necessary. The Nova Scotian Assembly had been elected in 1863, before ever the Confederation movement started, and that Assembly could run for four years. It did. In other words, Confederation had to come before that new provincial election, or there would have been no Confederation at all—or none with Nova Scotia in it. Only after July 1, 1867, when Confederation had become a reality, was there an election in Nova Scotia. Then there were two elections, federal and provincial, and in both the supporters of Confederation were badly defeated.

Nova Scotia after 1867 was bitter and resentful against those who had fastened Confederation upon her; even her loyalty to Great Britain suffered, as delegation after delegation, in 1866, 1867 and 1868 went to London to protest, and got no effective action. The better terms of 1869, and Howe's entry into the Macdonald government, eased the position slightly, and the prosperity of the years from 1869 to 1875, together with the completion of the Intercolonial railway in 1876, were powerful solvents of these bitter Nova Scotian attitudes. The best solvent of all would be time.

Even New Brunswick, which had had another election on Confederation in 1866, and which the supporters of Confederation won, still elected only eight supporters in the 1867 election against seven of the opposition, though not all these were opposed to Confederation à outrance. Both Nova Scotia and New Brunswick reacted adversely to the new rules and principles by which the Dominion government administered the new Confederation, and to some of the new legislation of the 1867-68 session of the new Dominion Parliament.

The civil service of the Dominion of Canada was that of the old Province of Canada writ large. There were of course Maritime appointments; but the tone of the new administration, its operating rules, were Canadian in the old meaning of that term, that is, stemming from the old civil service of the Province of Canada. And the new Parliament of Canada, in its first session, applied as new acts

for the whole Dominion laws that had been familiar to the old
Canadians living in the Province of Canada, but quite unfamiliar
to the new Canadians living in New Brunswick and Nova Scotia.
There was a stamp tax for cheques and official documents: that
was new to Maritimers. There was the imposition of postage on
newspapers: before 1867 newspapers in Nova Scotia and New
Brunswick had the free use of the mails. Almost the worst aspect
of that legislation was the way it was done, being passed through
second reading on December 20, 1867, when many Maritime members had left to go home for Christmas. Alexander Galt, still a
supporter of the government (though he had recently resigned from
it), appealed to Parliament's sense of equity, and asked the government to be reasonable, and not impose such taxes headlong on a
province as already aggravated as Nova Scotia was, and as New
Brunswick was coming to be. It made no difference. Almost as bad
was the application of the Canadian tariff. Canada had lowered
her 1859 tariff in 1866, but even at 15 per cent it was still higher,
by from 3 to 5 per cent, than the old tariffs of the two Maritime
colonies.

But the new tariff was expected. What was not expected was the
new administration of the customs. Here there was no compromise.
The Canadian customs was much more rigorously administered than
had been the old customs administrations of New Brunswick and
Nova Scotia. These had been rather lazy and easy-going. As the
Dominion Commissioner of Customs coolly remarked, "Experience
has taught us that . . . laws for the collection of our revenues can
hardly fail to be inquisitorial in their action."

"Tilley dances while New Brunswick weeps," said the Saint
John *Morning Freeman,* the day before Christmas, 1867. That
was doubtless the jaundiced view of an opposition paper. But the
newspapers that had supported Confederation were also unhappy.
The *New Brunswick Reporter* of Fredericton remarked in May
1868, "Whether too much was promised, or too much expected,
certain it is the facts fall far short of expectations, and the very
best friends of Confederation shake their heads ominiously." Tilley,
that very month, appealed to Macdonald. "Do strengthen my

hands. I want all the assistance I can get to allay dissatisfaction that exists in the province." Altogether it was to take a few more years yet to cement Confederation.

There began, too, the central Canadian business conquest of the Maritime provinces. Businessmen of the old Province of Canada seem to have known little or nothing of the possibilities of the Maritime market when the Confederation movement started. There was much talk of possibilities of this market by politicians; but businessmen distrust political oratory, and as a rule heavily discount it. But this time the politicians were right. Within a few years, the central Canadian businessmen were able to drive many American firms out of Saint John and Halifax. They sent their own manufactures—scythes, forks, threshing machines, clothing, even agricultural produce, to say nothing of the growing army of commercial travellers—down to the Maritime provinces, in the summers by ship to Gulf of St. Lawrence ports, in the winters by the Grand Trunk to Portland, and by ship from there. As yet this central Canadian economic conquest had not much affected Maritime business; but the easy-going ways of the Maritimes were soon put to the test by much more knowledgeable, aggressive, and price-conscious central Canadian businessmen. By the mid-1870s there were complaints about the too great efficiency of central Canadian techniques, driving Maritime manufacturers to the wall.

Confederation, like all great political changes, was productive of many things unexpected by those who proposed it, and, also, productive of both good and ill. But Nova Scotia and New Brunswick were powerless for the moment to repeal Confederation, and by the time they might have been in a position to do so, they had begun to accept it, and the value of the Intercolonial railway that went with it. It was a way of life that might, after all, give them a larger existence and a more purposeful sense of being themselves, than they had under the old colonial regime. Even Prince Edward Island was finally persuaded—by railways, and by hard cash—to join Confederation in 1873. By that time only Newfoundland was left out. Newfoundland's history, from 1869 to 1949, suggests what might have happened to Nova Scotia, New Brunswick and Prince Edward Island had they been left to themselves.

The 1860s were an end and a beginning; the last decade of British North America, the first of the Dominion of Canada. The building of this new Canada had just begun; it was not yet nailed together by railways, and as for the moral force of its new nationality, that hardly yet existed. The century since 1760 had seen a remarkable development of the several disparate colonies, often highly individualistic. Sometimes it seemed that they were linked by little more than their common loyalty to the crown. Each of them had had their own political experience, their own identity. Yet, they had confronted many of the same dangers, in 1775, in 1812. Some of them shared the struggle for responsible government. They had shared the Reciprocity Treaty of 1854, as they were now going to share Confederation. It was not inevitable, this union; but there was more in common between the colonies than they themselves realized. Despite their diversities, colonists and *Canadiens* had taken their own fate in their hands and set out together on the long voyage ahead.

INDEX

Acadia, 2, 7-8, 258
Acadians, 8-9, 24, 26, 86-90, 94, 125, 131
Act of Trade and Navigation, 54
Act of Union (1841), 213-214
Adams, John, 38
Agnew, Stair, 83, 85
Albert, Prince Consort, 256
Allan, John, 27-29
Allan, William, 145, 162
Alline, Henry, 30-33
American Fur Company, 139, 181
Anticosti Island, 8
Archibald, Samuel, 134
Arnold, Benedict, 37
Askin, John, 66
Astor, John Jacob, 103, 139
Aubin, Napoléon, 212
Aylmer, Lord, 181-182, 185

Bagot, Sir Charles, 215

Baillie, Thomas, 166, 176
Bailly, Bishop, 58
Baldwin, Robert, 190, 192, 198, 214-215, 217-218, 225, 238
Baldwin, William Warren, 169
Banks, General N. P., 263
Barclay, Major, 80-81
Baring, Thomas, 235
Bathurst, Lord, 127, 133, 138, 146
Bédard, Pierre, 112, 135-136
Bell, Alexander Graham, 254
Bibaud, Michel, 209
Bidwell, Marshall Spring, 169, 188, 191-192
Blanchard, Jotham, 165
Blanchet, François, 112
Boulton, D'Arcy, 145, 163
Boulton, Henry John, 145, 163
Bourdages, Louis, 183
Bourget, Ignace, 209-211
Bowie, William, 164

273

Bowring, Benjamin, 166
Briand, Jean Olivier, 12-13, 36
British North America Act (1867), 262
Brock, Isaac, 136, 142-143, 147
Brown, George, 239-243, 246-247, 260
Brown, John, 36
Buchanan, Isaac, 207
Burgess, Emmanuel, 160
Burgoyne, John, 39
Burton, Ralph, 4-5, 7
Butler, Ben, 263
By, John, 154
Bytown, 154, 160, 236. *See also* Ottawa

Caldwell, Henry, 71
Callbeck, Phillips, 25
Campbell, William, 26
Canals: Beauharnois, 211; Desjardins, 154; Erie, 154-155, 222, 236-237; Lachine, 72, 145, 153, 231, 236-237; Rideau, 145, 154, 160, 231, 236-237; Shubenacadie, 132, 151-152; Welland, 154-155, 162, 236-237
Cape Breton Island, 9, 26, 61, 88, 127, 134, 164, 229, 257
Carleton, Sir Guy, 11, 13-15, 18, 33, 35-39, 44, 52-54. *See also* Dorchester, Lord
Carleton, Thomas, 49, 82-85, 89
Carmichael, J. E., 170
Carson, William, 123-125, 166
Cartier, George Etienne, 233, 241-243, 246, 256, 260
Cartwright, Richard, 66
Cazeau, Félix, 222
Chapman, H. C., 252
Charlottetown, 25, 86, 125, 206, 228, 258, 261-262, 267-268
Chateau Clique, 110, 149, 161
Chauveau, Pierre, 247
Chiniquy, père, 210
Chipman, Ward, 83, 132
Clark, Thomas, 146-147
Colborne, Sir John, 162-163, 179, 187, 190, 197, 200, 204
Colclough, Caesar, 126
Colebrooke, Sir William, 219
Collins, Enos, 164
Colville, Andrew Wedderburn, 140
Confederation, 2, 226-227, 246-247, 250, 254-255, 259, 260-272

Constitutional Act (1791), 64-65, 67, 70, 72, 94, 117, 135, 191, 202, 204
Convention of 1818, 133, 151
Corn Laws (1815), 150, 222, 224
Costin, Thomas, 89-90
Council of Twelve, 150, 164-165, 175
Craig, Sir James Henry, 98-99, 104, 107, 109, 114-116, 118, 120-121, 135-136
Cramahé, Hector Theophilus, 5
Crémazie, Octave, 247
Cugnet, François-Joseph, 13
Cull, Henry, 70
Cunard, Samuel, 132, 205, 237

Dalhousie, Lord, 132-134, 139, 161, 166-167, 170, 182
de Forbin-Janson, Bishop, 210
de Lafayette, Marquis, 39
de Lanaudière, Charles, 58
de Lévis, Chevalier, 3
Denaut, Bishop, 63
de Salaberry, Charles, 136-137
de Tocqueville, Alexis, 178-179
Des Barres, J. F. W., 125-126
D'Estaing, Admiral, 39
de Vaudreuil, Marquis, 3
Dickson, William, 146-147
Dorchester, Lord, 54, 56-58, 60-61, 68, 89. *See also* Carleton, Sir Guy
Dorion, A.-A., 242, 246, 257
Douglas, James, 245
Doutre, Joseph, 209
Draper, William, 214, 243
Drawback Laws (1845, 1846), 222
Drummond, Sir Gordon, 137-138
Duncan, John, 159
Dundas, Henry, 67-68
Dunn, Thomas, 71
Durham, Lord, 198-205, 208, 218
Duvernay, Ludger, 212, 221

Eastern Townships, 70, 104, 108, 110, 113, 116, 212, 216
Eddy, Jonathan, 27-29
Education Act (1811), 129
Elgin, Lord, 216-219, 222-224

Falkland, Lord, 218
Family, Compact, 149, 161-164, 168, 187-188, 192, 198, 225
Fanning, Edmund, 86
Finlay, Hugh, 71
Finlay, James, 17

Fisher, Charles, 228
Fleming, Sandford, 258
Forbes, Francis, 124
Fothergill, Charles, 168
Franklin, Benjamin, 42
Franklin, John, 171
Fraser, Simon, 103
Fredericton, 84-85, 152, 176, 219, 229, 247, 258
Free Ports Act (1811), 128
Frobisher, Joseph, 71

Gage, General, 35
Gage, Thomas, 4, 7
Galt, Alexander Tilloch, 233, 245-246, 254, 270
Garneau, François Xavier, 209
George III, 10, 19, 29, 31, 51, 117
Gesner, Abraham, 253
Gladstone, William Ewart, 256
Glenelg, Lord, 190
Glenie, James, 84-85
Glyn, George, 235
Goderich, Lord, 189
Gore, Sir Francis, 107, 147
Gosford, Lord, 185-186, 190, 194-195
Gourlay, Robert, 147-148, 168
Grant, William, 71
Great Awakening, 21, 30-33
Grenville, William, 60-61, 91
Guarantee Act (1849), 218
Gurney, Charles, 207
Gurney, Edward, 207
Gzowski, Casimir, 233, 252

Hagerman, Christopher, 145
Haldimand, Frederick, 5, 39, 45-46, 53-56
Haliburton, T. C., 175, 201, 225
Halifax, 2, 9, 26, 29-31, 45, 48-49, 78-79, 81, 96, 99, 128-130, 132-133, 139, 151, 153, 155-158, 163-165, 175, 201, 205, 218, 223, 225, 229-230, 232-235, 237, 247-248, 251, 253, 255, 257-258, 267, 271
Halliburton, Brenton, 134, 164
Hamilton, Robert, 66
Harmon, Daniel, 76
Harrowby, Lord, 97
Hart, Moses, 70
Harvey, Sir John, 143, 218
Hastings, Warren, 45
Haszard, J. D., 170
Head, Sir Edmund, 219

Head, Sir Francis Bond, 190-192, 196
Hearne, Samuel, 18, 40
Hector, James, 265
Henry, Alexander, 17
Henry, John, 109
Hey, William, 37
Hincks, Francis, 198, 203-205, 214-215, 218, 223-225, 234-235, 238, 241
Holland, A. J., 133
Holland, Samuel, 5, 70
Holton, Luther, 233
Howe, Alexander, 81
Howe, Joseph, 165, 175, 198, 202, 206, 218-219, 225, 229, 234-235, 269
Hubert, Bishop, 58, 63-64
Hudon, Hyacinthe, 222
Hudson's Bay Company, 2, 17-18, 21, 40, 45, 55, 72, 76-77, 103, 137, 140-141, 152, 171, 174, 180-181, 220, 227, 242-245, 263-267
Huntley, Sir Henry, 219
Hutchinson, Thomas, 48

Indians, 3-4, 8, 16-18, 34, 37, 46, 51-52, 55, 68-69, 74-77, 96-98, 103, 134, 140, 143-144, 220, 247
Indian tribes: Beothuk, 159; Chippewas, 16; Hurons, 16; Iroquois, 51-52; Missisauga, 51-52; Ottawas, 16; Pacific, 77-78; Plains, 74; Senecas, 16
Intolerable Acts (c. 1775), 34
Irving, Paulus Aemilius, 5

Jameson, Anna, 180
Jay's Treaty (1794), 69, 75, 99
Jefferson, Thomas, 98, 100, 123
Johnson, Sir John, 57

Kane, Paul, 247
Keefer, Thomas, 232
Kempt, Sir James, 134, 156, 168, 181
Kingston, 65, 74, 104, 142, 145, 153-154, 160, 205, 207-208, 225
Knox, William, 47-48
Krieghoff, Cornelius, 247

Labrador, 8
Lachine, 36, 72
LaFontaine, Louis-Hippolyte, 204, 213-217, 223-225, 238
Lambert, John, 120

Lartigue, Jacques, 195, 202, 209
Legge, Francis, 26-28
Lincoln, Abraham, 249
Little, Philip Francis, 220
Liverpool, Lord, 117
Logan, Sir William, 247, 253
Loyalists, 41-57, 60-61, 65-66, 70-71,
  80-84, 88-89, 96, 100, 106-107,
  125, 128, 145, 157, 160, 165, 176,
  204, 228-229
Lymburner, Adam, 59
Lyons, John, 168

Mabane, Adam, 5, 56-57
McCulloch, Thomas, 129, 132, 165
MacDonald, John, 24
Macdonald, John A., 241-243, 246,
  256, 258, 260, 269-270
Macdonald, Sandfield, 257-258
Macdonell, Miles, 141
McDougall, William, 238, 246
McGee, D'Arcy, 261
McGillivray, William, 74, 141
McGregor, James, 79
McGregor, John, 155, 158, 163
Mackenzie, Alexander, 56, 73, 75
Mackenzie, William Lyon, 148, 168-
  169, 188-190, 193, 195-197
MacLean (poet, c. 1820), 157
McLeod, Norman, 157
McMaster, William, 207
MacNab, Sir Allan, 214, 241
Macpherson, David, 233
McTavish, Simon, 73
Magdalen Islands, 8, 88
Magee, Henry, 79
Maitland, Sir Peregrine, 148, 156,
  160-163, 168-170, 187
Malmros, Oscar, 266
Markland, George, 163
Maseres, Francis, 11, 14
Masson, Joseph, 211
Matthews, John, 168
Meilleur, Jean-Baptiste, 216
Melbourne, Lord, 201
Merritt, William Hamilton, 154-155
Métis, 140-141, 245, 265-267
Milbanke, Governor, 93
Mills, John, 222
Mills, Thomas, 5
Milnes, Robert, 113
Miquelon, 7, 88, 123-124, 127
Molson, John, 185

Monk, James, 137
Montgomery, Richard, 37
Montreal, 2-5, 9, 11, 17, 35-36, 40-
  41, 45-46, 54-55, 60, 63, 70, 72-
  75, 77, 96, 103-105, 114, 121, 137,
  139, 141-142, 144-145, 149, 152,
  159-160, 164, 177-178, 180, 183,
  185-186, 193-195, 197, 202, 205,
  209-212, 215, 217, 221-225, 230,
  232-233, 236-237, 240, 251, 256,
  259-260, 266
Montreal, Capitulation of, 3-4
Moodie, Susanna, 179, 208
Morin, A. N., 238, 241
Morris, Patrick, 124-125, 166
Mortimer, Edward, 79
Mountain, Jacob, 108, 113, 136, 169
Municipal Corporations Act (1849),
  218
Murdoch, Beamish, 80, 128
Murray, James, 3-16, 18, 53
Musgrave, Governor, 268

Negroes (in Nova Scotia), 50, 134,
  156
Neilson, John, 185, 202, 205, 208,
  213-214, 225
New North West Company, 75
Niagara on the Lake, 69
Nichol, Robert, 146-147
Noble, Seth, 27
Non-Intercourse Act (1809), 98
North West Company, 40, 55-56, 72-
  77, 103, 139-141, 152, 243

Oregon Treaty (1846), 220, 244-245
Ottawa, 236, 268. See also Bytown

Palliser, John, 265
Palliser's Act (1775), 91
Palmer, James B., 125-126
Palmerston, Lord, 255
Panet, Jean-Antoine, 112
Papineau, Louis-Joseph, 136, 138, 166-
  167, 169, 183-186, 191, 193-195,
  213-214, 224, 237
Parent, Etienne, 203-205, 209, 211,
  213, 215, 225
Parr, John, 45-46, 81
Parry, William Edward, 171-172
Patterson, Governor, 25, 86
Plessis, Joseph-Octave, 63, 119, 138
Pond, Peter, 40
Pontbriand, Bishop, 12

Pontiac, 4, 16
Pope, Joseph, 219
Portland, Duke of, 67
Power, Michael, 222
Prescott, Robert, 71
Prevost, Sir George, 129, 136-137
Proclamation of 1763, 7-16, 18, 34

Quebec Act (1774) 33-36, 39, 42-43, 48, 53, 56, 58
Quebec City, 2-4, 9, 11, 13, 33, 35-39, 98, 100-102, 104-105, 114, 120, 138-139, 142, 151, 159-161, 169, 181, 185-187, 194-195, 197-198, 200-203, 209-212, 216, 219, 221-222, 225, 233-234, 236-237, 240, 251, 255-256, 261-262, 268
Quebec Revenue Act (1774), 182

Rankin, Alexander, 128
Ready, John, 170
Reciprocity Treaty (1854), 231-232, 254-255, 272
Red River colony, 140-141, 171, 181, 220, 244-245, 263, 265-267
Reeves, John, 91, 93-94
Religions: Anglican, 22-23, 48, 64, 67, 84, 107, 117, 124, 131-132, 145-146, 162-163, 165, 169, 174, 190, 207-208, 218, 229, 238; Baptist, 117, 131, 229; Dunkards, 66; Jesuits, 6, 12, 111, 210; Ladies of the Sacred Heart, 210; Mennonites, 66, 117; Methodist, 117, 124-125, 169, 190, 207-208; Oblate Order, 210; Presbyterian, 64, 117, 125, 131, 146, 148, 165, 207-208, 229, 239; Protestant, 9-10, 12, 23, 60, 64, 84, 117, 159, 166, 174-175, 192, 208, 227-229, 239-240; Quakers, 66, 117; Roman Catholic, 9-10, 12-13, 18, 23, 33-34, 44, 59-60, 64, 86-88, 108-111, 113, 116-120, 124-125, 131-132, 159-160, 166-167, 174-175, 184, 192, 202, 207-208, 210-211, 214-215, 220, 225, 227-229, 238-240, 258, 266; Sisters of the Good Shepherd, 210; Sulpicians, 12, 211
Richardson, John, 71-72
Richelieu, Cardinal, 10
Richmond, Duke of, 138-139
Riel, Louis, 266
Robie, Simon, 134

Robinson, John Beverley, 145, 162-163, 201, 225
Robinson, Major, 234
Rolph, John, 190
Routh, Richard, 93
Rush-Bagot Agreement (1817), 144
Russell, Lord John, 186-187, 193-194, 218
Russell, Peter, 66
Ryerson, Egerton, 169, 208
Ryland, Herman W., 108, 116, 136

Saint John, 49, 78, 82-84, 89, 99, 128-132, 152, 166, 176, 206, 219, 228-230, 234, 237, 247-248, 251, 256-257, 271
St. John's, 22, 90-93, 123-125, 145, 158-159, 166, 221, 228, 268
St. Pierre, 7, 123-124
School Act (1850), 239
School Acts (1841), 208
Selkirk, Thomas, Douglas, Earl of, 140-141
Semple, Robert, 141
Seward, W. S., 264
Sewell, Jonathan, 108, 113, 116, 118, 137
Sherbrooke, Sir John Coape, 129-130, 132, 138
Signay, Joseph, 202
Sigogne, Jean-Mande, 88
Simcoe, John Graves, 64-69, 83, 94, 146
Simpson, Sir George, 244
Slick, Sam, 175, 180, 201
Smith, Charles Douglas, 126-127, 131-132, 170
Smith, D. W., 68
Smith, William, 56-58, 60-61
South West Company, 103, 140
Stamp Act (1765), 23, 29
Stearns, Jonathan, 81
Stewart, John, 170
Strachan, John, 145, 148, 162-163, 169
Sydenham, Lord, 200, 208, 215. *See also* Thomson, Charles Poulett
Sydney, Lord, 60

Taché, A. A., 266
Taché, E. P., 258, 266
Talbot, Thomas, 160
Taschereau, Jean-Thomas, 112
Tecumseh, 143

Tenures Act (1826), 183
Thom, Adam, 186
Thompson, David, 76, 103, 139
Thomson, Charles Poulett, 200, 204.
    See also Sydenham, Lord
Thorpe, Thomas, 107
Three Rivers, 4-5, 70
Tilley, Samuel Leonard, 228-229, 261,
    268, 270
Tomison, William, 77
Tonge, William Cottnam, 82
Toronto, 52, 68, 180, 190, 196-197,
    202-203, 205, 207-208, 210, 222,
    230, 233, 236, 238, 242-243, 246-
    248, 251. See also York
Traill, Catherine Parr, 179
Treaty of Ghent (1814), 131, 144
Treaty of Paris (1763), 1, 4-5, 7
Trois Rivières. See Three Rivers
Tupper, Charles, 229, 261, 267, 269

Uniacke, Crofton, 164
Uniacke, James Boyle, 164, 218
Uniacke, Norman, 164
Uniacke, Richard John, Jr., 164
Uniacke, R. J., 164

Vancouver, George, 73, 77
Victoria, 220, 245, 264
Viger, Denis-Benjamin, 111, 213, 217

Waldegrave, William, 92-93
Washington, George, 25, 28, 31, 36
Watkin, Edward, 252
Watson, Brook, 53
Wayne, Anthony, 69
Webster-Ashburton Treaty (1842), 43,
    219
Weekes, William, 107
Wells, W. B., 193
Wentworth, John, 78, 81-82, 128
White, Nathaniel, 151-152
Willcocks, Joseph, 107
Willis, John, 168
Wilmot, Lemuel, 219, 223
Winslow, Edward, 83, 89
Wyatt, Charles, 107

York, 66, 68, 76, 117, 142-148, 150,
    153, 160-163, 168, 180. See also
    Toronto
Young, John, 133
Young, William, 223

Zimmerman, Samuel, 232